Sept 2. 2000

Dear Jenn van Dyke

Thanks for everything, -
hope we'll stay in
touch! SL

D0935048

Science and politics in
international environmental regimes

MANCHESTER
UNIVERSITY PRESS

Issues in Environmental Politics

Series editors Mikael Skou Anderson *and* Duncan Liefferink

As the millennium begins, the environment has come to stay as a central concern of global politics. This series takes key problems for environmental policy and examines the politics behind their cause and possible resolution. Accessible and eloquent, the books make available for a non-specialist readership some of the best research and most provocative thinking on humanity's relationship with the planet.

already published in the series

Congress and air pollution: environmental politics in the US
 Christopher J. Bailey

Sustaining Amazonia: grassroots action for productive conservation
 Anthony Hall

The protest business? Mobilizing campaign groups
 Grant Jordan and William Maloney

Environment and the nation state: the Netherlands, the European
 Union and acid rain *Duncan Liefferink*

Valuing the environment *Raino Malnes*

Life on a modern planet: a manifesto for progress *Richard North*

Public purpose or private benefit? The politics of energy
 conservation *Gill Owen*

Environmental pressure groups *Peter Rawcliffe*

Governance by green taxes *Mikael Skou Andersen*

European environmental policy: the pioneers
 Mikael Skou Andersen and Duncan Liefferink (eds)

The new politics of pollution *Albert Weale*

Science and politics in international environmental regimes

Between integrity and involvement

Steinar Andresen, Tora Skodvin,
Arild Underdal and Jørgen Wettestad

Manchester University Press
Manchester and New York
Distributed exclusively in the USA by St. Martin's Press

The right of Steinar Andresen, Tora Skodvin, Arild Underdal and Jørgen Wettestad
to be identified as the authors of this work has been asserted by them in accordance
with the Copyright, Designs and Patents Act 1988.

Published by Manchester University Press
Oxford Road, Manchester M13 9NR, UK
and Room 400, 175 Fifth Avenue, New York, NY 10010, USA
http://www.man.ac.uk/mup

Distributed exclusively in the USA by
St. Martin's Press, Inc., 175 Fifth Avenue, New York, NY 10010, USA

Distributed exclusively in Canada by
UBC Press, University of British Columbia, 6344 Memorial Road,
Vancouver, BC, Canada V6T 1Z2

British Library Cataloguing-in-Publication Data
A catalogue record for this book is available from the British Library.

Library of Congress Cataloging-in-Publication Data applied for

ISBN 0 7190 5806 6 *hardback*

First published in 2000

06 05 04 03 02 01 00   10 9 8 7 6 5 4 3 2 1

Typeset in Sabon
by Northern Phototypesetting Co. Ltd, Bolton
Printed in Great Britain
by Bookcraft (Bath) Ltd, Midsomer Norton

Contents

Figures and tables

Figures

Tables

Preface

We began work on this study in 1993. A preliminary report was published in the internal series of the Center for International Climate and Environment Research (CICERO) and the Fridtjof Nansen Institute (FNI) in 1994. Encouraged by the positive interest expressed by practitioners as well as colleagues – including scholars outside our own discipline – we decided to update, extend and refine the analysis and make what we hope is a substantially improved version available to a larger audience.

In this process we have benefited greatly from comments and suggestions from a number of people, including Peter M. Haas, Edward L. Miles, and one of the editors of the Manchester University Press *Issues in Environmental Politics* series. Last but not least, numerous discussions over the years within the team itself have helped each of us to improve individual chapters and enabled us jointly to refine the overall design of the project. We are grateful to Susan Høivik, Lynn P. Nygaard, Kåre Rudsar, Ann Skarstad, Anne Christine Thestrup and Snorre Fjeldstad for valuable editorial assistance.

CICERO funded the first major phase of research. The final stage of rewriting was made possible through a grant from the Research Council of Norway. CICERO, FNI, and the Department of Political Science, University of Oslo, have all permitted us to set aside precious time to finish the study.

The full responsibility for the end product rests with the authors.

Steinar Andresen, Tora Skodvin,
Arild Underdal, Jørgen Wettestad

Abbreviations

ACMP	Advisory Committee on Marine Pollution
AGBM	Ad Hoc Group on the Berlin Mandate
AGGG	Advisory Group on Greenhouse Gases
ASMO	Environmental Assessment and Monitoring Committee
BAT	best available technology
BEP	best environmental practice
BIWS	Bureau of International Whaling Statistics
BWU	Blue Whale Unit
CCAMLR	Convention for the Conservation of Antarctic Marine Living Resources
CCOL	Coordinating Committee on the Ozone Layer
CFCs	chlorofluorocarbons
CICERO	Center for International Climate and Environmental Research
CMA	Chemical Manufacturing Association
CMS	Convention on the Conservation of Migratory Species of Wild Animals
CoP	Conference of the Parties (to the Climate Convention)
CO_2	Carbon dioxide
CVC	Group of Chairmen and Vice-Chairmen
EB	Executive Body
EC	European Community
ECE	Economic Commission for Europe (UN)
ECOSOC	Economic and Social Council
EMEP	Co-operative Programme for Monitoring and

	Evaluation of Long-Range Transmissions of Air Pollutants in Europe
EPA	Environmental Protection Agency
EQS	Environmental Quality Standard
FAO	Food and Agricultural Organisation (UN)
FNI	Fridtjof Nansen Institute
FRG	Federal Republic of Germany
GEAP	Group of Economic Experts on Air Pollution
GECR	Global Environmental Change Report
GEMS	Global Environmental Monitoring System
GHG	Greenhouse gas
GWP	Global Warming Potential
HCFCs	Hydrochlorofluorocarbons
IATTC	Inter-American Tropical Tuna Convention
ICES	International Council for the Exploration of the Sea
ICP	International Co-operative Programme
ICRW	International Convention for the Regulation of Whaling
ICSU	International Council of Scientific Unions
IGO	intergovernmental organisation
IIASA	International Institute for Applied Systems Analysis
INC	Intergovernmental Negotiating Committee
INC/FCCC	Intergovernmental Negotiating Committee for a Framework Convention on Climate Change
IO	international organisation
IPCC	Intergovernmental Panel on Climate Change
IUCN	World Conservation Union
IWC	International Whaling Commission
JMG	Joint Monitoring Group
LRTAP	ECE Convention on Long-Range Transboundary Air Pollution
MMP	Monitoring Master Plan
MSY	maximum sustainable yield
NAS	National Academy of Science
NASA	National Aeronautics and Space Administration
NGO	non-governmental organisation
NMP	new management procedure
NOAA	National Oceanic and Atmospheric Administration

NOx	Nitrogen oxide
NSC	North Sea Conference
NSTF	North Sea Task Force
ODP	ozone depleting potential
OECD	Organisation for Economic Co-operation and Development
OSCON	Oslo Convention on Marine Dumping
OSPAR	Oslo Convention for the Protection of the Marine Environment of the North-East Atlantic
OSPARCOM	Oslo and Paris Commissions
OTP	Ozone Trends Panel
PARCOM	Paris Commission
PARCON	Paris Convention for the Prevention of Marine Pollution from Land-Based Sources
PCB	polychlorinated biphenyl
PCT	polychlorinated triphenyl
POP	persistent organic pollutant
PP	precautionary principle
ppb	parts per billion
ppbv	parts per billion by volume
PRAM	Programmes and Measures Committee
PRIO	International Peace Research Institute
PWG	Policy Working Group
QSR	Quality Status of the North Sea report
RAINS	Regional Acidification Information and Simulation
RMP	revised management procedure
SACSA	Standing Advisory Committee for Scientific Advice
SBI	Subsidiary Body for Implementation
SBSTA	Subsidiary Body for Scientific and Technological Advice
SciCom	Scientific Committee
SO_2	Sulphur dioxide
SPM	Summary for Policymakers
SS-C	Scientific Sub-Committee
TAC	total allowable catch
TF	Task Forces
TOMA	trophosphoric ozone management area
TSU	technical support unit

TWG	Technical Working Group
UES	uniform emission standard
UN	United Nations
UNCED	United Nations Conference on Environment and Development
UNECE	United Nations Economic Commission of Europe
UNEP	United Nations Environment Programme
UNESCO	United Nations Educational, Scientific and Cultural Organisation
UNFCCC	United Nations Framework Convention on Climate Change
UNGA	United Nations General Assembly
VOCs	Volatile organic compounds
WCP	World Climate Programme
WG	Working Group
WGAS	Working Group on Abatement Strategies
WGE	Working Group on Effects
WGI	Working Group I
WGII	Working Group II
WGIII	Workimg Group III
WGN	Working Group on NOx
WGS	Working Group on Strategies
WGT	Working Group on Technology
WGV	Working Group on VOCs
WHO	World Health Organisation
WMO	World Meteorological Organization
WPAP	Working Party on Air Pollution Problems

1 *Arild Underdal*

Science and politics: the anatomy of an uneasy partnership

Without knowledge there is no (perceived) problem, no public awareness and consequently no policy process ... (Jänicke, 1997: 7)

A review of most of the international treaties negotiated since the 1972
Stockholm conference shows that scientific evidence has played a sur-
prisingly small role in issue definition, fact-finding, bargaining, and
regime strengthening. (Susskind, 1994: 63)

1.1 The research question

This book has grown out of a shared long-term interest in understanding why some attempts at solving or alleviating international
environmental problems 'succeed' while others 'fail'. Through a
series of projects we have, individually or together, been searching
for answers along two main paths of research. One focuses attention
on the *nature of the problem*, the basic argument being that some
problems are intellectually less complicated or politically more
'benign' than others, and hence easier to solve. According to this
line of reasoning, the most successful attempts will be those that
deal with the easiest problems. The other path of research focuses
on *problem-solving capacity*. Here, the underlying assumption is
that some institutions (regimes) or systems are more capable than
others of solving a particular kind of problem. This proposition suggests that the problems that are most effectively solved will be those
that are attacked with the most powerful institutional tools or with
particular skill or energy.

We know that both these propositions have considerable merit
(see Miles *et al.*, forthcoming). In recent years we have, however,
come to focus more and more on the latter, for the following reason:

it seems fair to say that research on collective action has made more progress in describing and diagnosing problems than in specifying what determines our ability to solve them. Thanks very much to the application of game theory constructs to the analysis of international co-operation we now know quite well what distinguishes 'malign' problems from those that are 'benign'. However, we tend to get into substantially greater difficulties if asked to specify what characterises those institutions or systems that are most capable of solving partic- ular kinds of problems, and what precisely makes these institutions or systems more capable. This should be a matter of concern to any social scientist who would like to see his or her findings and propo- sitions used as inputs into the search for solutions. The practitioner needs not only a diagnosis of the problem; as important is knowledge about effective cures. By implication, the practitioner is likely to be at least as interested in factors enhancing problem-solving capacity as in understanding what makes some problems more difficult to solve than others. The basic research question addressed in this book is premised on that argument.

Problem-solving capacity is an elusive and very complex concept, requiring further specification. Suffice it here to say that in the con- text of international co-operation, the capacity of an institution or system to solve a particular problem can be seen as a function of its capability to perform two main functions – one basically intellec- tual, the other essentially political in nature. The *intellectual* chal- lenge is to identify and diagnose problems and come up with effective response measures. The *political* challenge is to mobilise a group of states or other actors to undertake collective action in pur- suit of an effective solution. At the interface between the intellectual and political spheres lies the task of transforming knowledge into premises for policy decisions. This book focuses on the latter process. We are, in other words, not concerned with the *production* of knowledge *per se*; this is *not* a study of how science itself is con- ducted. Nor is this book about the aggregation of preferences into substantive policy decisions.[1] Our interest focuses on the *utilisation* of scientific knowledge as input for international environmental policy. Our basic objective is to understand better what determines 'success' and 'failure' in this process. Consistent with our interest in factors that can be deliberately designed and used as instruments, we focus primarily on the impact of *institutional* arrangements. The question we try to answer in this book can be formulated as follows:

to what extent and how is the utilisation of research-based knowledge as input for international environmental policy affected by the way the science–politics dialogue is organised?

1.2 From knowledge to policy

This study is premised on two basic assumptions. First, we assume that for all practical purposes, adequate knowledge about the problem itself and available response options is a *necessary* – although by no means a sufficient – condition for designing and operating *effective* international regimes.[2] Knowledge is a necessary tool for diagnosing problems as well as for prescribing effective cures. We furthermore assume that scientific research is, at the very least, one major supplier of '*advanced*' knowledge. Science is certainly not the only supplier of knowledge, but the more sophisticated the measurements required and the more complex and less transparent the systems in question, the greater seems to be the advantage of systematic research over more impressionistic modes of generating knowledge. Many of the environmental issues on the current international agenda would not even have existed as recognised 'problems' had it not been for inputs from research. Stratospheric ozone depletion and climate change are only two of the most prominent examples.

From these two assumptions we infer that rational or informed management of the environment requires that findings and insights from relevant research be transformed into, and actively utilised as, premises for policy decisions.

These formulations probably generate as many questions as they answer. Moreover, we have come to learn that they also tend to generate important objections. For one thing, they might be read as implying that we consider 'knowledge' to be a straightforward concept, and that knowledge is what comes out of science. This would indeed be a most simplistic view of what is in fact a very complex relationship. The everyday meaning of knowledge seems to be well captured in one of the definitions offered by the *Webster Oxford English Dictionary*, as something that we (or, rather, the most competent men and women in the field) 'hold for true or real with assurance and (what is held to be) an adequate objective foundation'. What qualifies as 'knowledge' in a particular field is normally a matter of continuous and sometimes intense discussion within the scientific community itself.[3] We should recognise that the outputs of research range from weak hypotheses and tentative observations to propositions that are incorporated into 'core knowledge'. Moreover, some of the uncertainty pertaining to environmental changes may be attributed to inherent characteristics of nature itself rather than to imperfections in the state of knowledge. There is no way in which science can ever remove the hard core of uncertainty that is inherent in stochastic processes of nature or man. To complicate things further, even some of the propositions that are, by general consensus, considered 'core knowledge' at a particular point in time will often be rejected or modified substantially in light of new findings. What all this amounts to is the sombre conclusion that scientists quite often do not have (reliable) answers to the questions decision-makers wrestle with. And sometimes the answers scientists think they have turn out to be wrong, perhaps leaving decision-makers to regret that they ever listened.

Second, to say that knowledge is a necessary basis for designing and operating *effective* regimes does not imply that decision-makers cannot, do not or should not *act* in the absence of 'firm' knowledge. In fact, environmental policies will almost always have to be made on the basis of imperfect information about important aspects of the problem itself and/or the impact of alternative options. Precautionary action will usually have to rely at least as much on tentative hypotheses and unsubstantiated beliefs as on 'core knowledge'; this is precisely what makes it so vulnerable to objections. Moreover, the proposition that knowledge is a basis for rational management raises the question of *how much* knowledge is needed. The answer depends on the complexity and specification of the decision model and the purpose for which the model is used. The more complex and precise the notion of social welfare, and the finer we can 'tune' the policy response, the more extensive and exact knowledge is needed. In negotiating international regimes decision-makers most often focus on rather crude choices among a small number of discrete options, such as whether to declare an unconditional ban on dumping of a particular kind of toxic waste or simply require a government permit.[4] Moreover, they rarely have a precise set of agreed criteria against which alternative options can be evaluated. If the policy options considered are few and crude, and the notions of collective 'optima' diffuse, the choice of 'cure' is likely to be rather insensitive to the fine print of the 'diagnosis'. Even though some remarkable exceptions exist, it seems fair to say that international regulations are most often *not* derived from a precise formula specifying what constitutes the optimal response to a particular state of environmental degradation.

One reason why the science–politics relationship is so tenuous is, of course, that policy cannot simply be *derived* from knowledge, however firm the knowledge base may be. Research findings rarely, if ever, speak for themselves; no documentation of damage to nature by itself prescribes the optimal cure. Only when interpreted in a particular context and related to some particular concerns, interests and values can knowledge be 'used' by decision-makers. Our focus on the mechanisms by which this transformation occurs is motivated by the assumption that this is a quite sensitive and vulnerable process with a substantial risk of 'failure'. Moreover, policy will always to a very large extent have to be based on premises that science can *never* deliver. Thus, environmental policy will have to be guided by some notion of social welfare and some normative decision-rules for dealing with uncertainty (e.g. the 'precautionary principle'). Research can help clarify relevant criteria and the dilemmas and trade-offs involved, but the basic question of what shall be considered 'good' or 'bad' cannot be answered by science. To say that knowledge is a necessary input in environmental policy-making, and that science is a principal supplier of 'advanced' knowledge, is, in other words, not to suggest that politics is generally *led* by science – nor that it can or should be. However useful, *knowledge can be neither the master of, nor a substitute for, politics*.

Third, we suspect that some of our readers might interpret the assumptions formulated at the beginning of this section to reflect a naïve conception of the nature of science and politics – one in which science is seen as carrying the torch of light, guiding what Plato referred to as 'philosopher kings' in their altruistic search for the common good. Let us therefore pause to emphasise that we do not perceive scientific networks to be insular communities of intellectual eunuchs devoted exclusively to the pursuit of 'eternal truth' – in splendid isolation from the mundane concerns that plague governments and all other segments of society. There is no reason to believe that the production of knowledge should be the only productive activity in society that does not generate its own stakes for those involved. Although the ultimate purpose and rationale of science is to enhance our knowledge and understanding of nature,

humanity and society, scientists also have and often pursue their
own private concerns and (professional) interests. One of these private concerns is to secure funding and status. In some cases such
professional concerns and interests may even be hard to reconcile
with the official purpose of their work. Thus, as pointed out by
Boehmer-Christiansen (1993a), the wish to secure funds and sustain
interest in one's work tend to imply a predisposition to keep an
issue on the agenda and to emphasise the need for additional
research and more knowledge. From this perspective, science can be
seen also as 'an independent political actor with interests, institutions, and strategies' (Boehmer-Christiansen, 1997: 113).

Similarly, nothing of what we have said above should be con-
strued as implying that we perceive politics to be simply the enlightened pursuit of 'the common good'. Decision-makers typically have
multiple and sometimes conflicting concerns and objectives, some
of which can be quite remote from those enshrined in their official
roles. Particularly in the highly decentralised international system,
most actors will be more concerned about the interests of their own
domestic 'clients' than with some notion of global welfare. Whenever these interests diverge – as they normally do – decision-makers
may very well turn to science not (primarily) in search of 'truth' but
rather in search of selective *arguments* for positions into which they
are already deeply entrenched. Particularly in situations characterised by intense conflict, science is not only 'used' but as often
abused – legitimising rather than informing policy.

The upshot of all this is that the relationship between science and
politics is a complex and precarious one, vulnerable to various kinds
of aberrations and perversions on either side. It is characterised first
by *interdependence*. Even the most cynical observer would have to
admit that international environmental regimes tend to rely heavily
– though not necessarily systematically – on inputs that originated
in science. This applies in almost any field – from fisheries management to the control of greenhouse gas emissions – and to problem-
diagnosing as well as the search for solutions. It is, in fact, hard to
imagine how international governance in these areas could function
without such inputs. In this sense our initial assumptions seem war-
ranted. Moreover, there is no doubt that new knowledge sometimes
leads governments to change established positions. Although, for
example, the sharp turn-around in 1982–83 of the Federal Republic of Germany (FRG) in negotiations about 'acid rain' regulations

in Europe seems to have a rather complex explanation (see Boehmer-Christiansen and Skea, 1991), findings from recent research played an important role. This is not to say that governments easily sacrifice national interests in response to new pieces of evidence about links between human activities and environmental damage; rather, what happens is that governments sometimes *redefine* the national interest in light of new information.

Dependence is mutual, however. Not only are international environmental regimes dependent upon input from scientific research; (regulatory) science is itself to some extent dependent upon funding and other kinds of support from governments and other important actors. And such support is in turn to some degree contingent upon what science can deliver (or make decision-makers believe that it can deliver). In this sense, research 'thrives on ignorance and uncertainty' (Boehmer-Christiansen, 1997: 141). It is precisely this matching of demand and supply that provides the basis for the science–politics interface.

The complexity and precariousness of the relationship stems from the fact that science and politics are not only interdependent, they are also *basically different* spheres of human activities – pursuing distinctively different purposes with different means (see Chapter 2). At least in democratic political systems, the authority and status of science very much hinges on its disengagement and autonomy *vis-à-vis* government and social interest groups (March and Olsen, 1995: 101). At the same time, science augments its service to society by helping governments and societal actors to improve their understanding of the problems they are struggling to solve. This dualism makes for a very delicate balance between disengagement and autonomy on the one hand, and responsiveness and involvement on the other. Constructive use of input from scientific research in the making of environmental policy decisions seems to require that we find some way to combine or balance the integrity and autonomy of the scientific undertaking with responsiveness to the needs of decision-makers for diagnostic and therapeutic knowledge and involvement in problem-solving processes. Conversely, it also requires that decision-makers find some way not only to utilise the knowledge and insights that science has to offer, but also to ask policy-relevant questions without ordering particular answers or in other ways undermining the professionalism that makes scientific research the major supplier of 'advanced' knowledge.

This book explores *how* such a relationship can be accomplished. More precisely, we explore to *what extent and how the use of findings from relevant research as inputs into decision-making processes is affected by the way the science–politics dialogue is organised.* Our dependent variable is the extent to which outputs (findings, hypotheses) from scientific research are utilised or *adopted* (undistorted) as (consensual) premises for policy decisions. As used here, 'adoption' refers to the end product of what may be a complex process through which outputs of science are transformed into inputs to the policy-making process. Our independent variables are certain aspects of the institutional setting; more precisely, organisational arrangements and procedures. Our reason for focusing on institutional arrangements is *not* an assumption that these are necessarily the most important determinants of the rational utilisation of knowledge, or account for most of the variance that we can in fact observe in a given sample of cases. Rather, we focus on organisational aspects partly because their impact in this context is yet poorly understood, and partly because they are political constructs that can, at least in principle, be deliberately designed and manipulated by the actors themselves. Organisational arrangements and procedures constitute one class of instruments that decision-makers can use to achieve a particular goal.[5] In order to tap the potential of institutions-as-instruments, we need to understand *how* different institutional arrangements actually work, and *what* makes one work differently from another. The purpose of this study is to contribute to answering these basic questions.

The remaining sections of this chapter first clarify our *de*pendent variable, i.e., what we mean by the 'adoption' or 'utilisation' of conclusions from research as decision premises, and how we determine to what extent such adoption has in fact occurred. Then we identify those aspects of the institutional setting that are examined in this study (i.e., our *in*dependent variables), and introduce three 'non-institutional' factors that we believe can affect the extent to which inputs from science are adopted by decision-makers. In our design, the latter factors are treated partly as control variables, and partly as background variables. Finally, we introduce our five empirical cases and add a few words about a couple of the methodological problems that we have faced in pursuing our research question.

1.3 The dependent variable

We propose to conceive of the 'adoption' of findings and hypotheses from research in terms of a cumulative scale with three levels.[6] At the first and lowest level decision-makers 'tune in' to science, i.e., they *recognise the relevance and usefulness* of the kinds of knowledge that scientists produce, and look to the scientific community for information, models and theories. Scientists are considered competent experts, and decision-makers have a substantial amount of (diffuse) confidence in science as an 'undertaking'. The more relevant and useful science is considered to be, the more likely that we will see some regular channels for communication being established. At the second level decision-makers also accept as valid or tenable the *substantive conclusions* that meet the standards of the scientific community itself. Whatever the transnational community of scientists considers, by general (though not necessarily universal) consensus, to be the best knowledge so far available is also by and large accepted as such by decision-makers. At the third level decision-makers accept not only factual conclusions but also what might be called the 'policy implications' of these conclusions, and respond positively to more explicit advice offered by the scientific community.[7] At this level inputs from scientists are adopted by decision-makers as to some degree *guiding policy*, not merely informing deliberations.

This scale can be considered *cumulative* in the sense that higher levels can be reached only through the preceding step(s). It is hard to imagine that decision-makers will accept the curative implications of a diagnosis they reject,[8] and it is equally hard to imagine that they will genuinely accept as valid the substantive conclusions offered by a particular scientific community unless they place a certain minimum of confidence in the professional competence and moral integrity of that community.

Even though we conceive of these as distinct levels of utilisation or adoption, we do recognise that at each level adoption is a matter of degree. Clearly, the amount of confidence in the validity of a certain proposition or diagnosis can vary significantly. Similarly, decision-makers may very well respond positively to a certain diagnosis or piece of advice without taking all the steps required to solve the problem. Quite often decision-makers respond by taking some limited steps to control emissions or reduce levels of exploitation without achieving what scientists would consider the 'perfect' solution. We shall here consider even a small step to cure or alleviate the problem as a positive response. In the empirical analysis we will not be able to measure 'degree of adoption' with high precision at any of the three levels. We nevertheless believe that this crude scale provides a useful conceptual grid for empirical research, enabling us to compare cases in soft, ordinal-scale terms that will make intuitive sense also to the practitioners concerned.

1.4 Independent variables

We have already suggested that a key to a constructive relationship between science and politics is to combine or strike an optimal balance between the autonomy and integrity of science on the one hand, and involvement and responsiveness to the concerns or 'needs' of decision-makers on the other. Seen from the perspective of decision-makers *as a group*, confidence in scientists and their findings seems to rest on two basic assumptions: competence and integrity.[9] The principal reason why decision-makers and the attentive public look to science for information and guidance is confidence in the competence of scientists as producers and custodians of advanced and reliable knowledge. Similarly, one main reason why they often collectively accept the conclusions produced by research as valid is confidence in scientists as 'truth-seekers', strongly committed to the professional methods and norms of scientific inquiry, and collecting and analysing evidence independent of any substantive interests that a government or other parties may pursue. Although some individual scientists may fail to meet these high standards, decision-makers may have confidence in the ability of the *community* of scholars through its pluralism, competitive structure, and procedures of critical peer review to correct such aberrations, at least in the longer run. All this suggests that confidence in the autonomy and integrity of science at least comes close to being a necessary condition for the *collective* adoption of inputs at all levels.

Confidence is not enough, however. For inputs to be utilised they must also be seen as *relevant* to the concerns of decision-makers. This is where responsiveness and involvement enter the equation. The standard reporting of research results rarely offers knowledge in the form of handy, ready-to-use modules. A substantial amount of translation and adaptation is often required before knowledge can be utilised by decision-makers. This applies at all levels of adoption, but it seems particularly critical at the third level. For decision-makers to respond positively to policy implications or explicit advice, they will want to make sure that factual conclusions are given in a frame of reference that they recognise as compatible with their own, or that recommendations for actions are framed to address *their* problems. A minimum of responsiveness to the concerns of decision-makers and some interactive dialogue are likely to help.

We may then ask: to what extent are autonomy and integrity compatible with responsiveness and involvement? Can autonomy and integrity be preserved only at the expense of isolation in the ivory tower of Academia? This question is a complex one, and calls for a somewhat different kind of analysis than we can offer here. We shall, however, return to this question in the concluding section. Suffice it here to say that our initial assumption is that, up to a certain level, responsiveness and involvement are indeed compatible with autonomy and integrity. However, we also believe that as we move beyond that level there is a price to be paid for strong and direct involvement in the policy-making process, and that some sacrifice of autonomy will be part of that price. Looking at the science–politics interface in this perspective, the optimal relationship seems to be one where science enjoys great autonomy and engages itself only to a *moderate* extent and perhaps only *indirectly* – i.e., through some intermediate 'agent' – in the policy-making process. And responsiveness should take the form of efforts to address the concerns and *questions* that decision-makers are wrestling with, not to accommodate any preferences that they might have with regard to the substantive contents of the *answers*.

1.4.1 Autonomy and integrity

The autonomy and integrity of a particular network or body of scientists may be conceived of as a function of multiple variables. The list below is by no means exhaustive, but we have found it useful as a checklist for the empirical case studies to follow.

1 Selection and funding of the scientists involved:
    a Who selects the scientists involved: (non-governmental) scientific organisation(s), independent of the *regulatory* body,

national governments, intergovernmental organisation (IGO)
(i.e., the regulatory body)?

b Who funds the research?

2 Principal criteria for the selection of participants:

 a Is entry open to any participant nominated by a member country, or subject to (firm) restrictions?

 b To the extent that entry is restricted, what are the principal
 criteria for appointment: scholarly merits v. other criteria
 (nationality, ideology, formal position, etc.)?

3 Operational autonomy:

 a To what extent are the scientists, considered as a group, free to
 organise their own work? Can they, for example, set their own
 agendas and decide on the division of labour and the allocation of specific roles such as principal investigators, rappor-
 teurs etc.?

4 Main function:

 a Production of new knowledge; participants are themselves
 actively conducting research.

 b Participants are mainly *co-ordinating* (and supervising)
 research.

 c Participants are essentially translating existing knowledge into
 decision premises; their main contribution is to elaborate
 'policy implications' of existing knowledge.

5 Unity and homogeneity of scientific body/network:

 a Does the network have its own 'institutional basis', i.e., some
 internal co-ordinating device?

 b Are all members scientists (i.e., people presumed to spend a
 substantial portion of their time in active research), or does it
 also include administrators and other non-scientists?

These dimensions may be combined to construct an index, as indicated in Table 1.1.

1.4.2 Responsiveness and involvement

We have so far used two words to describe this dimension: responsiveness and involvement. We conceive of 'responsiveness' as essentially an *attitudinal* variable, referring to the willingness and
readiness of the scientific community to address the concerns and
questions of policy-makers. We use the term 'involvement' to refer
to *behaviour*, more precisely participation in problem-solving
processes. Since attitudes tend to be more difficult to study than

Table 1.1   *Index of autonomy/integrity*

High autonomy/integrity	Low autonomy/integrity
Selected and funded by scientific organisation or the IGO itself	Selected and funded by national governments
Recruitment based on scholarly merits or role in scientific community	Recruitment based on political position or administrative office
High operational autonomy; sets its own agenda and organises its own work	Under effective instruction and control by governments
Participants engaged in active research, or at least in co-ordination of active research	Mainly concerned with policy implications
Independent internal co-ordination; scientists only	No independent institutional basis; mixed composition

manifest behaviour, we shall focus essentially on involvement. More specifically, we suggest that the *involvement* of the research community in the policy-making process can be seen as a function of the extent to which it is engaged in formulating policy advice (item 4 in Table 1.1), and the organisational variables listed below (and see Table 1.2).

6 Functional differentiation – coupling between research and advice:

   a To the extent that the formulation of policy advice is part of the scientists' agenda, do the same scientists that are supposed to *produce* knowledge also formulate explicit advice, or are the functions separated, i.e., performed by different experts?

   b To the extent that the functions are separated, how great is the 'organisational distance' between the actual research activities and the formulation of policy advice?

7 Formal links to decision-making body:

   a Does the scientific network or body have a regular channel for communicating findings and advice to the decision-making body?

   b Is there a regular channel whereby the decision-making body can put questions to the body of scientists involved?

   c Is there a regular dialogue about conclusions between scientists and decision-makers, or at least some kind of feedback

from decision-makers (in the form of requests for more information, follow-up questions, criticism or support, etc.)?

Table 1.2 *Index of involvement*

High involvement	Low involvement
Scientists formulate policy advice	Scientists engage in research and research management only
Little or no organisational 'distance' between research and advice functions	Great organisational 'distance'
Regular channels of communication, working both ways	No regular channels

Clearly, Tables 1.1 and 1.2 outline ideal-type constructs. For most
of the actual cases analysed here, scores will probably fall some-
where in between. For example, the specificity of policy advice provided may vary considerably. In some cases, scientists would only
indicate what would be required to achieve a certain hypothetical
goal, e.g., the stabilisation of CO_2 concentrations in the atmosphere
without actually *prescribing* the goal of stabilisation itself. In other
cases scientists may take steps towards recommending a certain
target and/or prescribing one particular strategy for achieving this
target. Other things being equal, we would consider scientists in the
latter category to be 'more involved' in the policy process than the
former.

Suggesting that the factors listed can be combined to form
indexes, as we have done in Tables 1.1 and 1.2, immediately raises
the question of whether or not all of these factors can be considered
equally important. In the comparative analysis we shall have to rely
heavily on aggregate assessments of each case, but in the individual
case studies we shall look also for evidence that might indicate that
one particular factor or mechanism was particularly important. An
even more intriguing question is whether two or more of these factors can *interact* to produce effects that cannot be attributed to any
of them individually. Can we, for example, point to one particular
combination of high *and* low scores on different dimensions of
autonomy that seems particularly productive? What if we have a

strong core of independent scientists and add a set of administrators or scientists nominated by governments to serve as their representatives? Would the former educate or 'socialise' the latter, or would the political agents 'contaminate' the scientific process? To the extent that the core of independent scientists dominates the interaction, we might see the development of a particularly potent 'epistemic community' (Haas 1990; 1992a), where the supervisors act as *de facto* agents of a transnational coalition, and by virtue of their links to their respective governments also exercise more influence on their domestic arenas. These are very complex questions that we cannot explore in depth here. The point we want to make at this stage is simply that the indexes outlined in Tables 1.1 and 1.2 should be considered primarily as crude *checklists* for comparative analysis, not used mechanically as finely calibrated instruments capable of providing cardinal scale measurements of autonomy/integrity and involvement.

1.5 Control/background variables

We have already explained that our interest in *institutional* arrangements is not based on an assumption that these are necessarily the most important determinants of how input from science is adopted as a premise for policy. A wide range of other factors may be equally or even more important. In an earlier article, Underdal (1989) pointed to nine factors that seem to affect the use of scientific knowledge as inputs into environmental policy-making processes (Table 1.3).

In this analysis we have decided to pay particular attention to two of these variables:

1 The *state of knowledge*; in particular the conclusiveness of available scientific evidence and the scope of uncertainty and ambiguity of findings reported in previous research. The general assumption is that other things being equal the less conclusive the evidence, the less likely that it will be utilised as a basis for joint policy decisions. If the state of knowledge is very poor, there is simply nothing for decision-makers to adopt.

2 The *political malignancy* of the problem itself (cf. Underdal, 1987). Other things being equal, the more politically malign the problem, the more conflict it tends to generate, and the less likely

Table 1.3 *Conditions affecting the impact of scientific inputs*

Impact likely to be strong	Impact likely to be weak
Definite or at least consensual conclusion	Tentative or contested hypothesis
Feasible 'cure' available	'Cure' unclear or not feasible
Effects close in time	Effects remote
Problem affecting social centre of society	Problem affecting periphery only
Problem developing rapidly and surprisingly	Problem developing slowly and according to expectations
Effects experienced by, or at least visible to, the public	Effects not (yet) experienced by, or visible to, the public
Political conflict: low	Political conflict: high
Issue linkage: none or on substantive merits only	Tactical issue linkage: Issue contamination
Institutionalised setting, iterative decision-making	Not yet institutionalised, *ad hoc* decision-making

Source: Underdal, 1989: 259.

that anything but the most conclusive evidence will be generally accepted as a basis for collective action.

A third variable that seems to interact with the latter is the *public saliency* of the problem. High saliency probably boosts the demand for knowledge and advice, but the impact on adoption seems to be contingent upon the kind of problem encountered. For benign problems high saliency is likely to have a (weak) positive effect, but for strongly malign problems saliency may very well serve to politicise the issue further, thereby creating a climate in which the rational use of inputs from science becomes very difficult. In brief, then, we expect saliency to *reinforce* rather than change the pattern hypothesised below.

These variables are expected to influence the adoption of inputs from research directly as well indirectly, i.e., through their impact on institutional arrangements.[10] In its most simple representation, our core model can thus be drawn up as shown in Figure 1.1.

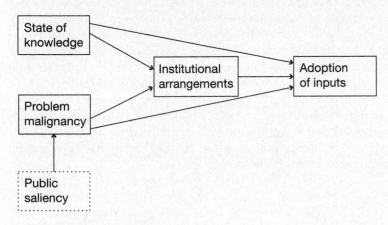

Figure 1.1 *The core model*

More specifically, we expect our two main control variables to affect level of adoption as indicated in Table 1.4.

Table 1.4 *Hypothesised impact of state of knowledge and problem malignancy*

Type of problem	State of knowledge		
	Poor	Intermediate	Good
Clearly malign	0	1 (0)	1 (2)
Mixed	0 (1)	1 (2)	2–3
Clearly benign	0–1	2 (3)	3 (2)

Note: figures in cells refer to levels of adoption (see p. 9). Figures in parentheses indicate 'second guesses', i.e., the direction in which we expect to see deviance from our hypothesised pattern.

We expect institutional arrangements to affect level of adoption primarily when the state of knowledge is good or intermediate. Moreover, we expect institutional arrangements to make less difference at the extremes (upper left-hand and lower right-hand cells) than in the middle; in particular, the combination of poor knowledge and strong malignancy is normally beyond rescue. We make modest claims on behalf of institutional arrangements. More precisely, we expect state of knowledge and type of problem to account for more of the variance in level of adoption. What we can realistically expect from a 'good' institutional set-up is that it will enable us to accomplish the *higher* rather than the lower score *within* the intervals indicated in Table 1.4. Finally, we expect state of knowledge and type of problem to affect the kind of institutional arrangements that are feasible. Basically, we expect problem malignancy to threaten autonomy and integrity (but enhance involvement), while a poor state of knowledge generates low demand and limited involvement (without threatening autonomy).

1.6 Cases

In subsequent chapters we present five case studies, all focusing on international regimes for management of natural resources and the environment:

- The International Convention for the Regulation of Whaling (ICRW)
- The Paris Convention for the Prevention of Marine Pollution from Land-Based Sources (PARCON) and the North Sea Conferences.
- The Economic Commission for Europe (ECE) Convention on Long-Range Transboundary Air Pollution (LRTAP)
- The international protocols on measures to prevent the depletion of stratospheric ozone
- The Global Climate Change Convention.

These five cases have been selected partly on pragmatic grounds (prior knowledge), and partly to provide a sufficient range of variance in terms of our dependent and independent variables. Pragmatic considerations spoke in favour of focusing on cases for which we already had a fair amount of data available and/or good secondary sources to build on. All five cases meet at least the former criterion; each case is fairly well known from previous research to at least one of us. In terms of variance we initially had three considerations in mind. First, we wanted to cover different kinds of reg-

ulatory problems, that called for the use of different kinds of regulatory instruments. The basic rationale here is that the demand for
scientific knowledge (and for various kinds of inputs) to some
extent depends on the purpose for which it is to be used. In operational terms we translated this concern into the coverage of both
resource use and pollution control regimes. Second, we wanted to
study regimes that are homogeneous in membership as well as
regimes that are more heterogeneous, the underlying assumption
being that the diversity of interests and the differences in capabilities to acquire and utilise scientific knowledge will increase with
heterogeneity. Our sample ranges from what started out as a small
'whalers' club' to the very heterogeneous global climate change
regime. Finally, we wanted to cover a time span of at least three to
four decades, the rationale being that we expect some amount of
learning to occur. In this sense the more recent cases may to some
extent have incorporated experiences accumulated through previous efforts. We are, in other words, interested not only in comparative statistics but also in patterns of historical development.

1.7 A brief note on method

The reader should recognise that all of our key concepts are hard to
measure accurately, and that the operational indicators we use do
not capture fully the contents of the concepts. For example, the concept of 'adoption', which is a key word in our definition of the
dependent variable, refers to a cognitive operation that is not
directly observable. We therefore have to base our scores on indirect
evidence, more precisely on what actors say and do. Clearly, this
approach is fraught with pitfalls; propositions and findings from
research may sometimes be invoked without being adopted in a gen-
uine sense. Similarly, the concepts of 'autonomy' and 'involvement'
will here have to be studied by means of structural and behavioural
indicators that do not tap the cognitive or affective aspects, which
determine an actor's own *sense* of being autonomous or involved.
The latter may in some respects be equally important. We have tried
to supplement documentary material with interviews to get some
rough impressions of actor perceptions and evaluations, but we
make no claims to have penetrated the cognitive aspects of our core
concepts.

Moreover, we should like to point out that although guided by a common research question and a common conceptual framework, this study should be read essentially as an exploratory venture into a poorly charted terrain rather than as an attempt at rigorous testing of a set of precise hypotheses. The fact that we start our empirical work without a well-developed model, let alone a coherent theory, explains why we have decided to provide rather 'thick' descriptions of each case, casting the net somewhat widely in a search for clues that can help us understand how the science–politics relationship has evolved and functions. The reader should, however, find a common analytical framework, and our main conclusions will be based on a systematic, comparative analysis.

Notes

1 This topic is analysed in another study to which three of us have contributed (Miles *et al.*, forthcoming).
2 In theory there is, of course, a possibility that 'optimal' solutions may be developed from a 'false' understanding of the problem, or that a particular problem can be solved as a side-effect of actions undertaken for other purposes. It seems equally obvious, however, that it would be foolhardy to *base* one's policies on such fortuities.
3 We have more to say about this process in Chapter 2.
4 There are some instances, though, where regulatory decisions are – at least in principle – supposed to be fine-tuned to the description and diagnosis of the problem. Regulations of fishing effort and catch – based on notions such as 'maximum sustainable yield' – and regulations tuned to the demanding concept of 'critical loads' (notably the latest ECE Convention on Long-Range Transboundary Air Pollution [LRTAP] protocol) are good examples.
5 We do realise that this instrumental perspective is open to serious challenges. Thus, Scott (1981) distinguishes three basic conceptions of organisations: organisations as 'rational', 'natural' and 'open' systems. In his words, 'Rational systems are designed, but natural systems evolve; the former develop by conscious design, the latter by natural growth; rational systems are characterised by calculation, natural by spontaneity' (Scott, 1981: 101). The description of 'natural' systems seems to apply quite well to the scientific community. We should also recognise that organisational arrangements may have considerable *symbolic* value for both sides. Even though our perspective is somewhat narrow in the sense that it focuses on only one particular aspect, we believe that the problem it addresses is real and important. We assume, in other words, that there is *some* scope for deliberate organisational

design, and that instrumental concerns provide important and legitimate design criteria.

6 In addition, there is, of course, the possibility of a 'zero score', i.e. complete neglect of science.

7 We shall have to ask our readers to accept a rather loose definition of the term 'policy implications' in this context. What we refer to here is the kind of *conditional* normative 'implications' that follows when a certain factual statement is linked to the official purpose of a particular regime. Take, for example, a regime for regulating marine fisheries. The official purpose of most such rgimes is to provide for 'rational' use of the resources, meaning – *inter alia* – 'sustainable' levels of catch. Coupled to this particular regime purpose, a factual statement saying that the current level of exploitation is rapidly depleting fish stocks can be said to imply the policy conclusion that *for the purpose to be achieved* the catch level will have to be reduced.

8 It is, though, conceivable that they will accept a piece of advice *for some other reason*, e.g. because it happens to coincide with the implications of another diagnosis to which they subscribe, or because it can be used to promote their own interests. In the latter case it is accepted as *tactically useful* rather than scientifically valid.

9 For each individual decision-maker, confidence may be based instead on a combination of competence and a belief that the expert is 'on our side' or at least 'sympathetic to our cause'. When we are dealing with 'malign' issues, however, this can hardly be a recipe for *collective* confidence, which is our concern here.

10 In such a case, they are treated as background variables.

2 Tora Skodvin and Arild Underdal

Exploring the dynamics of the science–politics interaction

2.1 Introduction

Science and politics constitute two distinct and different systems of behaviour. Some may even characterise the difference as one of opposite poles, where science is everything politics is not: pure, objective, governed by rational analytic reasoning and thus not hostage to subjective biases, manipulation tactics or coercive power – ingredients often associated with politics. According to this view the distinction between science and politics is clear-cut. The ideal relationship between science and politics is seen as one where knowledge – generated by competent, truth-seeking scientists working in accordance with stringent professional standards – is *communicated*, undistorted, to decision-makers who then *utilise* it as factual premises for policy decisions. In its interaction with politics, science must above all remain science and never blend with politics; any adoption of the modes of operation that characterise politics constitutes 'contamination' and will inevitably lead to the perversion of science. And if science is perverted, policy will suffer, at least in the longer run.

This 'purist' image of science and politics is extreme in the sense that it juxtaposes ideal-type constructs rather than real-world systems of activities. Experience from science–politics dialogues shows that the relationship between the two is far more complex than the purist view would indicate. It *is* true that science and politics constitute distinct and different systems of behaviour – each with its own constitutive norms and rules and its own internal logic. However, the process through which scientific knowledge is *transformed* into decision premises is neither pure science nor pure politics. It combines elements from both realms and adds its own distinctive characteristics. It is this process of transformation that constitutes the focus of this study.

This chapter explores briefly how distinctive features of science and politics, in their pure forms, are brought to bear on the process of transformation. Furthermore, it takes a first look at the unique dynamics that are generated when these elements are combined. We proceed in three steps. In section 2.2 we take a brief look at the internal dynamics of the process by which *science* produces *knowledge*. In section 2.3 we do a similar investigation into distinctive characteristics of the processes through which *politics* produce *decisions*. In the final section of the chapter, we use these two pictures as a background to explore the nature of the dynamics that are generated when science and politics *interact*. We should like to emphasise that our ambitions in this chapter are strictly limited; all we try to do is to offer a glimpse into the *dynamics* of the process through which research-based knowledge is transformed into inputs for policy. It should not be read as a study of the modes of operation of science or politics *per se*.

2.2 The internal dynamics of science

2.2.1 *What qualifies as 'knowledge'?*
An attempt to specify the internal norms and logic that characterise science is a fairly complex task that leads straight into the more fundamental question of what 'science' *is*. Each of the meta-scientific disciplines (philosophy, sociology, psychology, anthropology, etc., all with the postscript 'of science') have formulated their own answers, each emphasising different features and concentrating on different aspects, and each with a tendency to treat its own definition as self-sufficient (see Ziman, 1984).

The traditional view of science portrays research as a rational, rule-governed process, in which stringent implementation of 'the scientific method' is the main mechanism whereby established 'knowledge' is distinguished from mere knowledge *claims*. The scientific method constitutes, according to this view, the common framework within which hypotheses and theories are developed and tested, as well as functioning as the main arbiter of disputes over what is 'true'. 'Knowledge' is what the community of competent scientists holds to be 'true' on the basis of extensive scrutiny in accordance with demanding and discriminating methods. One important implication of this line of reasoning is that, in order to qualify as 'knowledge', a proposition must be *consensual* or inter-subjective in the sense that any competent scientist, applying the scientific method correctly, will reach the same conclusion. Should scientific disagreement occur, there are only two possible explanations: either at least one of the researchers is biased (i.e., not genuinely seeking the 'truth'), or at least one of them has applied the scientific method erroneously (see, for instance, Collingridge and Reeve, 1986). Accordingly, true knowledge can – with some reservations – be distinguished from mere knowledge claims by the operational criterion of *consensus* among competent and serious scientists.

The role of consensus in science has been subject to intense debate among philosophers[1] and sociologists[2] of science. This debate has demonstrated that the relationship between scientific consensus and 'knowledge' is not as simple as the traditional view would lead us to believe. Yet, the notion that consensus among competent scientists is an important feature of established knowledge seems to be firmly embedded within both of these research traditions. A common understanding seems now to prevail in which it is recognised that scientists do operate, at any given time, within frameworks of generally accepted theories and propositions constituting the basis for further research. At the same time, it is also recognised that these frameworks of corroborated theories and propositions are subject to continuous change, either as the result of an evolutionary process, or through abrupt 'revolutions'. What constitutes generally accepted knowledge at point T does not necessarily do so at point $T1$. The mechanisms at work in these shifts are debated. More generally, there is disagreement regarding the mechanisms by which knowledge becomes 'established' – that is, about the nature of the *process* by which consensus is developed and propositions acquire the status of 'knowledge'.

2.2.2 The development of consensus in science
In his seminal book *The Structure of Scientific Revolutions* (1970, first published 1962), Kuhn maintains that scientists operate within the framework of 'paradigms' – i.e. 'universally recognised scientific achievements that for a time provide model problems and solutions to a community of practitioners' (Kuhn, 1970: viii)[3] – and that in

the development of paradigms non-scientific and social factors may also determine scientists' choice of theory.

Kuhn's study became a catalyst in the development of the field known as social studies of scientific knowledge.[4] According to this school, Kuhn's analysis convincingly demonstrated that the criteria by which 'good' research is distinguished from 'poor' are constituted by scientific knowledge itself (see, for instance, Shapin, 1993), and hence that the process whereby consensus in science is established and maintained becomes open to sociological analysis (Mulkay, 1978). Building on Kuhn, some sociologists maintain that there is not one, but several social orders in science. Hence, there are also several sets of rules and norms employed by scientists both in the conduct of research and in the evaluation of knowledge (Shapin, 1993). This also has implications for the development of consensus. Mulkay argues that consensus only occurs under certain conditions: when 'scientists share a common scientific/technical background' and 'are able to select for attention problems which they judge to be solvable within their common framework' (Mulkay 1978: 111). According to Mulkay, therefore, 'scientific consensus … is seldom complete and its establishment may well depend on such socio-cultural factors as the selection of problems for which technically defined solutions appear likely as well as on the application of a relatively uniform scientific perspective' (Mulkay 1978: 111).

Another central proposition derived from this school of thought is a conception of the internal processes of knowledge production as processes of *informal negotiations* among scientists (see also Kuhn, 1991). Mulkay, for instance, argues that, 'scientific consensus in research networks seems to be achieved, at least partly, by processes of informal negotiation between participants who have certain shared as well as certain conflicting interests' (Mulkay 1978: 111). This perspective has also been developed in numerous studies of the nature of laboratory work – a tradition of which Latour and Woolgar's analysis from 1979 is representative. A major proposition in these studies is that social processes influencing the construction of scientific knowledge are at work not only in 'borderline' cases where science interacts with policy in more direct ways – such as, for instance, when scientific communities are called upon to give advice in processes of policy-making[5] – but also in the routine work of 'normal' science. Negotiation is, according to

Latour and Woolgar, one of several micro-processes whereby 'facts' are established or socially constructed and acquire the status of 'knowledge'.

The *implications* of this observation are, however, not at all obvious. Stephen Cole argues that while these studies of 'laboratory life' demonstrate that certain 'a-rational' or even 'ir-rational' features associated with what Kuhn has labelled the 'context of discovery' exist, they fail to demonstrate that these features have a significant impact upon the substantive *content* of the knowledge produced (Cole, 1992: 102). By failing to give an account of what happens to the knowledge claims of laboratory work in terms of *communal acceptance*, argues Cole, these studies also fail to demonstrate any causal link between social variables and specific propositions or conclusions.

Cole furthermore conceptualises scientific knowledge in terms of two types of knowledge; knowledge in the 'core' and knowledge at the 'frontier'. The core constitutes the starting-point, or the knowledge scientists take more or less as a given. The core is characterised by 'substantial consensus' and comprises what we normally refer to as 'facts': knowledge that is judged by the scientific community to be both true and important (Cole, 1992: 15). The research frontier, on the other hand, 'consists of all the work currently being produced by all active researchers in a given discipline' (Cole 1992: 15). In contrast to knowledge incorporated in the hard core, knowledge at the research frontier takes the form of 'soft' hypotheses and propositions with question marks attached. Hence, the crucial variable distinguishing core from frontier knowledge is that while the former is considered – at least for the time being – to be beyond dispute, the latter is still open to falsification and diverging interpretations.

This very brief survey cannot do justice to the richness of these traditions of research. None the less, it should suffice to demonstrate that while the notion of consensus as a criterion of core knowledge has a strong position among philosophers and sociologists of science, there is a continuous debate regarding the intellectual and social mechanisms at work in processes of consensus formation. Most importantly, it demonstrates that divergent interpretations among scientists are not necessarily a symptom of incompetence or lack of professional integrity; rather, confrontation between competing hypotheses and interpretations is an essential driving force for the development of knowledge at the research frontier. The kind of input that research can offer to the development of a proactive environmental policy will to a large extent be in the form of 'soft' frontier knowledge. This is exactly what makes this input and the scientific enterprise itself so vulnerable in the encounter with *politics*, a system of activities governed by different rules and generating its own internal dynamics.

2.3 The internal dynamics of politics

While the purpose of research is to produce *knowledge*, the purpose of politics is to produce *authoritative decisions* on behalf of a society or group. In some cases – notably those that can be considered 'benign' co-ordination problems – political decision-making can be described essentially as a question of finding 'good' solutions to promote common interests. In more 'malign' cases, characterised by some degree of conflict of interests or values, politics often turn into games of *bargaining*. In bargaining, one party's success to some extent depends on how well it can defend or promote its own interests *vis-à-vis* those of its opponent(s). This has profound implications for the way information and knowledge is viewed. In the realm of science, the ultimate criterion for evaluating hypotheses and propositions is *truth*.[6] The corresponding criterion in politics is *usefulness*. The relationship between these two concerns is not at all straightforward.

For one thing, the usefulness of knowledge as input into policy-making processes is not merely a function of its scientific merit, but as much a question of its *relevance* to the particular political objectives pursued. Truth and accuracy are, in other words, certainly not *sufficient* conditions for usefulness. More critical from our perspective is the question of whether truth is a *necessary* condition for usefulness. The answer is more complex than one might like to think.

As a point of departure, we can assume that each party will want *for itself* the best information available about the nature and causes of the problem and the effects of alternative solutions. It may not want all the fine print; for a decision-maker, knowledge will normally at some point become subject to the law of diminishing returns. Accordingly, beyond a certain level, further 'perfection' tends to be less highly valued by its prospective users than by its producers. There may even be circumstances of severe stress in which a decision-maker just does not want to know – at least not right *now*. Such circumstances can, though, safely be seen as exceptions; the general rule clearly is that decision-makers normally wants to know 'the truth' themselves. It is, however, not at all obvious that they will want *others* to have equally accurate information.

Consider, first, the 'benign' case where values and interests converge. Under such circumstances actors will probably want their partners to have a good understanding of the problem and alternative solutions. In more 'malign' situations where values and interests diverge, however, actors may well find that their own interests are best served if opponents possess *inferior* knowledge. More generally, actors may want their opponents to have inferior knowledge whenever (a) their own interests or values are in conflict with their opponents', and (b) accurate information is believed to favour one set of values or interests relative to another. In these circumstances, incentives for distorting or manipulating information are inherent in the strategic logic of politics and bargaining. Realising that this is so, parties often take some kind of precautionary measures, such as discounting information that they suspect may be manipulated. The fear of becoming victim to manipulation may sometimes be exaggerated and lead a party to discount also what is in fact 'solid knowledge'. Fortunately, the fact that the temptation exists does not mean that everyone will necessarily succumb. In most cases, there will be important constraints operating – in the form of internalised norms or fear of external sanctions. Moreover, even in situations of conflict, a party will usually also want its opponents to have a thorough understanding of the essential features of their common problem. The bottom line is none the less clear: in politics, information and knowledge become subject to *strategic* evaluation in terms of their value as *tools* for achieving political objectives. To the extent that this perspective penetrates the realm of science, it becomes *potentially* devastating. This is what makes the encounter between science and politics so problematic. Science is the more vulnerable party and therefore likely to become the first victim. But if science succumbs to politics, policy will suffer in the end.

2.4 The dynamics of science–politics interaction

If political controversy penetrates the realm of science it can effectively undermine the mechanisms by which the research community itself establishes 'knowledge'. As we have seen, research produces 'knowledge' by critically examining alternative hypotheses and propositions according to scientific standards of validity and tenability. Only propositions that survive prolonged and critical scrutiny by competent scientists can qualify as 'knowledge'. To the extent that the research community itself comes to evaluate a certain proposition in terms of its strategic 'usefulness' as a tool for achieving a particular political objective rather than in terms of its scientific merits, the process by which 'knowledge' is established becomes impaired, at least as far as politically 'malign' issues are concerned. Collingridge and Reeve even argue that,

> relevance to policy, by itself, is sufficient to completely destroy the delicate mechanisms by which scientists normally ensure that their work leads to agreement. Consensus on scientific questions which are more than marginally relevant to policy is therefore impossible. Science under these conditions leads not to agreement, but to endless technical bickering about an ever growing number of issues. (Collingridge and Reeve, 1986: ix–x)

To further complicate matters, the selective use of propositions or research-based knowledge as political tools may lead to a process in which each new policy argument that is introduced with a scientific justification generates efforts on the part of opponents to attack the legitimacy of that justification. As pointed out by Litfin, 'the cultural role of science as a key source of legitimation means that political debates are framed in scientific terms; questions of value become reframed as questions of fact, with each confrontation leading to the search for further scientific justification. Paradoxically, the demand for legitimation results in a process of delegitimation' (Litfin, 1994: 4).

In sum, we see that by interacting with politics science runs a risk of suffering a double loss. First, the mechanisms by which it produces 'knowledge' may be impaired. Second, when its results are invoked to promote the interests of one side in a political conflict, the other side may well try to undermine the status of these propositions as 'knowledge' and/or question the competence and integrity of the scientists involved.

Some argue that these risks pertain essentially to soft frontier knowledge.[7] According to this view, science can play a constructive role in policy-making only when it can offer established 'facts' as opposed to tentative hypotheses. Contamination and the justification –de-legitimisation spiral are both due to the fact that someone is trying to apply propositions which have not yet attained the status of core knowledge. If only policy-makers were willing to wait for the scientific process to run its course until broad consensus is reached within the scientific community, these problems would not arise.

This line of argument does not, however, address the real dilemma. As pointed out above, 'science for environmental policy' will to a very large extent *have to be* soft frontier knowledge. Policy-makers cannot simply wait for science to produce conclusive evidence; any *pro*-active environmental policy will have to be formulated in a context of uncertainty. Equally important: when research-based knowledge is used as input into policy-making processes, it will usually be taken out of its original context and (re-)interpreted within a new framework. Whether core or frontier knowledge, inputs for policy will always be an *interpretation* of the policy *implications* of conclusions that research itself produced. Very few, if any, pieces of (core) knowledge are readily available for policy-makers simply to 'apply' in a straightforward manner. One indication of this is that 'members of the same specialized and mature research community frequently reach different conclusions when they try to apply their expertise in practical situations' (Mulkay, 1978: 118). Mulkay interprets this to suggest that 'intellectual consensus in science is relatively loose and flexible, and that its content is open to interpretation in numerous directions' (Mulkay, 1978: 118). And only when *interpreted* in the context of a particular policy problem, can knowledge be utilised as policy premises (see also Jasanoff, 1990; Litfin, 1994; Sundquist, 1978).

We can now see why the optimistic view that consensus within the scientific community on 'facts' will foster consensus among decision-makers on policy is somewhat naïve (cf. Collingridge and Reeve, 1986; Jasanoff, 1990; Mulkay, 1978). It is true that open disagreement within the scientific community can fuel political controversy, and vice versa. It is also true that consensus within the research community on 'facts' can facilitate international negotiations on policy, at least as far as benign or moderately malign problems are concerned. But as there is no straightforward method of 'deriving' policy from knowledge, there is no simple, linear relationship between the state of knowledge in a particular issue-area and consensus on substantive policy measures. Research-based knowledge may in various ways *inform* policy decisions, but neither the scientific method nor the conclusions it produces can ever *resolve* conflicts over interests or values.

The combination of the features described above – the legitimating power of science and the indeterminacy and context dependency of scientific knowledge, especially in combination with political conflict – can generate a perverted dynamic in the science –politics interaction. On the one hand, policy-makers will be eager to find a way to couch a policy argument in scientific terms and delegitimate the scientific justification of the arguments of their opponents. On the other hand, the indeterminate nature of the policy implications of scientific knowledge makes it very vulnerable to this kind of manipulation. Scientific communities may become involved in disputes over method and interpretation ('endless technical bickering'), often not realising the political function that such disputes play in processes of policy-making. When they do realise the political role of such disputes, they may become tempted to conceal points of disagreement and perhaps exclude (at least from the science-policy dialogue) members of the community who hold divergent views. To the extent that the latter happens, the scientific community itself becomes involved in a kind of censorship that threatens the basic *modus operandi* of research as enterprise.

We assume in this study that the kind of pitfalls and problems that we have described above are inherent in the fact that science and politics constitute two very different systems of activities. Science –politics interaction is characterised by an immanent tension between impartiality and objectivity on the one hand, and strategic reasoning and tactical manoeuvres to promote particular interests on the other. We also believe, however, that while this tension cannot be removed, it can be successfully *managed,* for mutual benefit. Despite all pitfalls, a constructive relationship between science and politics *can* be achieved. The question is *how?*

As we have argued above, the critical challenge is to find mechanisms that can *transform* research-based knowledge into premises for policy decisions. This transformation process should meet a dual requirement: it should provide an *enlightened, consensual* and *user-relevant interpretation* of the policy 'implications' of a certain knowledge base – without distorting knowledge itself or impairing the practices through which it is produced and maintained. We know of no proven recipe for accomplishing this complex goal. It seems, however, that important keys can be found by searching along two different paths – one leading us to focus on *individual skills*, the other pointing us in the direction of *institutional design*.

The transformation of knowledge into policy premises is by no means a mechanical process; it is in a fundamental sense a social process, requiring a particular combination of intellectual, interpersonal and 'political' skills. Accordingly, much can be said in favour of the argument that the outcome depends on a fortunate 'matching' of tasks and human skills. This matching itself need not be a purely fortuitous event; the supply of relevant skills for a particular task can at least to some extent be influenced through careful selection and/or good training of people. At the most general level the recipe is clear and simple: find the right people, and train them properly.

The other path leads us to focus on *institutional arrangements*. This is what we will do in this study. The underlying assumption is that the outcome of the transformation process depends on how it is organised. According to this line of reasoning, the key to 'success' is a *conducive* organisational setting. The research question becomes: what makes a setting 'conducive' in this particular respect?

What we are looking for is an arena where scientists and policy-makers *together* can work effectively towards a *consensual interpretation* of relevant knowledge with reference to a particular policy problem. The line of reasoning we have outlined above leads us to suggest that such arenas will be most effective if they are constructed as *buffers* – coupling scientific knowledge with the concerns of policy-makers without penetrating and impairing the internal mode of operation of either system (cf. Miles, 1989). This proposition seems to be consistent with the findings reported by Sheila Jasanoff in her studies of 'regulatory' or 'advisory' science in the USA: 'negotiation – among scientists as well as between scientists and the lay public – is one of the keys to the success of the advisory process' (Jasanoff, 1990: 234). This, she argues, indicates that a strict separation between science and politics, in this context, is artificial:

> The negotiated and constructed model of scientific knowledge, which closely captures the realities of regulatory science, rules out the possibility of drawing sharp boundaries between facts and values or claims

and context ... Evidence from regulatory case histories suggest, further, that proceedings founded on the separatist principle frequently generate more conflict than those which seek, however imperfectly, to integrate scientific and political decisionmaking. (Jasanoff, 1990: 231)

The paradox is that although negotiations – both among scientists and between scientists and policy-makers – constitute an essential element of a successful scientific advisory process, it is equally important to draw clear *boundaries* between the realm of science and the realm of policy. These boundaries are themselves 'negotiated' by scientists and policy-makers during the course of the process (see also Jasanoff, 1990). In essence, then, negotiation is a necessary device for developing interpretations of knowledge that can be *generally accepted* as *valid* and *useful*. At the same time, clear boundaries are needed to enable the parties involved to preserve their different identities and place confidence in the outcome:

> By drawing seemingly sharp boundaries between science and policy, scientists in effect post 'keep out' signs to prevent nonscientists from challenging or reinterpreting claims labeled as 'science'. The creation of such boundaries seems crucial to the political acceptability of advice ... Curiously, however, the most politically successful examples of boundary work are those that leave some room for agencies and their advisers to negotiate the location and meaning of the boundaries. (Jasanoff, 1990: 236)

To the extent that these requirements can be combined as described above, '[w]hat emerges from a successful recourse to scientific advice, then, is a very special kind of construct: one that many, perhaps most, observers accept as science, although it both shapes and is shaped by policy ... When the process works, few incentives remain for political adversaries to deconstruct the results or to attack them as bad science' (Jasanoff, 1990: 234–7).

In Chapter 1 we formulated a set of hypotheses – summarised in section 1.5 – specifying more precisely *what* organisational arrangements we expect to be most conducive to fostering a constructive relationship between science and politics. As we now move on to present our empirical analysis, our goal is not only to 'test' these specific hypotheses; a more fundamental objective is to explore how well *the general line of reasoning* that we have outlined in these two introductory chapters stands up against evidence from the five international environmental regimes that we have selected.

Notes

1   The philosophical debate is best exemplified in the intense discussion between Thomas S. Kuhn and Karl Popper. While Kuhn views scientific consensus, or 'normal science', as a necessary condition for effective research (Kuhn, 1970), Popper (1970) views the phenomenon described by Kuhn as a 'danger to science'. Taking a closer look at Popper's (1963) arguments, however, we find that it is not really consensus as such that he resents, but an explicit aim on the part of the scientist to verify rather than falsify existing theories. Popper (1968), too, recognises that scientists operate within the framework of some sort of consensus, or 'structures of scientific doctrines'.

2   See for instance Cole, 1992; Gilbert, 1976; Mulkay, 1978; Ziman, 1968.

3   This is the initial definition provided by Kuhn. It should be noted that the concept is ascribed several meanings throughout Kuhn's text. Masterman, for instance, has traced no less than 21 definitions of the terms in Kuhn's own writing (Masterman, 1970: 61–5).

4   Some of the propositions associated with this school are not supported by Kuhn himself (see especially Kuhn, 1991).

5   A situation referred to by Latour and Woolgar as a situation in which, 'one can clearly identify the presence of some politician breathing down the necks of working scientists' (Latour and Woolgar, 1979: 23).

6   This is not to say that it is the *only* criterion. Clearly, the scientific enterpise evaluates its products by other criteria as well, such as nontriviality, accuracy, generality, etc.

7   This argument was, for instance, put forward at the 'Governing Science' conference held in Oslo, 17–18 November 1995.

The whaling regime[1]

3.1 Introduction: background and main institutional features

The first convention for the regulation of whaling was signed in 1931, and another one in 1937. The effect of these conventions was limited and although some scientists had expressed concern about the effect of whaling on stocks already early in this century, 'generally all sizes and species were fair game' prior to the Second World War (McHugh, 1974: 322). The large-scale industrialised whaling was highly concentrated geographically and by the end of the 1930s the Antarctic seas were producing some 85 per cent of the world catch. Traditionally whaling was a shore-based industry, but the introduction of factory ships initiated the *pelagic* phase of the whaling industry and processing was carried out at sea.[2] The peak was reached in 1938 with nearly 55,000 animals of different whale species caught. Although some 8–10 countries undertook pelagic whaling in the 1930s, the industry was dominated completely by Norway and the UK, which between them accounted for more than 95 per cent of total catches (Birnie, 1985; Tønnessen and Johnsen, 1982). As Japan and Germany, having demonstrated the strongest resistance towards international regulation of whaling in the 1930s, were no longer active players in the game just after the Second World War, according to one observer, 'the period following the Second World War marked a tremendous opportunity for whale conservation' (Scarff, 1977: 351). The ICRW was set up at an international conference in Washington in 1946, based mainly on a US draft. It came into force in 1948 and by 1950 16 nations, including all major pelagic whaling nations, had ratified the Convention.

The basic structure of the whaling regime is spelled out in Article

III of the Convention: 'The contracting governments agree to establish an International Whaling Commission ... to be composed of *one member* from each Contracting Government. Each member shall have *one vote* and may be accompanied by one or more *experts* and *advisors*' (emphasis added). As to decision-making procedures, decisions shall be taken by a simple majority of those voting. However, a three-fourths majority is needed to amend the Schedule (Art. V). The Schedule (Arts I and V) forms an integral part of the Convention. While the Convention as such is rather general, the Schedule is an instrument to secure its flexibility as it contains the actual regulations such as the length of the whaling season, catch quotas, which species to be caught, etc. Members have the right of objection to any amendment (Art. V.3) meaning that the amendment does not apply to the objecting party. It is also important to note that *any* state may become a member of the IWC, irrespective of its interest in whaling. Also, parties to the IWC may withdraw from the organisation, provided certain procedures are followed. As we shall see later, several members have availed themselves of this opportunity.

As regards the role of science within the IWC, there is no reference to a Scientific Committee (SciCom) or to other scientific bodies in the Convention. Still, it is recognised that science has an important role to play. For example, amendments of the Schedule 'shall be based on scientific findings' (Art. V.2.(b). Elsewhere (particularly Arts V and VI) the need for studies and analyses of whales and whaling is underlined.

According to Art. III.4. the Commission may set up 'such committees as it considers desirable' and at the first IWC meeting in 1949, a (joint) standing Scientific and Technical Committee was set up. In addition a Sub-Committee of Scientists was set up in 1949 and this group had separate meetings in the following years. In 1951 the 'Rules of Procedure' were changed and the three following standing committees were established: the SciCom, a Technical Committee and a Committee of Finance and Administration. While the Finance Committee was restricted to five representatives, the member nations may have any number of representatives they want in the two other bodies, but each nation has only one vote.[3] From 1955 on a new standing Scientific Sub-Committee (SS-C) was appointed. Although there has been a vast expansion of the IWC agenda and the number of working groups, subcommittees and special meetings on scientific issues etc., this is still the *basic* structure and organisation of the IWC, with *one* SciCom (no longer the SS-C) at the very heart of its activities. However, within this main structure a number of important institutional changes have taken place through continuous revisions of the Schedule and the 'Rules of Procedures'.

3.2 Scientific knowledge and political development: an overview

Have conclusions from scientific research been adopted as premises for policy decisions in the IWC, and how has this relationship developed over time? As the history of the IWC is so varied, it is quite common to split the history of the IWC into different phases. In this chapter, we basically apply a three-phase approach.[4] The first phase goes from the establishment of the IWC until the early 1960s, characterised by resource depletion and weak institutions. In the second phase, ending in the late 1970s, institutions are strengthened and a more conservation-oriented approach is adopted. The last phase of the IWC is characterised by a protectionist-oriented approach.

As scientists within the setting of the IWC provide *quantitative* advice on the size of the recommended total allowable catches (TACs), it is in principle possible to measure the distance between *suggested* quota, *adopted* TACs and the *actual catch*. This gives us a rough indicator of the extent to which scientific advice is adhered to – in contrast to many international environmental regulatory bodies which provide only more general 'status reports'. In principle, this is an important distinction, presumably offering us a more precise measuring rod when quantitative advice is given. As the early history of the IWC will show, however, the difference between quantitative advice and more vague status reports may not amount to much in practice when the scientific basis is very uncertain. Later, this is a very different story as advice has become much more precise and has a much better scientific foundation.

As a part of the planning process in setting up the ICRW, at an international conference in 1944, a total catch of 16,000 Blue Whale Units (BWU) was suggested by some scientists for the Antarctic region (one BWU equals one blue whale, two fins, two and a half humpbacks or six sei whales).[5] This figure was hardly more than a very rough 'guesstimate'; according to one of the three scientists behind it: 'the two others were pleased that I had suggested this figure instead of 15,000 or 20,000. It looked more reliable' (Tønneson and Johnsen, 1982: 157). It was up to the whalers to determine the species and stock composition of the total catch – which proved to be a very damaging management approach from an eco- logical perspective as the whalers switched to smaller species as the larger ones were successively depleted.

Just before the Second World War, on the one hand there were indications that the stocks of commercially important species like the blue whale and the humpback had been reduced. On the other hand there had been a *de facto* 'whaling moratorium' due to the Second World War. Against this backdrop, the suggested quota of 16,000 BWU in 1944, seemed rather modest compared to the aver- age catches in the two years prior to the Second World War (29,876 and 24,830 BWU) (McHugh, 1974: 322).[6] This figure was adopted as a total quota by the IWC from 1946 to 1953.[7] Moreover, for roughly the next decade in the history of the IWC (phase 1), quotas were in the range of 14,500–16,000 BWU.[8] Based on official IWC reports, there was a remarkably high match between quotas recom- mended and catch taken throughout this period. Until 1960, it was reported that actual catch exceeded quotas adopted by only 23 units on average per year.[9] Thus, *compliance* seemed remarkably high. However, already in the 1950s it was believed that considerable under-reporting was conducted by some of the whaling nations, most notably Panama and Russia. All attempts to establish an inspection regime, however, failed.[10] Beginning early in the 1950s, however, members of the SciCom, expressed serious concern that quotas were too high, but they had difficulty in quantifying the nec- essary reductions and not all the scientists were convinced that any reductions were necessary at all. So behind the seemingly precise advice there was much uncertainty as well as disagreement among the scientists, and the IWC chose not to pay attention to those sci- entists warning that catches were too high.

In the first half of the 1960s, the IWC received more specific and detailed scientific advice on the necessity of quota reductions. A total ban on the catch of blue whales was recommended and it was suggested that the BWU approach be abandoned and that individ- ual quotas be set by species. There was often a considerable time-lag between scientific advice and adopted regulations and some of the advice was not adhered to. Still, the IWC gradually reduced quotas as suggested by the scientists. The catch of blue whales was banned and in 1967 '21 years after it had been established, the IWC had agreed on a quota that was below scientific estimates of the sustainable yield of the stock' (Scharff, 1977: 366). By the end of the 1960s the quota was down to 2,700 BWU; that is about 10 per cent of pre-Second World War catches and less than 20 per cent of catches during the first phase in the history of the IWC.

Quotas were set for areas and species that had previously been unregulated and by 1976 all whale stocks had their own quotas. Finally, it was also agreed to abolish the blue whale unit and to set quotas by species. By the mid-1970s, the IWC adopted the so-called new management procedure (NMP). This consisted of a set of rules to be applied by the Commission on the basis of advice from the SciCom. The basic idea was that all whale stocks should be stabilised slightly above the level of maximum sustainable yield (MSY). According to one observer, the NMP 'marked the strongest and most specific commitment to conservation that the IWC had ever undertaken' (Scharff, 1977: 370). The *practical* significance of this approach should not be exaggerated as uncertainties and deficiencies abounded, and it has subsequently become clear that this new procedure did not work very well. Unfortunately, although the procedure looked very attractive in principle, the SciCom found that full implementation was difficult (Gambell, 1993). Still, there is hardly any doubt that the *intention* of this approach was to further enhance the significance of scientific advice in the IWC decision-making system. Despite some disagreement in the SciCom, weaknesses in the NMP as well as considerable time-lags between advice and adopted regulations, there is no doubt that scientific advice was indeed adopted as decision premises to a much higher extent than used to be the case in the first phase of the IWC history (Andresen, 1989).

Although the scientific effort was considerably increased throughout the 1970s, by the end of this decade it became increasingly difficult for the SciCom to agree on recommendations. It all started out with an understandable concern among scientists as well as environmental non-governmental organisations (NGOs) in the mid-1960s. Frustrated by the lack of progress within the IWC some scientists stated that: 'there is no justification for increasing the serious risk of extinction of the main stock of the largest living animal' (Røssum, 1984: 161). The outcry by the scientists triggered strong public concern and emotions over the whaling issue. This continued to grow and during the United Nations (UN) Conference on the Human Environment in Stockholm in 1972, a ten-year moratorium on commercial whaling was called for. The scientists were no longer the driving forces in this development as the whale was about to become a *symbol* for the international environmental movement: 'saving the whales is for millions of people a crucial test of their political ability to halt environmental destruction' (Holt, 1985: 12).

The IWC was not left unaffected by the changed perception and values concerning the whales. The crucial question in this connection is what the role of science has been in this process. The SciCom rejected the first call for a blanket moratorium in 1972 and continued to oppose it throughout the 1970s when different proposals to the same effect were made. The SciCom maintained that there was no scientific justification for a blanket moratorium, the management approach should be more refined and selective[11] Neither had the SciCom suggested a moratorium on commercial whaling when it was adopted in 1982. However, a number of scientists in the SciCom supported the moratorium. Thus, the SciCom was not able to agree on the scientific justification of a moratorium. In fact, the disagreement was quite fundamental as the Committee was unable to agree if the effect of a moratorium would increase or decrease the flow of information, whether whale biology would be hastened or retarded. (Andresen, 1989) Thus, although we will maintain that science was not a major force in the adoption of the moratorium, clearly any assessment of the impact of science on this decision is bound to be controversial considering the political temperature of the whaling debate at the time and the blurring of the lines between science and politics.

What about the role of science over the last few years in the IWC? As a means of increasing knowledge and improving management procedures, the Commission decided in 1982 (at the same time as the moratorium was adopted) to carry out a Comprehensive Assessment of potentially exploitable whale stocks by 1990 at the latest. 'This was defined by the scientists as an in-depth evaluation of the status and trends of all whale stocks in light of management objectives and procedures' Gambell (1995: 701). As part of the Comprehensive Assessment, research started to revise and improve the management procedure of 1976 (NMP). A revised management procedure (RMP) was adopted in 1991 by the SciCom (with a minority dissenting), and the Commission conditionally adopted the procedure that same year. In 1992, according to one observer, the IWC adopted a resolution that 'accepted the scientific engine that will calculate catch quotas, but added numerous features that need to be in place before the engine is used' (Cherfas, 1992: 11).

At the IWC meeting in 1993, the specifications for the RMP were now completed by the SciCom and recommended to the Commission for adoption and endorsement, but they were not accepted by the IWC.[12] After further adjustments, the Commission in 1994 formally adopted this procedure for the management of whales. Through this process it became clear that certain whale stocks could be harvested commercially without any danger to the status of the stock and 'The procedure is very conservative compared with anything that has gone before, and also by comparison with management regimes for other wildlife and fisheries resources' (Gambell, 1995: 701). The status of the north-east Atlantic minke whale stock was estimated by the Committee to be 86,700 animals in the early 1990s. Later estimates have been increased to more than 100,000 animals. According to the SciCom, the minke whale stock is much more plentiful in the southern Atlantic Ocean. Nevertheless, although the Commission has adopted the new procedure in principle, the majority of the IWC members have not been willing to implement it so that quotas could be set for a limited commercial catch of the most abundant species. What might seem a deliberate strategy of prolongation and neglect of scientific advice, caused the UK Chairman of the SciCom to resign. In his letter of resignation to the IWC Secretariat (26 May 1993), referring to the new management procedure, he wrote that 'the future of this unique piece of work, for which the Commission has been waiting for many years, was left in the air'. Another illustration of the lack of concern for the role of science and scientific advice, is the adoption of the Southern Ocean Sanctuary (Burke, 1996). According to a former US IWC Commissioner, John Knauss, 'after the 1994 meeting it was clear that it was only a matter of time before the IWC would be faced with either abiding by the implicit premises of the convention and award quotas to those nations that had chosen to continue whaling, or following the wishes of the significant majority of its members to continue the moratorium' (Knauss, 1997: 82). His advice is that limited commercial whaling should be permitted, but the fiftieth IWC meeting in Oman gave no indications that this would happen.

To sum up: initially the impact of science was dubious. Science had a strong impact in the sense that the quotas suggested by scientists were generally followed by the IWC. However, the basis for the recommendations was highly uncertain, the quota was in line with the interests of the whaling industry and the IWC paid little or no attention to the concern from the majority of scientists later on that quotas and catch were too high. In the next period, scientific advice was more precise and implied far greater restrictions on whaling. Yet, gradually the recommendations were to a greater extent adopted as decision premises. Although it may be difficult to assess the role of science in the IWC in the 1980s, in the 1990s, one can safely conclude that at least on the key issue of harvesting or non-harvesting, no attention is paid to advice given by the SciCom, although advice is much more precise and generally as consensual as one can for all practical purposes expect.[13] A number of delegates have declared that they are against commercial whaling, irrespective of scientific advice, putting in jeopardy the role of the SciCom and perhaps ultimately, the IWC (Andresen, 1998).

3.3 Institutional design: main features and evolution

What role, if any, has institutional design had in shaping the varying relations between science and politics within the development of the IWC?

The first phase: weak institutional basis Schweder (1993) has given a detailed account of the working of the scientific apparatus in the 1950s and to some extent also of its more recent developments, while Birnie (1985) has given an account of all IWC meetings from 1949 to 1983. We lean heavily on these two sources in parts of this presentation.[14]

As noted, each member nation had the right to one member on the SciCom, and he or she may also bring advisers. However, according to Schweder (1993: 6) 'The Composition of the SciCom was decided by the Commission ... (and) national members were named by the Commission.' However, the scientists were nominated by the respective governments, which for all practical purposes had the decisive say. The number of participating scientists was very limited in this initial phase. Although 14 countries were members of the Commission, at the 1949 meeting only four scientists are mentioned in the records, those from Canada, Norway, the UK and the USA (Schweder, 1993). In the SS-C, where most of the basic work was being done, the mean attendance per meeting

(1953–59) was seven scientists (Schweder, 1993). However, gradually participation increased and in 1959 altogether 11 nations were represented in either SciCom or the SS-C. According to Schweder, most of these were well qualified as scientists. Entry to the IWC SciCom was limited to scientists from member countries; no outside expertise was invited and contact with other relevant scientific organisations was also limited. Thus, it took time to build up the scientific apparatus, and initially 'it functioned somewhat irregularly' (Allen, 1980: 27).

The SciCom was explicitly subordinated to the Commission and: 'It should not hold any meetings until after the first plenary session at which appropriate matters will be referred to it' (Schweder, 1993: 13). However, this strict subordination of the scientific work was modified somewhat by the fact that the main scientific work was carried out in the SS-C *prior* to the SciCom meeting. Scientific work was undertaken and funded exclusively on a national basis. The Committee had no funds of its own for such purposes. In fact, the Commission itself was not empowered to conduct research. Article VI allows it only to recommend that its members conduct research. This provision, however, has not been considered a hinderance against the establishment of a research fund later on. The committee could also request funding from the Commission for specific purposes, but this was rarely done. The only exception for many years to come was the whale marking scheme. some £500 was spent on a yearly basis during the last half of the 1950s, but not without the 'grumbling' of some member countries as this meant higher fees on the part of the member countries. Publication procedures, or rather lack thereof, also underlined that the IWC was still a very young organisation. In connection with the IWC meeting in 1952 it is stated that: 'Its papers and proceedings remain private, apart from the publication of a brief annual report' (Birnie, 1985: 213) and the report of the SS-C was not published until the 1954 meeting. The scientific papers presented to the SciCom were only partly included in the records of the IWC and its records were very brief. Moreover, there was no independent secretariat associated with the IWC. Thus, the scientific institutional structure was both immature and weak in this initial period.

Independent scientists: better advice?   An important turning-point in the institutional development of the IWC was the introduction of

external and *independent* scientists to the work of the IWC. By the
end of the 1950s, the IWC was on the verge of a breakdown politically as key members were threatening to leave the organisation
and little progress was being made scientifically.[15] In an effort to
break the impasse, an initiative was taken to have the Commission
appoint outside scientists. Upon a formal suggestion of the UK, a
group of three (later extended to four) scientists was appointed to
undertake an assessment of the stocks. They had to be 'qualified in
population dynamics and drawn from countries not engaged in
pelagic whaling in the Antarctic' (Gulland, 1998: 42). Although a
number of objections were made on different grounds by several
members, the Committee of Three was appointed in 1960.[16] Still,
the reluctance on the part of some members was demonstrated on a
number of occasions during the years of its operation (1960–63)
through their unwillingness to finance the necessary research
activities proposed by the Committee of Three. This delayed
their work and it was less extensive than they had planned. Still,
this group of scientists, in close collaboration with the SciCom,
gave more detailed and precise advice than had previously been the
case.

There was general agreement in the IWC that after three years
this *ad hoc* committee should be abandoned. However, it was
agreed that the IWC was still in need of outside scientific expertise
in order to fulfil its functions. Alternative institutional models were
discussed, and it was decided to use the Food and Agricultural
Organisation (FAO) in such a capacity, and this was done for a few
years. The SciCom also considered the use of alternative outside
expertise and in 1965 it suggested that also the bio-economics of the
resources be studied 'by an impartial specialist committee of economists, perhaps assisted by FAO' (Birnie, 1985: 339). However, this
line of thought was not followed up at the time and has not been
pursued since.

Expanded agenda and increased administrative capacity   By the
end of the 1960s, the formal link to the FAO was broken,[17] but gradually the SciCom received increased input from a number of special
meetings and working groups reporting on specific areas and
species. Not least as a result of outside pressure, the scientific
agenda expanded continually with new questions raised, such as
procedures for scientific permits for whaling and the question of

including small cetaceans under IWC regulations. With every new issue, new working groups and new scientific sub-groups were established.

In light of the strongly increased activity, especially on the scientific side, the question of strengthening the administrative capacity was brought up in 1973. Until this time, the IWC had continued to operate from the UK Ministry of Agriculture and Fisheries, using part-time staff only. Now it was agreed that there was a need to strengthen the Commission by appointment of its own full-time staff, including as its Secretary the appointment of a scientist and the provision of its own premises.[18] When new suggestions were tabled with the purpose of strengthening the IWC, many members were concerned about increasing costs, although the member contribution was still only £500 per year. Thus, it took another two years before the Secretariat was in place, based on a modification of the previous flat contribution on the part of the IWC members.[19] According to Birnie (1985: 465): 'backed by the services of the improved Secretariat, both the meetings and the reports on them became longer and more detailed as the IWC expanded its role and tasks'. Moreover, this strengthening of institutional capacity was particularly important in an attempt – although not very successful – to accommodate the additional scientific work done nationally in connection with the adoption of the NMP.

Although the IWC's institutional basis had been considerably strengthened, pressures were mounting in the 1970s as a result of the development *outside* the IWC for a *new* convention stressing the need of an ecosystems approach, broader participation and the removal of the objection procedure. The ICRW was not regarded as a suitable instrument to protect the whales, as an increasing number of countries and environmental NGOs wanted to do.[20]

New procedures: new organisation? Although the Convention remained unaltered, important procedures were changed not the least as a result of external pressure. A main criticism was that most research was still done by some of the whaling nations, not always trusted to be impartial and not always supplying the information that was called for. Thus, there was increasing concern about the lack of international scrutiny and participation in the IWC's work by other independent scientists as well as independent scientific bodies. Research conducted by the IWC was still very modest; the whale-marking programme being the only concrete project, now increased to a modest £1000 a year. The many special scientific meetings arranged were usually sponsored by national sources. Thus, the whaling nations had a virtual *knowledge monopoly*. As a means to reduce their power, especially the USA worked actively to change relevant procedures (Andresen, 1998).

The problem of *data and information* became apparent in connection with the establishment of the NMP. This more ambitious management procedure with the more sophisticated categorisation needed more detailed data in order to work. The main sources of information necessary to implement this procedure had to come from the whaling nations, but member governments' obligations under the ICRW to supply the necessary information was rather weak. Member governments themselves decided both what information was available and whether it was practicable to pass it on. The members were welcome to interpret their treaty obligations broadly and supply the maximum information, but this was not always the case. At the thirty-first IWC meeting in 1979 a resolution was proposed requiring members to submit data, and the Commission should decide whether they were adequate. The resolution, however, was defeated and Birnie (1985: 507) concluded after this meeting that the failure of members to do this persisted, undermining the effectiveness of the NMP.[21] Disputes continued over what was a necessary and legitimate demand for information in the 1980s. An independent survey conducted over the extent to which Norway had supplied the necessary data in 1987, was not very flattering for the whaling nations: 'Over the years a total of more than 100,000 minke whales have been taken by Norway. However, very little data useful for the management of this species has resulted from this catch' (Anderson *et al.*, 1987: 68). In part as a response to this criticism as well as a call for a Comprehensive Assessment of whale stocks by the IWC, large research programmes were launched in the late 1980s and early 1990s, not the least by the (previous) whaling nations with the result that the flow of information and data to the IWC has improved dramatically. Somewhat paradoxically, this information is not put to much use due to the political opposition to commercial whaling by the IWC majority.

To strengthen the *independent scientific input*, in 1974 the USA proposed that observers from the FAO and the United Nations

Environment Programme (UNEP) should be allowed to participate in the discussions of the Committee. This was accepted, upon the discretion of the Chairman, and in 1977, for the first time scientifically qualified observers were permitted to attend the SciCom, and they have regularly availed themselves of this right. As to the observer status of *international non-governmental organisations* and *international organisations* (IOs), no criteria were laid down concerning the subject interests of these organisations. Traditionally, however, only a handful of the two categories – combined – used to participate as observers. As the question of NGO participation got more attention in the 1970s, it was decided that such organisations had to have offices in at least three nations. This rule was taken over from the United Nations Educational, Scientific and Cultural Organisation (UNESCO) as the definition of an international organisation. The intention was to restrict NGO observer status to international rather than purely national organisations, but this procedure had no effect as to restricting NGO participation which has increased sharply in the Commission meetings, particularly during the 1980s and 1990s.[22] Participation of relevant international organisations has increased as well, but not to the same extent. Usually approximately ten international organisations send observers.

Within the SciCom, the FAO and the UNEP were given a special status as *intergovernmental* organisations as they were explicitly mentioned in the Revised Rules of Procedure. They participated 'as scientists' with the status of advisors to the SciCom. Subsequently corresponding status has been given to Convention for the Conservation of Antarctic Marine Living Resources (CCAMLR), Inter-American Tropical Tuna Convention (IATTC), Convention on the Conservation of Migratory Species of Wild Animals (CMS) and similar intergovernmental organisations. Non-governmental organisations may also send qualified observers to the Committee, but they are not frequent participants here as they are within the Commission.[23] Over time the SciCom has become a much more open forum. Recall that the mean attendance of scientists in the mid-1950s was seven and as late as 1974, there were 24 representatives of the Committee In the 1980s and 1990s, however, some 100 scientists usually participated in the deliberations. Although much of the more basic work takes place in the various scientific subcommittees, the general discussions take place in the plenary and all meetings are open to those accredited to meet. Although the majority of scientists are still sent by national governments, more recently approximately one third of the scientists have not been appointed by the member states. The largest category among the 'independent scientists' is the category 'invited scientists'.[24] However, as the countries are free to send as many (or as few) scientists as they wish there are considerable variations in the size of the different delegations. During the 1990s, only about half of the contracting governments are represented in the SciCom. Of those represented, the majority send one or perhaps two scientists, while the two 'participatory giants', Japan and the USA 'have almost half of the total number of scientists participating' (Andresen, 1998: 437).

As commercial whaling was brought under increasing pressure, some NGOs as well as anti-whaling countries maintained that whaling nations increased their catch for *scientific purposes*, while the ultimate motive was commercial interest.[25] Thus, the procedures concerning scientific whaling came more to the fore in the latter half of the 1970s. This question had a bearing upon the need for more and better information as well as on the question of the competence between the IWC and its members. According to Article VIII of the ICRW, the IWC members may grant permits to: 'kill ... whales for the purpose of scientific research ... as the Contracting Government sees fit'. Thus, it is clearly within the realm of the Contracting Parties to decide whether to kill whales for such purposes or not. As a means to increase the role of the IWC in this respect, the SciCom in 1976 recommended that it should review permits prior to issue and make reports and recommendations on the proposed permits to the IWC. The Commission agreed to change the SciCom's Procedures to this effect.[26] Not until the mid-1980s, however, was this made compulsory and the Commission was given a broader mandate to evaluate the scientific criteria in relation to the SciCom, strengthening the role of the Commission *v.* the SciCom (Andresen, 1989: 113). Although the IWC can only give recommendations on this matter, it has no means of rejecting the issuance of such permits, practice having shown that the opinion of the SciCom and not least the Commission carries considerable weight when national decisions are taken as to whether or not to issue permits. While the Committee praised Iceland for its extensive research programme during the latter half of the 1980s, the Commission was strongly critical, passed resolutions against it and caused Iceland to reduce its programme in terms of scientific catch (Ivarson, 1994). In a similar vain, in the early 1990s the Commission adopted strongly critical resolutions against Norwegian research whaling even when it was down to a handful of animals. More recently it appears that Japan and Norway paid less attention to IWC resolutions on this account, probably in part as a result of the emerging consensus in the SciCom.

There was, however, no need for any procedural changes to allow for perhaps the most important institutional development in the IWC in the more recent period, the massive influx of new members that started in 1978/79. As will be recalled, the IWC is open to any country, but the number of contracting governments had been very stable (some 15 members) throughout the course of its 30-year history, all of them with current or previous connection to whaling. Within the span of four years (1979–83), membership increased to 41 member countries (Hoel, 1985). Thereafter, participation by state actors has stabilised.[27]

Partly as a result of changing access procedures (for scientists and NGOs), and partly as a result of using opportunities of existing procedures (open access for all states), the IWC has been transformed from a small closed whaling club to a very *open* and large organisation with increased transparency – much in line with the more general development of international regimes and generally welcomed by most students of international affairs. As a part of this process, and not the least due to the political controversy, there has been a strong call for more and better knowledge. Although the knowledge and management mechanisms existing today 'is something one could only dream of when the moratorium was discussed back in the early 1980s', the IWC majority has been very reluctant to put *some* of this knowledge to use.[28]

3.3.1 Internal organisation[29]

Autonomy, participation and funding As the SciCom is directly subordinated to the Commission, formally the degree of autonomy enjoyed by the SciCom is low. According to the present 'Rules of Procedure' the members of the SciCom shall be scientists, but in practice that decision is up to the preferences of each country. The question, however, is not only whether those appointed are scientists or not, but whether they are independent of their respective governments. It is obviously *possible* for governments, so inclined, to appoint scientists they are sure will support their official views on controversial matters while others who may also be highly qualified are avoided. According to information we have obtained both from participating scientists as well as from the Secretariat, the SciCom enjoys a considerable degree of *autonomy vis-à-vis* the Commission, and the large majority of the members of the SciCom are well-qualified scientists as well as quite autonomous in relation to their appointees. However, especially in the 1980s when polarisation was at its peak, the links of some very capable scientists to certain environmental organisations as well as animal rights organisations, may have contributed to making scientific consensus more difficult. Similarly, this polarisation may have contributed to strengthening the ties between governments of whaling nations and 'their' scientists (Andresen 1993). More recently, however, such links have been considerably weakened as the SciCom to a much larger extent operates as an independent and unitary body in relation to the Commission (Andresen , 1998; Mitchell, 1998.)

The Committee is autonomous in the sense that it defines its own agenda and is free to take up any question it wants, without any kind of approval from the Commission. The SciCom also elects its Chairman and Vice-Chairman independently of the Commission, and it establishes, organises and elects the chairmen of the subcommittees it finds necessary to accomplish its work.[30] Although quite autonomous from the Commission, it has been maintained that in the election of chairperson of various scientific groups as well as other important positions, there tends to be an 'inner circle' of key people, most often with an Anglo-Saxon background, who usually decide among themselves on these matters.[31] Conversely, the Japanese, despite their very large delegations as well as considerable research programmes and scientific expertise are less frequently elected. This may partly be due to language difficulties and according to information from the Secretariat, there are no deliberate biases on this account. However, considering the polarisation also within the Committee at times with, for example, Japan on the whaling side and the UK and the USA on the other side, although not done wilfully, it may at times have had some effect on the outcome of the scientific process.

The scientists in the SciCom do *not* represent their countries or for that matter the organisations that have nominated them; they act in their capacity as scientists. Nevertheless, as some of the key scientific people are also a part of their national delegations, there may be tacit or open pressures for the scientists to conform with national preferences. The change in procedures, paving the way for the permanent presence of scientists *not* linked to any specific nation was meant to remedy this problem. The large number of 'invited scientists' as well as a number of scientists from other international governmental organisations has probably also reduced polarisation between the two contesting sides and contributed towards increased legitimacy as well as more consensus within the SciCom. Experience has also shown that being independent of *national* interests does not necessarily mean that the scientists are independent of other types of interests or neutral to controversial political issues. However, the strong increase in the number of participants to the SciCom has created problems of its own. Its large size makes it somewhat unmanageable (Anderson *et al.*' 1987). It appears, however, that this problem is alleviated by the fact that smaller `core' groups play a quite decisive role, not surprisingly within such a large group

The communication *within* the SciCom between different groups of scientists has also posed certain problems more recently. Traditionally, the SciCom was quite dominated by whale biologists. Gradually, however, more quantitatively oriented scientists (statisticians and experts on population dynamics) have become more dominating, as a result of the elaboration of new and complex models in connection with the Comprehensive Assessment as well as the making of new management procedures. Thus, considering the increased focus on population dynamics and on statistical problems connected to the abundance estimation and stock assessment, this development is not surprising. Uncertainty present in the interpretation of data and the complexity of this task require extensive statistical competence. However, this has caused certain problems of communication within the Committee between the biologists and the more quantitatively oriented scientists (Andresen, 1989). It has also been maintained that the new models elaborated are so complex that only a handful of scientists truly comprehend them. This is said to have reduced the influence of some of the scientists with close links to the environmental movement.

The increasing dominance of the statisticians has also raised the question of what emphasis should be placed on uncertainty in interpreting available data for whale management. When uncertainty is high enough with respect to stock identity and abundance, it might be argued that whaling should not occur. In many ways this seems to be consistent with the *precautionary principle*, which has been adopted as a principle in connection with certain environmental agreements.[32] It has been argued that the uncertainty has from time to time been overemphasised in the SciCom, and that certain quantitative scientists have employed the disguised method of `maximum uncertainty'. This is opposed to the statistical method of 'maximum certainty' used to extract as much information from the data as possible (Schweder, 1993). If this is the case, it may have served as a means of delaying the scientific as well as the political process. In 1987 outside observers noted that they: 'Could not fail to detect the continuing existence of deep division and lack of mutual confidence between some of those involved in the affairs of the SciCom of the IWC ... [and] it would have been difficult for any scientific advisory body to have maintained a ... strictly impartial approach in such emotive circumstances.'[33] However, this quote is more representative of the late 1980s than the late 1990s.

An interesting concept was introduced in connection with the *development of the revised management procedure*. Five separate teams were set up and they met twice a year over a five-year period to discuss their work. Some teams consisted of scientists from whaling nations, others from the group known to have close connections to the anti-whaling movement. According to Schweder (1993: 29): 'The process of mutual learning and competition has turned out to be productive [and] despite the great differences in technique ... the five candidate procedures improved and ended up with broadly similar performance.' Thus, this approach seemed productive towards reaching increased scientific consensus.[34]

As regards *funding* of research, this is still mainly provided by the member states and the bulk of the primary research is conducted by the (previous) whaling nations, most notably Japan, Iceland, Norway and the USA.[35] No doubt, the IWC has been extremely important as an instrument to increase domestic research on the part of these nations in connection with the Comprehensive Assessment. The large domestic research programmes launched by, for example, Japan, Norway and Iceland would hardly have come about had it not been for the IWC. Moreover, there is little doubt that these large research programmes, scrutinised by the whole

SciCom, have been instrumental in bringing about the emerging scientific consensus. Thus, the moratorium, though politically driven, also resulted in more research to reduce uncertainty, and this in turn has reduced the scientific legitimacy of the same moratorium.[36] It should, however, also be noted that at the SciCom meetings, researchers from some other countries (like Australia, New Zealand, The Netherlands and the UK) also play a very active part – while others tend to be bystanders, or not represented at all. Thus, the key scientific state parties are relatively few. However, a fair amount of theoretical work and statistical analysis is carried out by the invited scientists. Thus, although truly 'independent' IWC research is limited, it provides the international institutional and legitimising framework for the domestic research, and arranges the necessary procedures for peer review and publications. It seems that practically all the relevant scientific expertise internationally on the various issues related to management of whaling is assembled in the SciCom, which in itself is no small achievement. As to research done by the IWC as such, there is a research fund, part of which has been used for the comprehensive assessment and the elaboration of the new management procedure. The Secretariat may also hire scientists to do specific research.[37] Canada is not a member of the IWC, but does conduct aboriginal whaling and is heavily engaged in scientific research. It does, however, co-operate with and provide information to the SciCom.

3.3.2 Communication between the Scientific Committee and the Commission

The communication between the SciCom and the Commission goes both ways. The SciCom gives advice, partly on its own initiative and partly as a result of questions and demands from the Commission. No particular body within the SciCom is designed especially for giving advice. Thus, in principle, the same scientists that do the research also give advice, in contrast to some environmental regimes where specific advisory or 'intervening' bodies are set up. The most important piece of information from the SciCom to the Commission is the Report of the SciCom, produced as a result of their two-week meeting prior to the meetings of the working groups, the Technical Committee and the Commission meeting. The recent reorganisation of the IWC meeting procedures was designed to allow major agenda items to be discussed twice, most extensively in a working group or subcommittee, and then in the plenary.[38] Although most of the basic scientific work is done in between sessions, this has often not been circulated to the wider group before the Committee meets. Current practice is for the Chairperson of the SciCom, in consultation with the conveyors of the various subcommittees, to send out a workplan for the Committee after the IWC meeting and take account of the decisions of that meeting. Still, the process is bound to be a very hectic and demanding task for those key persons having the responsibility for putting this together in one report.[39]

The report of the SciCom shall be completed and available to all Commissioners by the opening date of the annual Commission meeting. According to Birnie (1985: 179): '[this] rule is not always adhered to because of the infrequent meetings of the SciCom, the growing expense of convening them and the immediate proximity of its meetings prior to that of the IWC annual meeting'. The argument about the infrequent meetings of the SciCom no longer holds true, but closeness in time between the SciCom and the Commission meeting may still be a very real problem. It might be worth considering separating the scientific and the political process in time, both as a means to reduce political control over the scientific process as well as giving more time for communication between decision-makers and scientists at the national level.

The most important direct and informal channel for communication is between the scientists and the respective Commissioner and delegation from the same country, and the head of the national scientific delegations accompanying their respective Commissioner to the Commission meeting. The scientists outline and explain what conclusions have been reached in the SciCom. Most Commissioners will not be experts *per se* on the whaling issue; it will usually be one of many issues they are dealing with at a rather general level in their respective Foreign (or other) Ministries. In addition, however good the scientists are at *their* scientific work, the conveying of complex scientific work to (more or less) laypeople, is not usually a part of their scientific training.[40]

Apart from this informal communication at the more personal level, there is of course also formal communication at the Commission level. The chairperson of the Committee presents the main results of the scientific report to the Commission as such. In addition, scientific presentations are given on a number of more specific points during the Commission meeting by other scientists. This may result in further questions and demands from the Commission, wanting more and new scientific questions dealt with before the next annual Commission meeting. Thus, there is a true dialogue between the two bodies. For communication to be effective, we would expect that there is a need for more continuous dialogue between the scientists and the 'managers' between sessions. Such communication is close in traditional whaling nations like Norway and Iceland, owing to the significance of the issue, and it is probably likewise in other activist countries like Japan and the USA.[41] For the majority of the less involved parties without scientific representation, this question has less relevance and quite a few of the Commissioners must be assumed to base their decisions on a rather slim scientific basis.

3.3.3 How far from the optimal combination?

Assuming that the 'ideal' is to combine scientific integrity/autonomy on the one hand and responsiveness to decision-makers' questions and 'needs' on the other, how does the IWC score on this account? As noted, in a formal sense the autonomy of the SciCom is low as it is directly subordinated to the Commission, while the score on responsiveness should be expected to be high as its aim is to serve the Commission's need for management advice. Thus, we would assume that the greatest challenge for the Committee would be to obtain a high score on the autonomy dimension. Looking at the practical functioning (of the interface between science and policy-making), a main observation is that polarisation has upset this ideal balance in large parts of the history of the IWC, both within the Scientific Committe, in the Commission and in the relation between the two. In fact, this has been more the rule than the exception within the IWC. To a large extent this has reduced the integrity of the Committee and made the process of giving impartial advice very difficult. In other words, too much involvement in the political process by science has been the problem rather than the 'independent ivory tower ideal'. The exception from this picture is primarily the intermediate phase of the IWC's history when knowledge was increasing and polarisation was yet to start.

More recently a number of institutional and procedural measures have been introduced, as a means of getting around the politicisation of science as well as a means to reduce scientific uncertainty, linked to, for example, involving more independent scientists and not least through a massive increase in domestic research effort by the previous whaling nations – inspired as well as supervised by the IWC. Over time, this has generally had a positive effect as to reducing polarisation of science, but it has not been possible to eliminate – or even reduce – the differences of opinion in the political game, where strong elements of (differing) *values* are key ingredients (Mitchell, 1998). Infusion of a 'rational' element that science represents has limited effect when bargaining is over values and not numbers. Although a rather good balance between the need for autonomy and involvement has been attained in the late 1990s, the value of this balance has been discounted due to the polarisation over the whaling issue.

3.4 Institutional impact: 'real' or 'spurious'?

As discussed in the introductory chapter, institutional design can only be expected to explain a small part of the weight attributed to scientific premises. Running briefly through the history of the IWC, how much of a difference has institutional design made, and what weight should be attributed to other factors such as the nature of the problem, the status of knowledge and public saliency?

First, did institutional design matter for the acceptance and weight of scientific evidence in the process of depleting the large whales in Antarctic waters? Birnie answers this question in the affirmative. According to her analysis, parts of the reason for the failure of the IWC in this initial period was of an institutional nature: 'its determination to have a minimal budget limited to small members' contributions and its limitation of scientific advice and research to *national* efforts, without the addition of international *independent* research, or research conducted by the IWC' (Birnie, 1985: 203). She also maintains that 'the SciCom itself, being composed only of *government* scientific advisers, was over-willing to temper its recommendations to conform to so-called 'practicalities' (Birnie, 1985: 261).[42] Schweder (1993) has a somewhat different perspective in his description and analysis of the work of the scientists until 1960. He claims that 'It is probably safe to say that from a point of view of whale biology, the SciCom mustered the main competence available at the time. However, in other fields, like statistics and population dynamics, the competence ... was much weaker than it could have been at the time.' This was partly due to the fact that links to other relevant scientific organisations, having such competence, were weak or non-existent. On the question of the *independence* or *autonomy* of the SciCom, according to Schweder, this was primarily a problem in relation to a small minority of scientists.[43] Thus, there are varying opinions both on the nature of these 'institutional defects' as well as over what consequences they had. On balance, we would tend to conclude that they have at least *some* consequences for the depletion of the large whales in this initial period. Moreover, the *immaturity* of the organisation, characterised by low administrative capacity and irregularity of formal procedures, not the least on the scientific side, weakened the institutional basis.

However, these scientific institutional features were by no means the *main* reason for the policies adopted. Other institutional features, linked to *access rules* were more important. The fact that IWC did not restrict entry into the whaling operations and the use of an overall quota system set in the undiscriminating BWU approach, reflecting the philosophy of liberalism and competition inherent in the ICRW, were important factors in causing the 'whaling Olympics'. More fundamentally, the problem-structure of the whaling issue in this initial period was of a *malign* nature, characterised by externalities as well as competition (Andresen, forthcoming). The common property nature of the whale is known to generate the so-called 'tragedy of the commons' within a system of free competition and the way the IWC was set up did not reduce this competitive element, rather the contrary. Considering the strength of this industry in this period and its excess capacity, any serious attempt to constrain it would have been met with fierce opposition. Moreover, some of the most important negotiations between the whaling nations at the time took place *outside* the IWC. As the ICRW did not allow national quotas, discussions on this issue had to take place elsewhere (Tønneson and Johnson, 1982). Some whaling nations simply did not want a stronger science-based organisation, which could be a way to curtail their activities. Thus, the combination of a 'malign' problem with certain institutional defects, most of them not directly related to the science–policy interphase, were the main reasons for the depletion of the large Antarctic whales. Overall the knowledge base was also weak. It should be borne in mind, however, that the very perception of whaling in this period was completely different from what it is now. Whaling was considered a blessing in a period characterised by unlimited need for food and fat, and whaling was also seen as a rather 'heroic' and daring adventure, so public opinion tended to *reinforce* rather than curtail whaling. Although a stronger scientific institutional basis might have made it more difficult to neglect scientific advice, in part it was unrealistic to expect it at the time, in part it probably would not have made much difference owing to the strength of other forces.

Did institutional design matter for the acceptance and weight of scientific evidence in the more conservationist-oriented management of the latter half of the 1960s and the 1970s? Again, as a point of departure, we can answer this question in the affirmative, the main reason being the institutional innovation of bringing in external and independent scientists through the Committee of Three/ Four and the FAO (in the 1960s) which also brought with them new and necessary scientific qualifications. According to Birnie (1985: 304): 'The scientific advice given to the IWC at last began to point in the right direction with the authority of independent scientific opinion.' The general opinion among a number of different analysts of the history of the IWC seems to be that this institutional innovation, however constrained by economic difficulties, represented a turning-point in the history of the IWC.[44]

More generally, the considerable strengthening of the scientific administrative capacity through the establishment of the new Secretariat in the 1970s and the increased frequency of special (scientific) meetings etc. worked in the same direction. Budgetary constraints did serve as a limiting factor on the scientific effort throughout this period also. Nevertheless, there seems to be a close link between the strengthened institutional basis and the weight attributed to science.

However, by looking at the change in the nature of the problem associated with whaling, the link between institutional strength and adherence to scientific advice may – at least in part – be a spurious one. As we moved into the 1960s, the whaling issue gradually became much more 'benign' because the number of main actors were strongly reduced and so are the economic stakes involved.[45] It is also a fact that quotas and catch were not reduced in accordance with scientific evidence until the whaling nations were unable to catch their quotas.[46] These changes implied that it was much easier to follow scientific advice since the economic costs of following them were considerably reduced for key parties. An increased and better knowledge basis also played a role, as did public opinion. Whales were no longer, in key Western countries, regarded in terms of 'food and fat'. They had to be protected, thus strengthening the forces that wanted to restrict whaling in the IWC. Nevertheless, we think the process of turning the IWC into a more conservation-oriented body was smoothed by the institutional change and development within IWC. A positive circle was created through the *interaction* between a more benign problem and strengthened institutional capacity.

During the last stage of development within the IWC, the organisation has been opened up for new actors. This has been done, at least in part, to get a ban on commercial whaling as the organisation has become 'packed' with anti-whaling members.[47] The fact that the IWC is open to all states has no direct bearing upon the scientific institutional framework. However, the procedures for participation by non-state actors, including scientists, have been gradually charged to open up for new participants. In this way the active use of existing rules and the creation of new ones have been essential elements in creating a 'new' IWC. This development also contributed to broaden and improve the scientific basis, but it also increased polarisation. As accounted for, conflict over values undermined the role of science for improvement in the 1980s, and even more so in the 1990s. Innovative scientific institutional procedures had little effect on the policies adopted in the 'new' IWC.

Thus, the nature of the problem has again turned 'malign'. In fact, in a sense it may have been even more difficult in this last phase compared to the first phase, as bargaining over values has proven even more difficult than the bargaining over numbers that took place in the first phase of the IWC. Although it seems reasonable to coin the conflict in terms of values, the dimension of *unilateral power* must also be added. Had it not been for the political, economic and legal pressures asserted on the (previous) whaling nations by the USA, it is doubtful whether most of them would have quit commercial whaling (Andresen, 1998). The vocal public opinion, mostly in the USA, Germany and the UK also tended to reinforce the pressure to stop commercial whaling. In this setting, improved knowledge as well as better procedures have – so far – had little impact on decisions taken.

3.5 Concluding remarks

What is the 'score' regarding the adoption of findings and hypotheses from research in terms of the cumulative scale with three levels accounted for in Chapter 1? The answer is simple in relation to the first level: the relevance and usefulness of science has been acknowledged by the decision-makers ever since the IWC was established. As science was considered necessary for management purposes, regular channels for communication was established early on. The score varies, however, on the latter two dimensions. The substantive conclusions of the SciCom was not accepted by everyone during the first phase of the IWC as some nations preferred to listen to a minority of dissenting scientists. In the second phase of the history of the IWC, however, the decision-makers accepted the main conclusions by the scientists. In fact, the dominant trend was also that the third-level requirements were met in the sense that the scientific advice was to some degree also guiding policy. This has changed in the most recent period. The first two criteria are still generally met, but overall the policy of the majority is guided by criteria other than science.

Although the formal bodies and main rules have been unaltered during the 50 years of history of the IWC, *de facto* the IWC has become a new organisation. A quite small and exclusive 'whalers club' with a weak and *ad hoc* oriented institutional apparatus has been transformed into a rather large professional organisation, including in excess of a hundred scientists participating in the SciCom meetings. This development is partly the result of the general growth of international regimes over this period, although the growth has probably been stronger in the IWC than in most international organisations. In this case, there have been both inside and outside forces pressing for growth and institutional strengthening. Apart from the quantitative growth, perhaps the most impressive growth in more qualitative terms is the increased knowledge and understanding of sizes and behaviour of various whale species. The new management procedure has also been described as the most advanced that has been developed for the management of marine resources.

The relative simplicity of the institutional 'science–policy set-up' is in itself a virtue; to assemble all relevant scientific expertise internationally beneath one scientific umbrella is no small accomplishment. Thus, the advice given is an expression of the 'best' scientific advice there is. There are small chances that diverging scientific opinions with much weight will be voiced from other relevant scientific bodies as used to be the case in the early history of the IWC. The IWC was also a pioneer by introducing the idea of bringing in experts other than those associated with the member countries, or whaling parties, to secure a place for research independent of economic interests. The fact that there are not only positive experiences associated with this procedure, does not necessarily reduce the value of this idea. Rather, it illustrates how difficult it is, if at all feasible, to find truly 'independent' research, especially when issues are highly politicised.

If we look at the scientific institutional set-up over time, there has been a steady growth and refinement, but there has not been a corresponding steady increase in the weight attributed to science. This fact may shed some light on under what circumstances policy-makers pay attention to scientists and how this may be linked to the way the process is organised. The first period is characterised by a *vicious circle*; the combination of large economic stakes, poor knowledge and weak institutions could not halt the depletion of whales. Correspondingly, the second period is characterised by *good circle*; more knowledge, stronger institutions and reduced stakes, moved the IWC in the 'right direction'. While the IWC has continued to grow regarding strength of institutions and increased knowledge, the good circle was broken when conflicts over values and unilateral coercive power were brought in; seemingly leaving little or no room for science, however well organised.[48]

The question is how we should interpret this development. The more pessimistic version would be that there is no point in wasting the valuable time of very competent people and scarce economic resources to make advanced management procedures when they will never be put to use anyway. A more positive interpretation would be that increased knowledge and understanding has a value of its own and may have various kinds of direct or indirect long-term benefits. It is also important to point out that had it *not* been for the conflict over the issue, we would have known far less than we do today about the status of the various stocks of whales. However, the improved knowledge has tended to undermine the position of those who called most eagerly for more research – the countries opposed to commercial whaling. This may constitute some of the background for efforts that have been made more recently to bridge the gap between the whaling nations and the anti-whaling nations. (Gambell, 1997) A process of more exclusive intersessional meetings has been initiated. The basis for these negotiations has been the so-called 'Irish proposal', suggesting a ban on all high-seas (pelagic) whaling, and on all trade in whale products, but allowing for limited coastal whaling for local consumption. Initially some progress was also noted. This may be seen in light of an attempt to break the impasse by the fiftieth IWC meeting in Monaco in 1997, but this was not successful and the parties are once more back to their original trenches. The Irish proposal, however, in itself acknowledges the scientific consensus that limited commercial whaling may be conducted. Based on previous experience with the IWC, there is no reason to be optimistic in terms of solutions to the political conflicts in the short term. Nevertheless, it illustrates that when science is consensual, produced legitimately and communicated effectively, it *may* still have an impact in the long run even when polarisation is high, but interplay with other factors is crucial.[49]

A final remark on the relation between institutional development and the interests of the dominating players. To some extent the institutional development is driven by its own internal logic; it tends to grow and expand over time as a result of learning, maturing and perceived organisational needs. On the other hand, the institutional basis also seems to be a reflection of 'outside' forces in the sense that institutional changes do not seem to run counter to the preferences of the dominating power coalitions, if any. Initially, the weak institutional basis may be seen as a reflection of the dominating pelagic whaling nations. In the middle period, no such dominating coalition existed, perhaps allowing for more independent institutional growth. In the third phase, rules and procedures to a large extent have been created and used in line with the perceived interests of the dominant anti-whaling coalition. In this perspective the more recent development in the IWC is also interesting as it may break this pattern and show the *independent* effect that institutions may have under certain conditions.

Notes

1 As with all the other chapters, this is a revised version of the 1994 publication. It is updated until 1997 and quite considerable changes have

been made. In this process the author has benefited considerably from participation in two international research projects where a number of other international regimes have been studied, including the International Whaling Commission (IWC), resulting in two publications: Andresen (1998; forthcoming). Some of the research done on the whaling regime during a sabbatical (1997–98) at Princeton University is also included in this chapter.

2 For a precise definition of pelagic, or modern whaling, see Tønnssen and Johnsen (1982: 6).

3 The Technical Committee was intended to function as a bridge between the Scientific Committee (SciCom) and the Commission. While the SciCom should consider scientific criteria only, the Technical Committee had a broader mandate and put forward proposals to the Commission with a simple majority. More recently, the role of this committee has been reduced as a result of the establishment of a number of more specialised working groups.

4 This is based on previous work by the author, most notably Andresen (1993). Other analysts of the IWC have also split the IWC development into phases, but not necessarily based on the same criteria and turning-points. See, for example, Birnie (1985) and Mitchell (1998).

5 The BWU was originally worked out to limit whale oil production in the 1930s, but now it became the standard regulative measure. As we shall see, when it was first adopted, it was not easy to abolish, although it did not take very long to find out its detrimental consequences for important whale stocks, see Tønneson and Johnson (1982).

6 According to Schweder (1993) this level was chosen as two-thirds of the average catch 1933–39, and was believed to be sufficiently low to give adequate protection to the blue whale stock, as this stock was considered most important to protect. Later on, however, it has been argued that the quota should have been no more than 3,000 units. (McHugh, 1974) Attempts, based on scientific advice, to reduce the BWU catch limit before the Second World War were resisted by the whaling companies because of their massive investment in factory ships and catcher vessels. As much of the whaling materiel was sunk during the war, it was easier in the post-war resumption to reduce the catch limit while still maintaining the BWU per operation at about the previous level. However, it did not take long before capacity was in excess of the quota.

7 For further details, see the reports of the IWC covering the period 1948–53. The level of 'detail', however, is rather slim. The first report was published in 1950. The substantive text was six pages long.

8 The level of detail for catch as well as other factors, increased considerably throughout this decade. While the substantive report was still short, there was numerous scientific appendixes. Altogether the four-

teenth report, covering 1962–63, was 122 pages long.

9 This was reported by the Director of the Bureau of International Whaling Statistics in Norway (BIWS) at the IWC meeting in 1959 (Birnie, 1985: 249).

10 Later on the revelations have showed that cheating on the part of Russia in this period was much more extensive than was believed at the time. Independent Russian scientists confirmed this, but official Russian sources later denied it. See IWC reports covering the forty-fifth to forty-eighth IWC meetings, 1993–96. See also Stoett (1995).

11 A standard phrase was that 'the Committee considered that there was no biological requirement for the imposition of a blanket moratorium on all commercial whaling and that the majority considered that there was at present no biological justification for such a moratorium' (ICW, *Twenty-Fifth Report of the Commission*, 1975: 6).

12 In Glasgow in 1992 the IWC accepted the so-called annex H, giving the technical specification for the RMP, although it was not quite finished. Thus an incomplete version was accepted in 1992, but not the complete version in 1993. This was stated by the (former) chairman of the SciCom, Dr Hammond, in a letter to the IWC, 26 May 1993.

13 In this period there has usually been a dissenting minority in the SciCom. It has been small (a handful), and it has been diminishing over time. It appeared to be consensus in the scientific group estimating the status of the north-east Atlantic minke whale stock in 1996, but one scientist suddenly changed his mind (Justin Cook), causing an usually harsh reaction in the SciCom. See IWC Report of the forty-eighth annual meeting, 1996.

14 As to the more recent development, the author of this chapter participated in parts of the IWC meetings in 1989 and 1990. Interviews have also been conducted with key participants at the last meetings, for example, Professor Lars Walløe, head of the Norwegian scientific delegation, Professor Tore Schweder, member of the SciCom and Alf Håkon Hoel, member o the Norwegian delegation and with the Secretary of the IWC, Dr Ray Gamble, as well as with members of the USA delegation. As to the use of written sources, mostly secondary sources are referred to here, but all relevant IWC documentation (1950–96) has been checked.

15 In 1959 Japan, Norway and The Netherlands gave notice of their withdrawal from the Convention and Norway and The Netherlands ended up withdrawing. They withdrew owing to disagreement over national quotas as well as total quota. To bring The Netherlands and Norway back into the Commission – and they re-entered shortly after – it was decided to remove the total quota so that in the 1960/61 and 1961/62 seasons, there were no restrictions on whaling.

16 Of particular interest is the initial objection raised by the USA, maintaining that: 'the best way to conserve a living resource was through the operation of a Convention in which only nations directly concerned with the resources participated' (Birnie, 1985: 257). Considering the more recent history of the IWC, this organisation would obviously have been quite a different one had this principle been adopted as the massive influx of new members without whaling interests would not have been possible. Based on the US position in the IWC over the 1980s and 1990s, this principle is no longer adhered to.

17 The FAO had been represented in the IWC already in the 1950s. It stopped its direct involvement in whale stock assessment in 1970 because it took the view that sufficient expertise was now available within the SciCom. The FAO's limited resources could then be reallocated to less well-researched fisheries problems.

18 The 1972 UN Conference on Human Environment in Stockholm had suggested that the administrative capacity of the IWC should be strengthened (Andresen, 1999).

19 The new procedures called for a flat rate contribution by all member states of 50 per cent, with additional contributions of 25 per cent each, based on areas in which each state had undertaken whaling in the previous 20 years and on catch the previous year. This meant that only 10 out of the 15 members paid for this organisational reform. More recently, the membership fee has been graded even more, based on shares, depending upon the degree of involvement in whaling activities as well as the size of the delegations. See IWC Report (IWC, 1992: App. 8, 50) and Provisional Estimates of Financial Contribution 1996/97 and 1997/98, 23 April 1996

20 We will not deal with the attempts to revise the Convention. It was a long process in part taking place outside the formal IWC meetings and it failed to result in a new convention.

21 In a comment, professor Tore Schweder maintains that this conclusion probably is too simple as the main discussion to a larger extent dealt with *how* data should be interpreted rather than lack of data. Moreover, catch data were regularly reported, but there was a greater lack of effort-data.

22 As late as 1965 only five international governmental and non-governmental organisations participated as observers. Especially from the late 1970s, the number of participating NGOs has increased very strongly and now some 100 NGOs participate at the yearly meetings. For an elaboration, see Andresen (1998).

23 Non-Governmental organisations sending an observer to the IWC might also nominate a 'scientifically qualified observer' to take part in the SciCom meetings. However, his or her scientific qualifications were

to be determined in advance by the chairperson of the SciCom. More recently few NGOs have sent observers to the Committee meetings. The World Conservation Union (IUCN) occupies a curious intermediate position, as it is not wholly intergovernmental in make-up and has some NGO characteristics. For further details, see Birnie (1985) and 'Rules of Procedures'.

24 The total number of scientists in the Committee as well as the different types of scientists from late 1970s to 1996 are accounted for in Andresen (1998: 436).

25 Greenpeace has calculated that, by 1990, commercial whaling countries had killed 13,000 whales under scientific permits or objections to the moratorium (Mitchell, 1998).

26 Some members protested and said this was a violation of the Convention. However, this was rejected by an expert legal opinion. A proposal to make this *mandatory* in 1979 instead of *recommendatory*, however, failed to pass.

27 As to the question of *why* all these new nations wanted to become members of the IWC, see Spencer with Bollwerk and Morais (1991) and Andresen (1998). Suffice it here to say that some joined to improve their green image at small costs, some saw it as a new chance to increase the influence of developing countries in managing common property resources, some were recruited by activist and wealthy NGOs and some are said to have been recruited by Japan. After the moratorium was adopted, many of the newcomers have left the organization.

28 Quote from interview with Dr M Tillman, former Commissioner from the USA as well as chief US scientist, La Jolla, April 1997.

29 Focus will primarily be on the last phase of the IWC history in this section.

30 Some directions as to the subcommittees are given: according to the Rules of Procedure of the SciCom, the SciCom shall include standing subcommittees by area, or species etc. However, this can hardly be seen as a limitation upon its freedom in this regard.

31 Interview with T. Schweder, spring 1994. There has been a strong IWC link to the UK throughout its history through the location of the Secretariat and the fact that the working language is English. The code of conduct is also said to be Anglo-Saxon and the strong US position accentuates this tendency in a number of ways. However, this does not mean that the persons elected to the various positions are not qualified, but that it is easier for some scientists than it is for others to obtain such positions. Most chairpersons are elected by acclamation.

32 In general terms the precautionary principle means that one should act with caution and not wait till there is conclusive scientific evidence between cause and effect before action is taken. While this principle is

of little practical significance within most international environmental regimes, it has certainly been very rigorously applied within the IWC.

33 This was the group of British and Norwegian scientists appointed by the Norwegian government in 1986. Although the scientific standing of this group may have been no less than the 'Group of Three/Four' (Schweder, 1993), the fact that it was appointed not by the IWC as the former independent group but by the whaling nation Norway, may have contributed to reducing the influence and legitimacy of this report. However, the fact that the report was very critical to previous Norwegian whaling illustrates the scientific integrity of the group.

34 Finally the SciCom decided to choose Justin Cook's procedure. Cook is known to belong to the 'anti-whaling' faction. In the final discussion he and some other scientists objected to this choice, and he proposed to forward all the candidate procedures to the Commission for it to make the choice, thus contributing to weakening the emerging scientific consensus.

35 What countries are previous and present whalin nations is a matter of definition. The USA is still a whaling nation in the sense that it conducts aboriginal whaling and so is Denmark through aboriginal whaling on Greenland. No commercial whaling was conducted between 1988 and 1992, but Norway, Japan and Iceland were conducting whaling for scientific purposes. After 1993 Norway has conducted commercial whaling, Japan has increased whaling for scientific purposes and aboriginal whaling continues.

36 One reason that Mitchell (1998) operates with four stages in the IWC history, rather than three as used here, is the emerging scientific consensus of the 1990s. However important this may be, as long as it has not resulted in a different management practice, we tend to conclude that we see the *seeds* of a fourth stage, not yet materialised.

37 Of a total staff of some 15 people, three are professionals. The main function of the Secretary is of a procedural nature, having the main responsibility for organising the IWC meetings as well as managing the Secretariat on a daily basis. Editing and refereeing the scientific publications is also a key function of the Secretariat. Needless to say, it is extremely important for the Secretariat to be neutral to scientific and political conflicts in the IWC. More recently, however, the IWC Secretary has stated publicly that from a scientific standpoint limited commercial whaling could take place on some species. The Secretariat has a budget in approximately £1.2 million, a strong increase over time (*Green Globe Yearbook*, 1997). The administrative core budget amounts to approximately GBP £800,000. A fair amount of routine computing has been carried out in the IWC Secretariat, but the extra costs incurred in connection with the many extra meetings neede in

connection with the elaboration of the RMP, were paid by the host countries.

38 It has also been pointed out that four weeks, the time it takes from the start of the SciCom to the end of the Commission meeting was too long for those having to stay for the duration of these meetings (interview in the Secretariat). However, a significant number of state parties only show up at the four-days Commission meeting.

39 The fact that this is a very hectic process again brings up the point about the Anglo-Saxon 'bias'; as scientists with such background often have key positions and a mastery of procedures as well as language, they may often have a decisive impact on the wording of the report. This tendency is strengthened by the fact that reporters from the various bodies are often Anglo-Saxons. It is possible to amend the report in the final meetings, but this requires a mastery of the English language which only few non-Anglo-Saxons muster.

40 Having witnessed such processes, it is indeed a tall order for both parties – in a hectic atmosphere of negotiations.

41 For a more detailed discussion of the whaling policies of Iceland after the adoption of the moratorium, see Ivarson (1994). For a comparison between Iceland and Norway in the same period, see Andresen (1998). Iceland left the IWC in 1992 as the stock estimates presented by Iceland were accepted by the SciCom, but the Commission refused to allow resumption of catch. Norway resumed limited commercial catch of minke whales in 1993, the only IWC nation to do so. Although legally entitled to do so, as Norway objected to the 1982 moratorium, and although stock estimates were approved by the SciCom, the Commission is strongly against Norway's resumed commercial whaling.

42 In 1956 New Zealand claimed that the SciCom took into account extra-scientific considerations such as the effects of catch reductions on the industry and the possibility that governments might not accept them, instead of presenting the facts, however unpleasant. The chairperson of the SciCom accepted that they were influenced by such 'other' factors when giving advice (Birnie, 1985: 236).

43 The thrust of his argument is captured in the title of his article: 'Intransigence, incompetence or political expediency? *Dutch* scientists in the IWC in the 1950's: injection of uncertainty'. (Schweder, 1993; emphasis added).

44 In a personal comment Schweder has added an interesting 'footnote' to this general interpretation. He maintains that key members of the SciCom in the 1950s and the 1960s (Ruud, Laws, Otterstad) were just as able scientists as the Committee of Three, and had pointed to the same problems for a long time without being heard. The real difference was that in this case, the IWC decided that these scientists were given a

role as independent 'referees', who should be paid attention to, under-
lining the fact that institutional design might make a difference.

45 By the end of the 1960s only two nations continued their Antarctic
whaling operations, Japan and the Soviet Union. Norway, the UK, The
Netherlands and South Africa had all left the scene. Moreover, due to
the strong depletion of major stocks and the subsequent small quotas,
Antarctic whaling lost much of its economic interest (Tønnesen and
Johnsen, 1982).

46 During the 1962/63 season less that three-quarters of the quota of
15,000 BWU was caught. Although the quota was reduced to 10,000
BWU for the subsequent season, less than 9,000 BWU were taken and
during the latter half of the 1960s, the whaling nations were not able to
fulfil their highly reduced quotas. (McHugh, 1974: 310, Table 13.2.
Blue Whale Unit catch limits established for the Antarctic since the
1945/46 season compared with actual catches.)

47 In many international co-operative ventures it is quite self-evident who
and how many shall participate, like the truly regional agreements as
well as the truly global ones. Although the ICRW is a global convention,
participation has never been universal. Within most international fisheries arrangements as well as within the Antarctic Treaty System a much
more *exclusive* approach has been chosen, based on direct and manifest
interests in the area (Stokke and Vidas, 1996). Had similar provisions
been adopted for the IWC, there would have been no room for the
large number of newcomers in the 1980s.

48 This particularly relates to the key political issue of whether to reopen
commercial whaling or not. On other less controversial issues, like aboriginal whaling, scientific influence has increased over time.

49 For a discussion on the future of the IWC, see Friedheim, forthcoming.

Dealing with land-based marine pollution in the north-east Atlantic: the Paris Convention and the North Sea Conferences[1]

4.1 Introduction.

It was the ocean dumping issue that gave the main impetus to the establishment of international conventions to regulate marine pollution in the North Sea and the north-east Atlantic in the early 1970s. The Oslo Dumping Convention (OSCON) was signed in 1972. As the 1984 Oslo and Paris Commissions (OSPARCOM) 10th Anniversary Book notes: 'After the signing of the Oslo Convention, international opinion in environmental matters was favourably disposed towards the conclusion of agreements to establish rules for the prevention of pollution' (p. 6). On the initiative of the French Government, a first diplomatic conference was held in 1972 to establish a convention on land-based marine pollution. The Convention for the Prevention of Marine Pollution from Land-based Sources (PARCON) was signed in Paris in 1974 and entered into force in 1978. In view of the more comprehensive and analytically challenging character of issues related to land-based marine pollution compared to dumping issues, and the general need for a workable delimitation of the empirical focus, this chapter will focus on science–politics issues within the *land-based* context.[2]

The main, initial goals of the regime were stated in Articles 4, 5 and 6 of the Paris Convention, which can be summarised as follows: (a) the elimination of pollution by 'blacklisted' substances (organohalogen compounds; mercury and mercury compounds; cadmium and cadmium compounds; persistent synthetic floating materials; persistent oils and hydrocarbons); (b) strict limitation and, as appropriate, elimination of pollution by 'grey-listed' substances (organic compounds of phosphorus, silicon and tin; elemental phosphorus;

non-persistent oils and hydrocarbons; the following elements and their compounds – arsenic, chromium, copper, lead, nickel and zinc); (c) prevention and, as appropriate, elimination of pollution by radioactive substances. To attain these objectives, the Contracting Parties should, with regard to substances on the black and grey lists, 'jointly or individually as appropriate' implement programmes and measures, taking into account the latest technical developments, fixing time limits for their completion and including 'as appropriate, specific regulations or standards governing the quality of the environment, discharges into the maritime area, and the composition and use of substances and products'. Moreover, Article 11 called for the establishment of a monitoring system to enable assessment of the effectiveness of reduction measures.

As PARCON has covered the north-east Atlantic area, the participating states in the annual Commission (PARCOM) meetings have been, in addition to the North Sea states, Ireland, Portugal, Spain and Iceland. In September 1992, the Oslo and Paris Conventions were merged into one revised convention, the *Convention for the Protection of the Marine Environment of the North-East Atlantic* (OSPAR Convention), which entered into force in March 1998. In terms of land-based issues, central new elements were the incorporation of the precautionary principle into the Convention, and also the obligation to use the best available technology (BAT) and best environmental practices (BEP). Moreover, the 1992 Convention does not distinguish between black- and grey-list substances – a uniform regime for all substances has been established.[3]

Dumping and land-based pollution have also been discussed at four regular ministerial *North Sea Conferences* (NSCs): Bremen 1984, London 1987, The Hague 1990 and Esbjerg 1995. In addition, intermediate meetings have been held in Copenhagen in 1993 and in Bergen in 1997. As the work of these two entities – PARCON and the NSCs – has been so closely interwoven, it seems natural to consider the various institutions connected to these entities as part of one, comprehensive regime.

Given this point of departure, let me briefly introduce the scientific–political complex. On the *scientific/technical* side, the regime has from the late 1980s on contained four main groups of bodies, three more formally connected to the regime and one in more of an outsider position. The three 'insider' bodies have been : (1) the scientific/technical working groups connected to PARCON, i.e. the *Technical Working Group* (TWG), with subsidiary working groups. In the wake of the 1992 OSPAR Convention, the technical working groups related to PARCON and OSCON (the TWG and the Standing Advisory Committee for Scientific Advice [SACSA]) have been merged into a 'Programmes and Measures Committee' (PRAM). As the effects of this reorganisation process are of a recent character and really require a new, in-depth study not feasible in this context, the main focus in this chapter will be on the functioning of the scientific–political complex *prior to* this reorganisation. This also applies to (2) the *Joint Monitoring Group* (JMG), which has been reorganised into an 'Environmental Assessment and Monitoring Committee' (ASMO),[4] incorporating the work of (3) the *North Sea Task Force* (NSTF), established in the wake of the London 1987 North Sea Conference. Membership of the NSTF included the eight North Sea states, representatives of the Commission of European Communities, under the co-sponsorship of the OSPARCOM and the 'outside' fourth body within this structure, the *International Council for the Exploration of the Sea* (ICES). Initially, ICES input into the work of the Commissions consisted of some limited advice on monitoring questions and a general briefing on the work of the ICES at Commission meetings.

On the *decision-making side*, there have been two main bodies: first, the annual *Commission meetings* (PARCOM) composed of the Parties to PARCON. These meetings have adopted legally binding decisions and 'morally binding' recommendations.[5] Second, there have been *Ministerial North Sea Conferences* (NSCs). These Conferences have produced political Declarations, normatively binding upon the participants.[6] In addition, the organisational structure has consisted of, first, the *Group of Chairmen and Vice-Chairmen* (CVC), which has carried out some preparatory work inbetween Commission meetings. In addition, a London *Secretariat* has served the Conventions and the NSTF (1988–93). The main tasks of the Secretariat have been quite traditional: to organise and prepare meetings of the Commissions and other bodies, distribute and translate documentation, issue reports from the annual meetings of the Commissions.[7] The administrative capacity has increased in the 1990s – from six staff members in the mid-1980s to almost twice that at the end of the 1990s.

4.2 The increasing acceptance and changing role of scientific knowledge in marine pollution policy-making

4.2.1 Introduction

Have policy-makers accepted conclusions from scientific research as legitimate advice,[8] and given weight to and acted upon this advice? How has this relationship changed over time? These questions form the point of departure for this section. I will first briefly assess the political/regulatory development of the co-operation, before turning to the science–politics relationship.

Political development: from inertia to action   The development of co-operation on north-east Atlantic marine pollution can be divided into two main phases: a low-key and rather passive first decade, then some clearly more vigorous recent years in the wake of the 1987 NSC.

The first decade: a slow start   The early years of PARCOM were marked by a conflict mainly between the UK and the continental states over regulatory philosophies and instruments. The crucial question was: should PARCOM decisions be made as 'Environmental Quality Standards', focusing on the 'assimilative capacity' of the marine environment, i.e. a level up to which emissions could be allowed to take place freely? This was the view favoured by the UK. Or should decisions be made as 'Uniform Emission Standards', focusing more on emissions and technology than absorptive capacity? This was the approach favoured by the continental states. A compromise solution was reached in 1978, when it was decided that both approaches should be regarded as valid for the time being.[9] During the period 1978–85, PARCOM adopted 12 binding decisions and 14 recommendations. Many of these regulations contained emission standards and water-quality standards, but some were cast in the form of recommendations to phase out entirely certain substances, for instance aldrin, dieldrin and endrin. Overall, however, the regulations had a vague and non-committal character.[10] Nor did the first North Sea Conference (Bremen, 1984) produce many specific new measures.[11]

After 1987: more international and national action   The 1987 *London* NSC can be characterised as a turning-point in the protection of the North Sea environment. Regarding land-based issues, the most important targets decided upon at this Conference were emission reductions of nutrients and toxic substances 'of the order of 50%', to be achieved within 1995 and with 1985 as the baseline. Of special interest in the science–politics context, the principle of precautionary action was endorsed. The 'correct' interpretation of this concept has been the subject of considerable discussion,[12] but a core notion is that abatement measures may be undertaken *before* a causal link to ecological damages can be conclusively and scientifically proved – as proof may come too late or never be established at all. In addition, and no less important in this context, it was decided to establish a specific North Sea Task Force (NSTF) for the general enhancement of scientific knowledge. The work of the NSTF will be further elaborated later on in this chapter. At the *1990 The Hague* NSC, the 1987 measures were made more specific. First, 36 pollutants were specified for the 50 per cent cuts; in addition it was decided to reduce emissions of particularly threatening substances (i.e. dioxins, mercury, cadmium and lead) by 70 per cent or more. It was also agreed that the 50 per cent targets should apply to atmospheric emissions of 17 of the 36 substances by 1995–99. Finally, at the *1995 Esbjerg* Conference, a new and important step was taken by the adoption of a 25-year target for eliminating the input of hazardous substances. In addition, it was decided to reduce hazardous substances (especially organo-halogen substances) to non-harmful levels by the year 2000, as well as to implement several European Community Directives and Regulations.[13]

In a similar manner, and in part directly related to the NSC measures, *PARCOM activity was vitalised*. Between 1986 and 1989, just as many recommendations were adopted as during the whole first eight years of the co-operation, 1978–85. PARCOM had an average of 3.8 decisions per year through 1985; this increased to an average of 5.7 from 1986; after 1990, the increase has been up to around 7.5 decisions a year.[14] Furthermore, from the late 1980s, PARCOM decisions have increasingly been cast in the form BAT process requirements – as against the earlier use of emission standards and water-quality standards.

All in all, then, the outcomes and general activity of PARCOM and the North Sea Conferences were clearly strengthened in the 1990s.[15] What role did scientific evidence play in this process?

4.2.2 The increasing acceptance and changing role of scientific evidence

Some caveats   Issue-specific differences between fishery/marine mammals management and pollution management[16] make less feasible the quantitative measurement of the acceptance/adoption of scientific conclusions in studies of pollution management. For instance, there are no quota recommendations on the scientific side, so there are also no quota decisions on the management side. This means that assessments of the degree of acceptance/adoption of conclusions from scientific research will have to be based mainly on qualitative interpretation of scientific reports and policy decisions, supplemented by interviews with scientific and political actors.[17] As, however, very few of the current decision-makers have been involved in the co-operation from the start, the interviews conducted first and foremost shed light on the 'vitalised' period in the wake of the 1987 NSC. My interpretation of the first formative years – based on scattered written sources – should be seen as a modest first step in the assessment of the science–politics relationship in this period.

The discussion will be structured in the following manner: first I will establish a very rough scientific baseline, describing the scientific state of knowledge at the time the co-operation started. Second, I discuss the science–politics relationship in the first decade of the co-operation, focusing on the scientific background for the decisions on emission limits and water-quality standards, and the 1984 Bremen NSC. The third and final section will discuss the more recent developments, with particular focus on the North Sea Conferences of 1987, 1990, and 1995.

The starting-point: high uncertainty, little conflict   Several other international environmental co-operative efforts, such as the acid rain and the ozone layer regimes, were established largely because of alarming scientific reports (see Chapters 5 and 6 in this book). Was this the case also with regard to the north-east Atlantic marine pollution co-operation? To some extent, yes. The Oslo dumping regime, the first north-east Atlantic marine pollution regime, was established due to concern over dumping activity. Part of the background were ICES reports in the late 1960s, indicating that large amounts of waste were being dumped in the North Sea.[18] By contrast, the background for the establishment of the Paris land-based marine pollution regime seems to have been a more general concern for the North Sea and north-east Atlantic environment, rather than any specific, alarming reports about the quality of the marine environment.[19] On the one hand, the absence of critical reports meant that the level of scientific disagreement probably was quite low. On the other hand, scientific uncertainty was quite clearly high. For instance, the main international marine scientific organization – ICES – had long been concerned chiefly with fishery science; its Advisory Committee on Marine Pollution (ACMP) was not established until 1972, only two years before PARCON. However, this does not mean that a scientific input into the regime's formation processes was entirely lacking. For instance with regard to the Oslo Convention process, it has been noted that 'the co-operation between the experts in international law and the experts in marine pollution was really excellent' (The Oslo and Paris Commissions, 1984: 4). There is nothing to indicate that the situation was very much different regarding the Paris Convention process.

The first decade: decision-makers clearly 'tuned in' to science   Concerning the first decade of the co-operation, let us first briefly look at the background for PARCOM decisions, centred around emission limits and water-quality standards. Here we should bear in mind that the initial establishment of the black and grey lists of substances was a scientifically based process. As these lists heavily influenced PARCOM's agenda in the following years, it follows that the priorities regarding PARCOM's agenda were fundamentally scientifically based. Second, the emission limits and water-quality standards decisions were based upon recommendations from the TWG, which also ensured a certain scientific influence. However, in these first years, the scientific part of the TWG's work was hampered by lack of data on usage, discharges, environmental effects and existing controls on the group of substances given priority.[20] For instance, a report on cadmium, mercury and polychlorinated biphenyls (PCB) inputs, produced by an Ad Hoc Working Group on Input Data in 1984, concluded that 'there were large gaps in the geographical coverage of the Convention area as a whole, and for PCBs the data were either missing or sparse. There was a general lack of information about the methodologies used by the Contracting Parties in measuring inputs and the analytical limits of detection varied markedly' (Oslo and Paris Commissions, Sixth Annual report: 2). Moreover, the progress of the JMG's monitoring work was slow – a point to which we will return later.

On the whole, it is thus reasonable to assume that this shortage and poor quality of data weakened both the acceptance and the weight of the TWG's recommendations, at least the scientific parts. But this does not mean that scientific uncertainty was a central issue in PARCOM decision-making in this period. PARCOM's Annual Reports for these years indicate that scientific uncertainty did occasionally turn up in the discussions. But this was first and foremost related to lacking national input data and hence reporting deficiencies, and not to scientifically bolstered assessments and proposals introduced by the scientific and technical bodies. In fact, these Annual Reports clearly show that reluctant Parties tended to cite other arguments than data inadequacies and scientific uncertainty. Such arguments included economic difficulties, legal obstacles to the implementation of measures (for instance the discussions on PCBs and polychlorinated triphenyls, PCTs), the lack of available substitutes (for instance the discussions on aldrin, endrin and dieldrin), and EC-related problems (PCBs and PCTs) – to mention only a few.

Regarding the 1984 North Sea Conference in Bremen, we should begin by noting that part of the background for the German initiative to hold this conference was a 1980 report published by the German Council of Experts for Environmental Affairs, indicating North Sea pollution problems. Moreover, under the leadership of Germany, a specific 'Quality Status of the North Sea' report (QSR) was produced in connection with the Conference. Were the contents of the QSR accepted and given weight at this Conference? Some claim they were. For instance, as stated in the *ENDS Report* just after the Conference: 'Demands by German environmentalists in 1984 for sweeping cleanup measures ... were rejected by ministers, not least because of a major scientific effort by the UK which showed that serious pollution is mostly confined to the major estuaries and is not a threat to the North Sea as a whole' (*ENDS Report 141*). However, as the report was completed just in time for the actual Conference, and had not been discussed by the delegations in advance, parts of the report were disputed at the Conference.[21]

The upshot of all this is that although decision-makers were clearly 'tuned in' to science, there were some controversies over existing evidence, but not with any high degree of drama. In general there was an agreed basis for determining which substances were to be given priority and for the decisions adopted, but in no way were these decisions directly derived from science.

After 1987: increasing acceptance, changing role   Let us now turn to the most recent phase in the co-operation, with the 1987 London NSC as an important turning point with regard to policy. Have the acceptance and weight given to scientific evidence in the first decade changed in recent years? In my view, some factors indicate that the acceptance of scientific evidence has increased, while other factors would indicate that the role of scientific evidence has changed rather than that the weight given to scientific evidence has unambiguously increased.

Judging by the treatment of the 1987 and 1993 QSRs at the respective NSCs, acceptance has gradually increased. First, participants at both the 1984 and 1987 NSCs have indicated that the longer and more extensive 1987 report was more accepted and given more weight in the negotiations than the somewhat more sparse 1984 QSR.[22] This development was further strengthened by the 1993 Intermediate Ministerial Meeting, which featured an assessment of the 1993 QSR as a central agenda item. At this meeting, the decision-makers' response was very positive. In the Statement of Conclusions adopted, the ministers congratulated the NSTF on the successful completion of the QSR.

Can the NSC reduction measures agreed to in 1987, 1990 and 1995 then be interpreted as direct effects of increased weight given to scientific evidence? The answer is probably no. First, my impression is that many natural scientists regarded the initial 50 per cent reduction measures adopted at the 1987 NSC as heavily politically motivated and only loosely 'scientifically justified'.[23] As the contents and main message of the 1984 and 1987 QSRs are not very different (see Wettestad, 1989), such a view is understandable. The 1987 QSR painted a quite moderate picture, emphasising the heterogeneity of the pollution situation. An important concluding passage goes like this: 'In general, deleterious effects, at present, can only be seen in certain regions, in the coastal margins, or near identifiable pollution sources. There is as yet no evidence of pollution away from these areas.'[24] In light of this 'heterogeneous' assessment, the 'homogeneous' common percentage-cuts approach was criticised.[25]

Such a crude approach ignored variations in toxicity between substances, and variations in degree of pollution between the various parts of the North Sea. However, and more as a footnote, the subsequent adoption at the 1990 The Hague NSC of a common list of 36 priority hazardous substances and a 70 per cent reduction target formulated for a smaller group of substances (e.g. dioxins, mercury, cadmium and lead), may be said to have contributed to a somewhat more nuanced approach.[26]

In this connection, we should note the added weight given to the *precautionary principle* (PP) as a decision-making tool in this period, as for instance witnessed in the formal inclusion in the 1992 OSPAR Convention. Does this in fact signal a weakening of the weight given to scientific evidence within the regime? The scientific and political implications related to the PP are of course a long and complicated matter, and I will only briefly touch upon the issue in this connection. Let us first quickly repeat the core of the PP: abatement measures may be taken even if there is no 'conclusive evidence' of a causal relation between inputs and effects.[27] At first glance, this may look like a weakening of the weight of scientific evidence. However, it may just as probably be seen as a change in the role of scientific evidence. First, increased weight given to this principle signals an increasing recognition of the formidable task of establishing 'conclusive evidence' of causal links in the marine environment. In some cases, waiting for such evidence may mean that policy-making proceeds far too slowly. Repairing damage can also be far more costly than anticipatory action. Moreover, scientific evidence will still play an important part in pinpointing areas for regulation and, not least, in providing the crucial background material needed for setting decision-making priorities.[28] All of this would indicate a change of function and role rather than one of 'weight'.

At least two points relevant in this connection can be noted about the 1993 QSR: first, the development with regard to clarification of the degree of uncertainty involved has continued in relation to the earlier QSRs. Moreover, we can see a slightly more 'alarmist' development with regard to issues of concern. Hence, in practice, not least the 1995 NSC decision on a 25-year target for eliminating the input of hazardous substances can be interpreted as a general response to the increased clarity about uncertainties and issues of concern with regard to the development of the North Sea environment. There has been increasing acceptance and utilisation of the precautionary principle, with more weight being given to other parts of the scientific evidence. But there is no sign of any radical change in the degree of literal 'adoption' of scientific evidence.

With regard to PARCOM decision-making, the turn towards increased reliance on BAT requirements has, naturally enough, further increased the relevance of technological knowledge as a basis for decision-making, in relation, for example, to monitoring data. However, again it seems far less controversial to say that emphasis *within* the 'family' of scientific knowledge has changed than to conclude that the general weight of scientific evidence has increased.

Summing up Have conclusions from scientific research been accepted and adopted as premises for policy decisions, and has this changed over time? The answers to these questions have to be qualified in several ways. As indicated earlier, an exhaustive answer to such questions would necessitate a far more detailed study of the 20 years of PARCOM and NSC decision-making. Thus, for the sake of simplicity, I have given much attention to the relatively few and more 'visible' NSC, in relation to the more complex and elusive decision-making activities of the Paris Commission.

Given this caveat, my assessment is, first, that conclusions from scientific research have influenced decision-making from the establishment of the black and grey lists at the very beginning and onwards. However, they seldom seem to have been decisive for the outcomes. Second, judging especially by the response to the various QSRs, the acceptance of scientific evidence has increased over time. On the other hand, this issue area has never been characterised by really fierce conflicts over the scientific evidence. Third, it is tempting to conclude that the weight of scientific evidence has increased accordingly. However, this is less obvious. For instance, the NSC reduction measures must be seen more as a general response to increasingly revealed uncertainty and hence potential pollution damages, and less as a more literal 'adoption' of implications of scientific knowledge. The increased importance attached to the precautionary principle and BAT requirements as decision-making tools represents more a change in the function and role of scientific evidence than any change in weight.

How does this development relate to the evolution of the institutional setting? The next section will describe the evolution of the institutional setting. Then, in section 4.4. we turn to the question of institutional impact.

4.3 Institutional design: main features and evolution[29]

Also with regard to institutional design, I will distinguish between two main phases, with the 1987 North Sea Conference and the related establishment of the NSTF as the main turning-point.

The first decade: establishing the Convention machinery   We begin by taking a closer look at PARCOM and related bodies as noted in the introduction, the two main scientific/technical bodies were the TWG and the JMG. First, the *Technical Working Group*. The TWG's terms of reference were set out in the first annual PARCOM report. These terms included open entry for all Contracting Parties 'which wish to send representatives'. Hence, appointment and funding of delegates were up to the Contracting Parties. In practice, the Contracting Parties have generally sent delegates considerably closer to the administrative than the scientific pole, but the type of representation and disciplinary background have varied from country to country.[30] Moreover, the TWG's main task was initially described as 'giving advice on technical and scientific questions remitted to it by the Commission', taking into account various scientific and technical knowledge.[31] However, at the second PARCOM meeting, it was agreed that also the political consequences should be taken into consideration (PARCOM II/11/1, para. 71).

In practice, the main tasks of the TWG were: (1) to produce more general technical inputs/reports to the discussions of the commission, (2) to recommend specific courses of action, and (3) to give technical assistance in the implementation process of measures. Regarding its place in the scientific–political communication chain, the role of the TWG can be described as an *interpretative buffer*, i.e. it translated and synthesised the work of the various, partly *ad hoc*, (sub)working groups into usable information and specific proposals for the Commission to decide upon. Its intermediate position indicates *medium autonomy*: it received from the Commission specific tasks to carry out, but also generated information and advice more or less independently. The TWG's main reporting was in the form of an annual report presented and discussed at the PARCOM part of the annual OSPARCOM meeting.

As to the *Joint Monitoring Group*, its mandate was given in Article 11 of the Paris Convention. Here, the Contracting Parties agreed to set up a permanent monitoring system allowing 'the earliest possible assessment of the existing level of pollution; and ... the assessment of the effectiveness of measures for the reduction of marine pollution from land-based sources taken under the terms of the present Convention'. This was to be done through 'pursuing individually or jointly systematic and ad hoc monitoring programmes'. In practice, the work of the JMG was dependent upon national monitoring programmes. As with the TWG, entry was open, and participants in the JMG were appointed and funded by their national governments. Its main function must be characterised as *co-ordinatory*, although participants clearly conducted research as well. Hence, JMG participants seem to have been considerably *closer to the scientific pole* than in the case of the TWG. The JMG also seems to have enjoyed greater autonomy than the TWG. As for communication and formal links to the decision-making body, the JMG reported both to the TWG and the annual Joint Commission meeting. Both groups also reported to the Secretariat and the Commission concerning their elections to the office of chairperson etc., but this was a mere formality. And with regard to publication of reports, all material was published with the permission of the Commission.

The role of the *International Council for the Exploration of the Sea* within this structure should also briefly be commented upon. The ICES is the oldest intergovernmental organization concerned with marine and fishery sciences (established in 1902). Up until quite recently, recruitment of scientists to its working groups on marine pollution was based mainly on scientific merit.[32] On the whole, the ICES played a quite limited role within the PARCON scientific–political complex in the first decade, mainly giving some assistance to the JMG's monitoring work. There were several reasons for this. First, the ICES itself accorded higher priority to fishery issues than to marine pollution issues. Second, PARCON decision-makers found ICES reports too technical and not sufficiently relevant to their practical decision-making needs.

The first NSC, held in Bremen in 1984, deserves some specific comments in this connection. As indicated earlier, prior to this conference, a specific Quality Status of the North Sea report had been produced, under the leadership of the Federal Republic of Germany.

This work was based partly on reports from the TWG, the SACSA and the ICES, and partly on national reports.

After 1987: the NSTF and reorganised Convention machinery   In the late 1980s, the most interesting organisational changes were initiated within the NSC context. First, the preparatory process for the 1987 London NSC was organised somewhat differently than the 1984 process. Work on the new QSR not only commenced earlier but was also more thorough than in 1984, and the QSR was completed well in advance of the Conference itself.[33] Second, an important part of the outcome of the 1987 conference was the establishment of the *North Sea Task Force*.[34] The NSTF comprised delegates from the eight North Sea states and the Commission of the European Communities, under the co-sponsorship of OSPARCOM and the ICES. Its main objective was formulated in the declaration from the London NSC: 'to carry out work leading, in a reasonable time scale, to a dependable and comprehensive statement of circulation patterns, inputs, and dispersion of contaminants, ecological conditions and effects of human activities in the North Sea'. It was funded by the participating states. The NSTF secretariat was based in the OSPARCOM office in London, and there was close co-operation with ICES.

The NSTF had two main functions: (1) the preparation of a new QSR of the North Sea in 1993, and (2) the co-ordination of monitoring, modelling and research activities. Some of the background material for the 1993 QSR came from a specific Task Force monitoring programmeme (Monitoring Master Plan, MMP) which utilised newly developed measurement techniques. Although the monitoring work experienced funding problems, the 1993 QSR clearly came up with new knowledge. The second task points to the co-ordinating dimension in the work of the NSTF. For instance, several NSTF workshops were organised in the field of modelling. Regarding disciplinary background and internal autonomy, the picture is a mixed one. As further described by the Secretary of the NSTF, there was a two-tier system (Ducrotoy, 1997). The compilation of scientific information was prepared by a '*ground level*' of *practising scientists*, with nominations simply 'confirmed' by governments. The five panels on geography, oceanography, chemistry, biology and ecology indicate the broad range of marine scientific disciplines involved. Moreover, close co-operation with ICES has been emphasised as a crucial factor in strengthening the validity and reliability of the scientific work of the NSTF.[35] Hence, autonomy at this level was probably quite high. With regard to the *core NSTF*, delegates were mainly scientific/technical senior administrators who represented their governments. This group having the prime responsibility for the two final QSR chapters on conclusions and recommendations, discussions naturally took on a more political flavour. Hence, autonomy at this level was probably lower. Still, according to Ducrotoy (1997: 188), conclusions reached by the research scientists were not altered in any significant way. The main formal reporting was obviously in the form of the 1993 QSR, but the Task Force also produced preliminary working papers, and reported to the joint OSPARCOM meetings.

Let us then briefly turn to the organisational changes that took place in the wake of the establishment of the 1992 OSPAR Convention, especially the establishment of the new ASMO and PRAM committees. Judging by the terms of reference for the two groups, the changes in the functioning of the scientific–political system initiated by the establishment of the NSTF has been strengthened. The terms of reference for *ASMO* clearly indicates that basic features of the NSTF organisational model and way of working has been retained: close co-ordination with ICES; the publication at regular intervals of reports on the quality status of the marine environment; the development of analytical tools such as modelling for assessment procedures etc. On the reporting side, in line with the more explicit advisory NSTF, the work of ASMO places greater emphasis on advisory and communication issues than did the old JMG. Regarding *PRAM*, which has replaced the earlier technical working groups, a more action-initiating role is signalled in its first obligation: 'in accordance with the priorities established in the Action Plan of the Commissions, prepare proposals for Decisions and Recommendations for consideration by the Commissions to prevent and eliminate pollution of the maritime area' (Annex 24, point 2.a). In comparison, the terms of reference for the TWG only contained what is now formulated as a second obligation for PRAM: to 'advise the Commissions on technical and scientific questions remitted to it by the Commissions'. However, as the TWG in practice also performed action-initiating functions, the new terms of reference may to some degree be a codification of practice so far. Definitely new is the obligation to 'review reports for assessing compliance with, and the effectiveness of agreed Decisions and Recommendations' (Annex 24, point 2.e). As this aspect will influence the science–politics interface only marginally, I do not assess its practical implications in this connection.

How far from the 'optimal' combination? If the ideal is to combine high scientific integrity/autonomy on the one hand, and high involvement in the political process and responsiveness to decision-makers' questions and needs on the other, how should we then assess the development of the quite complex system described in the preceding sections? During the first decade, the TWG enjoyed a strong position within the co-operation. Here the TWG was basically a 'low autonomy/high involvement' type of body, whereas the JMG, being much more 'high autonomy/low involvement', played a far less significant role. Hence, on the whole, the approach was more characterised by high involvement than high autonomy – although neither of these functions was performed very successfully.

With the establishment of the NSTF in 1987/88, the situation started to change somewhat. Over time, the NSTF combined 'quite high autonomy' with 'quite high involvement', with its multi-tiered system and assisted by substantial inputs from ICES. Moreover, the PARCON system started to change, with the 1992 OSPAR Convention approach explicitly building upon the mode of operation of the NSTF, including closer co-operation with ICES. Although the practical effects of the more recent and action-oriented PRAM and ASMO OSPAR bodies could not be verified in this context, it seems reasonable to conclude that the overall balance between involvement and integrity within this system is clearly improving.

4.4 Assessing institutional impact: from mild impediment to positive force?

The first decade Did *institutional factors* play a role for the decision-makers' 'tuning in' to scientific evidence in this period? The scientific and technical work of PARCON received some words of praise. Participants in the co-operation emphasised monitoring, reporting and generally the scientific work carried out in the TWG/ICES as positive aspects in this period (Sætevik, 1988: 109–10) However, there were also several weak points in the organisational model. First, as indicated by Sætevik (1988), the marked national/administrative element in TWG recruitment spurred some complaints about politicisation of the TWG. One example here is that the European Community in 1985 pressured a member country to withdraw a proposal put forward for discussion in the TWG, and instead give this the status of an information document (Sæte-vik, 1988: 116). Second, the work of an important independent marine scientific organization like ICES was only to a marginal extent integrated into the Commission context (Wettestad, 1989). Third, as indicated earlier, the work of the JMG had several flaws. It covered only the major estuaries and coastal zones of the partici-pating states, and no open sea sites. Moreover, although it was based on the already existing monitoring programmes of the con-tracting parties, very little methodological co-ordination/adaptation took place.[36] According to Norwegian participants in the PARCON bodies, the JMG's action-initiating function (related to its 'continu-ous assessment of pollution levels' mandate) was virtually non-exis-tent.[37] Thus, the institutional picture in this period is *mixed*. Although there were clearly weak points in the organisational set-up, the participants themselves seemed quite satisfied. Moreover, given that the design and operation of international institutions very much reflect national priorities, one may of course wonder if the institutional flaws were only reflections of moderate national prior-ities given to these issues at the time. This indicates that it is rea-sonable to look at some other background factors that might be of importance.

Turning first to the *state of the scientific evidence*, as already men-tioned, the initial situation was one of high uncertainty and a low level of scientific disagreement. Although we may assume that this uncertainty reduced the acceptance and weight of scientific evi-dence somewhat, we have also noted that scientific uncertainty was not a particularly important issue in PARCOM decision-making in this period. Moreover, there were several *interplay* effects at work. One reason that scientific uncertainty was scarcely reduced during this first period could be the inefficient organization of monitoring work within the JMG. However, as hinted at, the lacklustre perfor-mance of the JMG was probably first and foremost a reflection of the generally low priority which the co-operating states accorded to PARCON matters in this period.

This brings us over to the issue of *public saliency* related to marine pollution issues. After the initial environmental enthusiasm of the early 1970s, public awareness of land-based ocean pollution issues seems to have remained rather constant at a quite *moderate* level during the late 1970s and early 1980s, at least in most north-east Atlantic states. There were no dramatic marine incidents similar for instance to the German 'Waldsterben' uproar within the acid rain context which could have increased the interest in and weight given to scientific evidence by decision-makers. However, by the early 1980s, German concern also over marine pollution was on the rise, and this provided a major impetus to the holding of the first NSC, which in turn set in motion a very important process within the co-operation.

The fundamental *political malignancy* of land-based marine pollution problems was *high*. The general anti-clockwise circulation pattern in the North Sea indicated that 'export' and 'import' of pollution was taking place, but little more seems to have been known. What was certain was that abatement measures would affect the international competitive situation of the industrial actors concerned and, in the final instance, the national economies. Compared to dumping activities, the industries and activities that were contributing to land-based pollution problems were generally far more important for the states.[38] In addition came the differences in regulatory philosophies and in level of development among the northeast Atlantic states. Regarding regulatory philosophies, there was a fundamental controversy between the UK and the continental states: the UK favoured an 'assimilative capacity' approach focusing on Environmental Quality Standards (EQSs), while the Continental states favoured a more technologically-based 'uniform emissions standards' (UESs) approach. This conflict was not made easier by being fought out on the turf of the European Community as well as in several other environmental arenas. Add then to this picture the difference within the co-operation between the quite 'wealthy' North Sea states and the poorer Spain and Portugal, where the latter were inclined to give priority to other issues than marine pollution. Hence, the many basic economic and political issues to be clarified in these first years easily overshadowed the rather diffuse and uncertain scientific evidence. Nor was there any recognised approach for dealing with this uncertainty.

Briefly turning to the context of the NSC then, did organisational factors influence the acceptance and weight of scientific evidence at the Bremen 1984 NSC? To some extent, yes. According to participants, the late completion of the QSR reduced its value in discussions at the Conference. Few of the participants had managed to read or discuss the report beforehand. This led to some confused debates over scientific matters at the Conference itself.[39] On the other hand, in view of the various background factors mentioned above, (noting, however, that public awareness of pollution problems was on the rise in some countries), it is questionable whether more efficient organization would have made a substantial difference to the outcome of the 1984 Conference.

After 1987   My assessment was that this phase witnessed increasing acceptance of the scientific evidence, without necessarily implying a corresponding increase in the weight given to the evidence. Can changes in institutional factors account for this development, then? With regard to the Commission context, the answer is on the positive side. However, as the effects of the more recently established ASMO and PRAM bodies within the OSPAR context are uncertain, it is *the establishment and functioning of the NSTF* that stands out as the most important organisational change in this period. Now, as has been described, there was a governmental and potentially political dimension to the appointment and functioning of the 'core' NSTF. Although heated discussions took place, (Ducrotoy, 1997: 1888–9), the decision-makers' response at the 1993 Intermediate Ministerial Meeting was on the whole very positive. It may very well be that the organization and functioning of the NSTF – with a successful balancing of scientific and national/political concerns – contributed to increase the acceptance of scientific evidence. Before drawing such a conclusion, however, we will need to look at the development of other factors.

Regarding the *state of the scientific evidence* itself, uncertainty had been reduced somewhat, due not least to the work of the NSTF. Hence, if reduced uncertainty contributed to the increased acceptance and perhaps greater weight accorded to scientific evidence in this period, this will further point up the causal importance of the NSTF.

However, there have been potentially important changes in other factors as well. First and foremost, this applies to the issue of *public saliency*, which changed considerably throughout the 1980s, on both the general and the specific level. On the general level, the dramatic crisis-like development of environmental issues such as the

German 'Waldsterben' related to acid rain in the early 1980s, while the Chernobyl nuclear accident and the discovery of the 'hole' in the ozone layer over Antarctica contributed to a general heightening of environmental awareness from the mid-1980s on. On the more specific level, the late 1980s saw several North Sea headline-grabbing occurrences: these included other things, fish diseases and mysterious seal deaths linked to pollution, and plankton/algae blooms that killed off fish. Such events – at least temporarily and in some countries – considerably increased the demand for scientific information on North Sea pollution. For instance, Norwegian newspapers, which otherwise tend to mention the North Sea in passing every third month or so, devoted whole pages almost daily to the state of the North Sea in the 'algae' spring of 1988. It is reasonable to believe that this atmosphere also influenced the decision-makers and increased their interest in and openness to new scientific findings. Hence, it is also reasonable to assume that these events helped in making the precautionary principle and scientific evidence more and more salient.

The changes related to the precautionary principle and the role of scientific evidence were also influenced by slight changes in *political malignancy*. I am here primarily referring to the *reduced fundamental schism* between the UK and the Continent over regulatory philosophies in the late 1980s, with the UK increasingly accepting the UES approach that was otherwise dominant within the European Community (see Boehmer-Christiansen, 1990). The change in the British position paved the way for a greater acceptance of a precautionary approach.

4.5 Concluding comments

I have here distinguished between two main phases in the development of PARCOM and the North Sea Conferences, with the 1987 London North Sea Conference as a rough turning-point. Conclusions from scientific research have influenced decision-making from the initial priority-setting of the PARCON black and grey lists and onwards. However, for the first decade, decision-makers' 'adoption' of findings and hypotheses from research was assessed as being at the first and lowest 'tuning in to science' level. This may have had something to do with the organisation of the science–politics interface. The advisory TWG was staffed with nationally appointed scientific/technical bureaucrats, and there were some scattered complaints of 'politicisation'. Moreover, the progress of the JMG was slow. On the other hand, several factors indicate that these institutional features had little independent impact on the acceptance and weight given to scientific evidence. First, despite the weaknesses, participants were, on the whole, satisfied with the scientific and technical aspects of the co-operation. Hence, it makes more sense to see the limited acceptance and weight given to scientific evidence as being related to political background factors in this period. Although there were differences in how marine pollution affected the various states, such issues did not rank high on the states' agendas in this period. Moreover, differences in regulatory philosophy among the north-east Atlantic states still had to be clarified. My thesis is that these factors reduced the decision-makers' interest in scientific evidence. The malfunctioning of the JMG and to some extent the broader science–politics communication chain in this period can also be seen in this light: as a result of the generally rather low priority accorded to marine pollution issues by the co-operating states.

For more recent years, I postulated an increase in the acceptance of (if not necessarily weight given to) scientific evidence. Institutional innovations like the NSTF and a gradually improving science–politics communication chain have probably contributed to this increase in quality and acceptance. However, we should note that the basic organisational approach has not changed radically, as the core NSTF also was staffed mainly with nationally appointed scientific/technical bureaucrats – as was the case with the PARCON TWG. But this understandable, but potentially complicating, national dimension became better balanced than earlier, not least through stronger involvement of ICES. Political background factors also underwent major change in this period. First and foremost I am thinking about the appreciable increase in the public awareness of marine pollution issues. This was brought about both by a general greening of public opinion in the wake of dramatic events like the Chernobyl accident and the discovery of the 'ozone hole', and also by more specific marine pollution events in the late 1980s, like seal deaths and algae blooms. Thus, although we have identified several factors indicating an independent 'North Sea Task Force effect' on the increased acceptance of and possibly also the weight given to scientific evidence in recent years, there are clearly also other forces at work, quite independent of the organisational changes that have taken place.

A concluding reflection: the OSPAR reorganisation of the PARCON scientific and technical advisory bodies indicates that the closer co-operation with ICES and the more 'independent' marine scientific community, established by the NSTF, continues. This is probably a reflection of the fact that ICES has changed, now giving higher priority to marine pollution issues, and to the greater accessibility of its work. On the other hand, although the initial PARCON organisational approach, with a strongly national/administrative tinge in its scientific/technical work, seemed to function without much conflict, the closer integration of ICES in the recent decade may also be interpreted as the result of increased awareness of the fundamental legitimacy problems inherent in such an 'administrative' science–politics model.

Notes

1 This is a revised version of Wettestad (1994B; 1994C). Thanks to Susan Høivik, international Peace Research Institute, Oslo (PRIO), and Snorre Fjeldstad, FNI, for language and editing assistance.
2 PARCON originally covered marine pollution from land-based sources such as emissions via watercourses, directly from the coast and from offshore installations under the jurisdiction of the coastal states. It was amended in 1986 to include pollution of the sea from atmospheric sources as well.
3 For a discussion of this Convention, see for example, Hey, Ijlstra and Nollkaemper (1993).
4 In addition, ten permanent working groups have been established to assist PRAM and ASMO.
5 This is discussed by, e.g., Hayward (1990: 93).
6 See for instance Mensbrugghe (1990).
7 However, the Secretariat has also at times contributed more actively to decision-making processes. See Wettestad (1999a).
8 'Scientific knowledge' here refers to 'knowledge on inputs, concentrations and effects of contaminating substances in the marine environment'. This is in line with the 'Quality Status of the North Sea' reports produced in connection with the North Sea Conferences.
9 For more information on the EQO–UES controversy, see for instance Sætevik (1988, ch. 5); and Boehmer-Christiansen (1990).
10 See for instance Sætevik (1988) and Pallemaerts (1992). Pallemaerts's overall assessment is very similar to that of Sætevik: 'Finding itself

unable to adopt more than a few binding decisions of limited significance, the Paris Commission has resorted to making non-binding recommendations on various policy-matters relating to emissions of
dangerous substances. Apart from their non-binding nature, these recommendations are generally so vague and non-committal in their
wording that their real significance may equally be questioned' (Pallemaerts, 1992: 17).

11 See for instance Wettestad (1989: 22).
12 See for instance Gray (1990), Hey (1991), Nollkaemper (1991; 1993)
and Boehmer-Christiansen (1993b).
13 More specifically, the 1991 Urban Waste Water Treatment Directive,
the 1991 Directive on Nitrate Losses from Agriculture, and the 1992
Regulations on Agro-environmental Measures.
14 See Haas (1993b) and Andresen (1996).
15 For a more thorough discussion of the effectiveness of co-operation to
combat land-based marine pollution in the north-east Atlantic, see for
instance Wettestad (1992; 1999a), Haas (1993b), Andresen (1996) and
Skjærseth (1996; 1998).
16 Albert Weale introduces the useful distinction between 'common-pool'
resources (e.g. fisheries) ad 'common-sink' resources (e.g. environmental goods). See Weale (1992, ch. 7).
17 I have touched upon these issues in several rounds of interviews with
participants in the north-east Atlantic/North Sea co-operation and
researchers/observers during the late 1980s and the 1990s. Here special
mention should be made of Jens H. Kofoed and Lars Otto Reiersen of
the Norwegian State Pollution Control Authority, Per W. Schive of the
Norwegian Ministry of the Environment, John Gray of the University
of Oslo, Claire Nihoul, formerly with the OSPARCOM Secretariat and
Jean-Paul Ducrotoy, former Secretary for the North Sea Task Force.
18 The Oslo and Paris Commissions: (1984: 1). See also Skjærseth (1991).
19 In S. Sætevik's PARCOM study, PARCOM delegates were asked to state
the motives of their country for joining the regional cooperation. Sætevik summarizes the delegates' answers in the following manner: (1) a
wish to obtain more information and a better knowledge concerning
the connection between emissions and environmental damage; (2) a
wish to obtain more control over the emissions, especially from industry; (3) none had any particular reason for not participating in the co-
operation. See Sætevik (1988).
20 For further elaboration, see for instance Boehmer-Christiansen (1984).
21 Interviews with Norwegian civil servants in 1989.
22 Interviews with Norwegian civil servants in 1989.
23 Interviews with Norwegian scientists and civil servants in 1989 and
1991.

24 'Quality status of the North Sea', Summary Report (1987: 1).

25 See for instance Thaulow (1989).

26 However, according to *Marine Pollution Bulletin* (1990: 223), the scientific justification for this selection was also questioned: 'The reason for the singling out of these four substances is not clear ... Criticism was voiced to the effect that certain other substances are by far more hazardous than the four mentioned.'

27 For a discussion of the precautionary principle and its role within the 1992 OSPAR Convention, see Hey, Ijlstra, and Nollkaemper (1993).

28 This is explicitly stated in the Esbjerg North Sea Conference Declaration (1995: 18, emphasis added): 'The guiding principle for achieving [a healthy North Sea ecosystem] is the precautionary principle ... *The Ministers agree that in this work scientific assessments of risks is a tool in setting priorities and developing action programmes*'.

29 For a more comprehensive overview and discussion of PARCON institutional design, see Wettestad (1999a).

30 Interview with C. Nihoul, former Secretary of PARCOM, April 1992.

31 More specifically, the initial terms of reference of the TWG were as follows: It (1) was open for membership for those contracting parties wishing to send representatives; (2) should advise on technical and scientific questions submitted to it by the Commission, taking into account the information and advice received under the provisions of points(3) and (4) below; (3) make suitable arrangements to keep under review the progress of scientific and technical knowledge insofar as this may assist the work of the Commission; (4) seek advice on specific questions from the appropriate international or technical organizations (*First Annual Report on the Activities of the Paris Commission*, Annex II).

32 For more information on the ICES and its research on marine pollution, see Wettestad (1989: 13–15). See also Fløistad (1990). With regard to ICES recruitment criteria, more weight has relatively recently been given to national representation. For a brief discussion of this change within the ICES, see Andresen, Skjærseth and Wettestad (1993: 22).

33 In addition to the 'Scientific and Technical Working Group' that produced the QSR, there was also a 'Policy Working Group' (PWG). Although the PWG may have helped to clarify the positions of the various participants prior to the conference, the impression is that very little time was spent on discussing scientific matters.

34 For general accounts of the work of the NSTF, see Reid (1990) and Ducrotoy (1997).

35 For instance, monitoring data were assessed by ICES expert groups, and ICES also played a major part in reviewing the texts of the 1993 QSR.

36 This is based on the OSPARCOM Secretariat's own assessment in the

paper 'Measurement Campaigns of the Oslo and Paris Commissions', produced for the first meeting of the North Sea Task Force, The Hague, 7–9 December 1988.

37 Interviews with Norwegian civil servants in the State Pollution Control Authority and Ministry of the Environment, 1991.

38 However, according to Skjærseth's 1991 thesis on the effectiveness of the Oslo Convention, the importance of dumping activities differed from country to country. For countries like the UK, the dumping option has probably been seen as nationally quite important, given perceptions of alternative options.

39 Interviews with Norwegian civil servants in 1991.

The ECE Convention on Long-Range Transboundary Air Pollution: from common cuts to critical loads

5.1 Introduction: background and development of co-operation

In 1968 the Swedish scientist Svante Oden published a paper in which he argued that precipitation over Scandinavia was becoming increasingly acidic, thus inflicting damage to fish and lakes (Oden, 1968). Moreover, it was maintained that the acidic precipitation was to a large extent caused by sulphur compounds from British and Central European industrial emissions. This development aroused broader Scandinavian concern and diplomatic activity related to acid pollution, and played a part in the adoption of 'Principle 21' at the 1972 Stockholm UN Conference on the Human Environment. This principle pointed out that states have an obligation to ensure that activities carried out in one country do not cause environmental damage in others, or to the global commons. The specific background for formal negotiations on an air pollution convention was the East–West détente process in the mid-1970s, in which the environment was identified as one potential co-operation issue. Due to the East–West dimension, the United Nations Economic Commission for Europe (UNECE) was chosen as the institutional setting for the negotiations.[2]

The LRTAP was signed by 33 Contracting Parties (32 countries and the European Community Commission) in Geneva in November 1979. Four main aspects of the 1979 Convention may be discerned: a) the recognition that airborne pollutants were a major problem; b) the declaration that the Parties would 'endeavor to limit and, as far as possible, gradually reduce and prevent air pollution, including long-range transboundary air pollution' (Article 2); c) the commitment of Contracting Parties 'by means of exchange of infor-

mation, consultation, research and monitoring, develop without
undue delay policies and strategies which should serve as a means of
combating the discharge of air pollutants, taking into account efforts
already made at the national and international levels' (Article 3); and
d) the intention to use 'the best available technology which is economically feasible' to meet the objectives of the Convention (Nordberg, 1993). The Convention did not specify any pollutants, but
stated that measures should start with sulphur dioxide (SO_2).

The Convention has been in force since 1983 and has a current
membership of 42 Parties and the European Community (EC).
Moreover, the Convention was to be overseen by an Executive Body
(EB), which included representatives of all the Parties to the Convention as well as the EC. Furthermore, the ECE secretariat was
given a co-ordinating function. The institutional structure has also
included several Working Groups (WGs), Task Forces (TFs) and
International Co-operative programmes. One of these is the Co-
operative Programme for Monitoring and Evaluation of Long-
Range Transmissions of Air Pollutants in Europe (EMEP). Rooted in
the Convention's strong initial focus on knowledge improvement
and monitoring, a specific financing Protocol for the EMEP monitoring programme was established in 1984. The more specific
development of this 'scientific–political complex' is described in
more detail in Section 3.

The first main regulatory step in the co-operation was the 1985
Protocol on the Reduction of Sulphur Emissions. At the third meeting of the Executive Body of the Convention in Helsinki, July 1985,
21 countries and the EC signed this legally binding protocol. The
Protocol stipulated a reduction of emissions/transboundary fluxes
of sulphur dioxide (SO_2) by at least 30 per cent as soon as possible,
and by 1993 at the latest, with 1980 levels as a baseline. However,
some major emitter states chose not to join the agreement, among
them the UK, the USA, and Poland. The Protocol entered into force
in September 1987 and has been ratified by 21 Parties.

In the 1988 Sofia Protocol on Nitrogen Oxides (NOx), the signatories pledged to freeze NOx emissions at the 1987 level from 1994
onwards and to negotiate subsequent reductions. Twenty-five countries signed the Protocol, including the UK and the USA. Moreover,
12 European signatories went a step further and signed an additional (and separate) joint declaration committing them to a 30 per
cent reduction of emissions by 1998, with a flexible baseline

between 1980 and 1986.[3] The Protocol entered into force in February 1991 and has been ratified by 26 Parties.

The next step was the 1991 Geneva Protocol on Volatile Organic Compounds (VOCs). VOCs are a group of chemicals which are precursors of ground level ozone. The Protocol called for a reduction of 30 per cent in VOC emissions between 1988 and 1999, based on 1988 levels – either at national levels or within specific 'tropospheric ozone management areas' (TOMA). Some countries were allowed to opt for a freeze of 1988 emissions by 1999.[4] Twenty-one Parties signed the Protocol in 1991; Portugal and the EC joined in 1992. Russia and Poland chose not to sign. The Protocol entered into force in September 1997 and has been ratified by 17 Parties.

Then, the Protocol on Further Reductions of Sulphur Emissions was signed in Oslo in June 1994 by 28 Parties. The Protocol is based on the 'critical loads' approach. The aim of this approach is that emissions reductions should be negotiated on the basis of the (varying) effects of air pollutants, rather than by choosing an equal percentage reduction target for all countries involved.[5] Hence, the Protocol sets out individual and varying national reduction targets only for the year 2000 for half of the countries, and additional 2005 and 2010 targets for the other half – with 1980 as base year. The Protocol entered into force in August 1998 and has been ratified by 18 Parties.

As the most recent steps, two new Protocols on heavy metals and persistent organic pollutants (POPs) were signed by 34 Parties in Aarhus in June 1998. Negotiations on a new combined NOx and VOC Protocol will start in early 1999.

5.2 Did scientific evidence count? A rough overview

Have conclusions from scientific research been adopted as premises for policy decisions in this field? How has this relationship changed over time? These questions form the point of departure for this section. As indicated in the chapter on PARCON and the North Sea Conferences, at least before the quite recent political utilisation of the critical loads approach, it is difficult to measure the degree of acceptance/adoption of scientific conclusions. This means that assessments of the degree of weight given to scientific evidence also in this case have to be based on qualitative interpretation of scientific reports and policy decisions, supplemented by interviews with scientific and political actors.[6]

The discussion will be structured in the following manner: first, a very rough 'scientific baseline' will be established, describing the scientific situation at the time the co-operation started. Second, the role of scientific evidence in the process leading up to the 1985 SO_2 protocol will be discussed. Third, the role of scientific evidence in the process leading up to the 1980 NOx protocol and the 1991 VOC protocol will be discussed, with special weight on the NOx process. The fourth section will discuss the role of science in the second sulphur protocol negotiations.

The starting-point: high uncertainty, and also some controversies
Let us first turn to the scientific situation as it was at the time the co-operation commenced. As indicated in the introductory section, in the late 1960s and early 1970s, the main scientific input on acid rain and international air pollution came from Swedish and Norwegian researchers. However, in 1972, the Organisation for Economic Co-operation and Development (OECD) launched the 'Co-operative Technical programme to Measure the Long-Range Transport of Air Pollutants'. Eleven European states participated in this programme. Results of the programme were first published in July 1977. Concerning the question of long-range transportation, the report affirmed that such transportation was taking place. The report concluded that there was 'strong evidence' that the sulphur dioxide pollution caused the acid rain and snow that appeared to be killing salmon and trout, for instance in Norway and Sweden. However, the degree of scientific uncertainty related to all these aspects of the problem must also be characterised as quite high. For instance, the OECD stated explicitly that owing mainly to uncertainties surrounding emission data and dispersion models, the programme's findings were only accurate to within plus/minus 50 per cent (Wetstone and Rosencrantz 1983: 136). In addition to high uncertainty, there was also some scientific controversy, especially between Scandinavian and British researchers. However, according to researchers who participated in this debate, it was not as heated as the political rhetoric at the time may lead one to believe.[7]

Having established the rough scientific 'baseline' let us then turn to the role played by scientific evidence in the process leading up to the 1985 SO_2 Protocol.

The sulphur process: increasing scientific acceptance, but marginal effects on specific protocol design   First, compared to the situation when the co-operation started, there is no doubt that scientific evidence with regard to the transnational transportation of sulphur and nitrogen compounds was becoming much more accepted in the early 1980s than it had been in the mid-1970s. A certain scientific 'consolidation' was witnessed at the 1982 Stockholm Conference on Acidification of the Environment. The Conference's final statement concluded that 'the acidification problem is serious and, even if deposition remains stable, deterioration of soil and water will continue and may increase unless additional control measures are implemented and existing control policies are strengthened'.[8] This Conference also witnessed the very important scientific and political shift of West German positions, related to the domestic media and political 'Waldsterben' uproar.[9] Moreover, Park (1987: 177) maintains that 'by this time [i.e. 1983/84] … beyond doubt was the transfrontier character of the problem, in which some countries gained whilst others lost'. He further states as an example that when the European Parliament Committee on the Environment, Public Health and Consumer Protection held a public hearing on acid deposition in 1983, 'all agreed that the adverse effects of acid rain were clear, and the debate centred *not* on whether or not to reduce emissions but on how it should be done and who should pay for it' (Park, 1987: 174). Studies of the development of national perceptions of the acidification problems also clearly indicate shifting perceptions in countries like The Netherlands, Austria and Switzerland in the wake of the Stockholm Conference and the important German shift in positions.[10] Thus, we have good reason to assume that the existing scientific evidence was very much accepted and given considerable weight by the states choosing to sign the 1985 SO_2 protocol. Among the important non-signers (Poland, the UK, the USA), it was only the USA that seemingly gave very much weight to scientific uncertainty in its explanation for not joining the agreement (McCormick, 1989: 85).

However, this does not mean that the 30 per cent target was in itself 'directly derived' from scientific evidence. Both the baseline of 1980, the target date of 1993, and the 30 per cent reduction target itself have been characterised as arbitrary (Haigh, 1989). This being said, my own interviews have confirmed the impression that most scientists still saw the 30 per cent reduction as a significant step in the right direction.

The NOx process: more regime-driven – and politically sobering – knowledge improvement   Nitrogen oxide emissions stem from both power plants and automobiles. They are responsible for some acid deposition, and also contribute to the formation of ground-level ozone, a gas that is toxic to humans and harmful to vegetation (Levy, 1993: 94). The NOx negotiation story is somewhat different from the SO_2 story. On the one hand, the process was scientifically underpinned in the sense that the initiative to formal negotiations on a NOx protocol was a reflection of the growing recognition that the causes of air pollution problems were multifaceted and complex – and henceforth that the problems were far from 'solved' by the establishment of the sulphur protocol. On the other hand, at least in the first phase of the negotiations, scientific understanding of the NOx problem was much less developed than in the case of the SO_2 negotiations. For instance, a Norwegian observer claims: 'Here the politicians decided to go ahead with actual negotiations before the necessary scientific basis had been established' (Bakken, 1989: 202). However, scientific knowledge improved a good deal during the negotiations. Thus over time, the acceptance of scientific evidence seems to have become quite high.[11] According to Levy, 'the scientific consensus now is that ozone is just as harmful to forests and agricultural crops as sulphur deposition. It is also a public health problem in many urban areas. *All this was accepted during the negotiations of the nitrogen protocol.* There was dispute over the magnitude of the damage, though' (Levy, 1993: 94; emphasis added). More as a footnote, it is also interesting to note that the concept of critical loads was gaining increasing attention during the negotiations.[12] Hence, it was explicitly stated in the Protocol to base further international measures in this issue area on the critical loads approach.

It is very hard to say if the weight given to scientific evidence was lower or higher than in the sulphur process. What we can say is it that the role of science and technology was different within the NOx process. First, it seems that *technological considerations* played a more significant role in the NOx process than in the sulphur process, partly related to the question of automobiles and catalytic converters.[13] Moreover, increasing scientific and technological knowledge played an overall more *sobering* role in this context.[14] In the sulphur process, increasing knowledge led to increasing political support for an international 30 per cent reduction target. In the NOx process, increasing knowledge led to reduced political support for the initial political ambition of a similar 30 per cent reduction target.

Some notes on the VOC process: high complexity and regime-driven knowledge improvement[15]   In addition to NOx, VOCs are important contributors to groundlevel-ozone. Although West Germany's call for combined NOx and VOC requirements in 1986 was rejected, a TF on 'Emissions of Volatile Organic Compounds from Stationary Sources and Possibilities of their Control' was established. In 1988, on the initiative of Germany, France, the Netherlands, and Switzerland, the Working Group on VOCs (WGV) was established, in order to lead up to a VOC protocol. The initial work of this group clarified the emission picture. Emissions stemmed mainly from three sources: motor traffic, the use of solvents in industrial and household appliances, and the oil and gas industries. Geographically, emissions stemmed mainly from the highly industrialised and densely populated countries of Western Europe. Knowledge was further improved through among other things EMEP and a 'governmentally designated' expert group. Reflecting the complexity of this issue, several protocol approaches were launched in the negotiation process, combining 30 per cent flat-rate reductions with technological standards. Important actors like Canada, the USA, the Soviet Union, the EC and Norway were all sceptical towards the 30 per cent target. Gradually, consensus on the basic 30 per cent reduction commitment increased, sweetened by elements like a flexible base year (between 1984 and 1990), a freeze option for small polluters, and that some countries would only have to reduce by 30 per cent within specific TOMAs. This became the basic structure of the 1991 protocol.

So what about the role of scientific evidence? Overall, the VOC process entails several similarities with the NOx process, as a rapid knowledge production took place in a quite short time period and primarily within the regime context. The general impression is an overall acceptance of the scientific evidence at hand, but also a general recognition of the remaining considerable uncertainty and

complexity. This recognition is reflected in the unprecedented flexibility and complexity of the protocol's commitments.

*The 1994 sulphur protocol and the 'critical loads' approach: science
moving centre-stage?*   As indicated above, the concept of 'critical
loads' was introduced already in the NOx negotiations. However, it
was not before the negotiations on a new and revised sulphur protocol that this approach really moved centre-stage. Let us first
briefly describe the critical loads approach.

   A 'critical load' is most commonly defined as 'a quantitative esti-
mate of an exposure to one or more pollutants below which significantly harmful effects on specified sensitive elements of the
environment do not occur according to present knowledge'. This
approach was launched by Swedish scientists and government officials in the early 1980s.[16] An accepted element of the approach is the
generation of so-called 'target loads' from critical loads, target loads
taking into account economic factors especially, but also considering technological, social and political factors. More specifically, to
use the critical loads approach, the following information is needed:
a) inventories of current emissions and projections of future emission rates; b) estimates of the potential for and costs of emission
reduction; c) long-range transport models; d) maps of critical loads
and target loads; e) integrated assessment modelling. (Nordberg,
1993).

   However, in the pre-negotiation phase 1989–91, the extent to
which the second sulphur protocol could be based on critical loads
was open. For instance, Germany favoured flat-rate reductions,
combined with technical requirements. When the formal negotiations started in 1992, the basic approach was a combination of the
critical loads approach and technology standards. Early in the negotiations, it was recognised that it would be impracticable to reduce
sulphur depositions below critical loads by the end of the century.
Based on inputs from the 'Regional Acidification Information and
Simulation' (RAINS) model developed at the International Institute
for Applied Systems Analysis (IIASA), it was instead agreed to
reduce by (first 50 per cent, then in May 1993) 60 per cent the gap
between current levels of sulphur deposition and critical loads in
most of Europe, except for the most acid-sensitive areas. The
RAINS model then came up with tentative country-specific emission
reduction targets. As the model indicated that the most cost-

effective way was high reductions in a number of central European high emission countries, quite ambitious targets for these countries landed on the table. For some countries (like Austria, Finland, Germany, The Netherlands, Norway and Russia), existing reduction plans were adequate to meet the model requirements. For other countries (like Belgium, Denmark, France, Ireland, Italy, Spain and the UK), existing plans were insufficient. Hence, a period of sometimes intense bargaining followed. Old political conflicts reappeared, with for instance the Norwegian Environment Minister, Thorbjørn Berntsen, calling his British counterpart a 'shitbag'. The final Protocol was decided upon in Oslo in June 1994, and sets out individual and varying national reduction targets only for the year 2000 for half of the countries, and additional 2005 and 2010 targets for the other half – with 1980 as base year.

With regard to the 'adoption' of scientific evidence, this process comes close to our third and highest level. A widely shared view is to hail this protocol as something special with regard to the relationship between science and politics in international acid rain politics.[17] However, as indicated above, this certainly does not mean the 'abolishment' of politics in this issue area. Moreover, it should be noted that there were several conflicts along the way, for instance related to somewhat differing targets coming out of different models.[18]

Summing up Have conclusions from scientific research been adopted as premises for policy decisions, and has this changed over time? Noting the complexity of this question, the overall assessment is that the role of scientific evidence has varied somewhat. In the sulphur negotiations, the assessment is that the acceptance of scientific evidence was markedly increasing over time – even though the 30 per cent target adopted in the Protocol was clearly based on political judgement rather than scientific evidence. In the NOx and VOC negotiations, scientific evidence developed over shorter time periods and more within the regime context. Although scientific evidence seemingly became highly accepted, inherent uncertainty and complexity were also emphasised. Hence, the role of science was at least different and of a more sobering character in these processes – if not necessarily less important. However, related to the adoption scale focused in this book, the assessment for all these three processes would be a second-level score. Decision-makers accepted the substantive conclusions produced by the scientific community, but the targets discussed during negotiations and final commitments were only remotely related to science. In the case of the 1994 sulphur protocol, based on the critical loads approach, scientific evidence played a very important role. With regard to the majority of the countries, the general acceptance of the scientific evidence seems to have been quite high. Moreover, and this distinguishes this process from the foregoing ones, decision-makers also to a large extent accepted and literally adopted the policy implications inherent in the model predictions. This points towards the highest score in our scientific evidence adoption scale.

How then has this development been affected by the institutional setting? This is the main theme of the next sections.

5.3 Institutional design: main features and evolution[19]

5.3.1 Introduction

It should of course be noted that the following is a quite static presentation of a dynamic process, where new bodies have been established (and other abolished) in relation to changing scientific and political needs within the regime. Space does not allow the diachronic full story, though. Still, the presentation can at least distinguish between two main phases in the development of LRTAP institutional design: before and after the reorganisation that took place in 1991.

Let us first turn to the initial, 'formative' phase. A first thing to note is that part of the LRTAP scientific–political complex lingered on from pre-Convention days, namely the Working Party on Air Pollution Problems (WPAP). The WPAP was initially under the ECE body 'Senior advisers to ECE Governments on Environmental and Water Problems.' Other parts of the scientific–political complex grew out of the aforementioned OECD monitoring programme, namely the EMEP. The rest of the complex was established in connection with the Convention, with sub-groups gradually being added to the structure. Up until 1991, the structure was roughly as follows: on the administrative, political side, the main bodies were the Executive Body (EB) of the Convention, with the parties meeting annually since 1983, and the Working Group on Abatement Strategies (WGAS), an important forum for continuous negotiations. On the scientific/technical side, important subsidiary bodies under the EB were the Working Group on Effects (WGE); the Working Group on NOx; the WGV; the EMEP Steering Body; the Group of Economic Experts on Air Pollution (GEAP); and the aforementioned WPAP. Under these bodies, several International Co-operative Programmes (ICPs) and TFs were established.

This set-up was reorganised in November 1991. The current organisational structure is somewhat simpler: on the administrative/political side, in addition to the EB, there is a Working Group on Strategies (WGS). On the scientific/technical side, in addition to the Working Group on Effects (WGE) and the EMEP Steering Body, there is a Working Group on Technology (WGT). Current ICPs under the WGE are forests (Germany), freshwaters (Norway), materials (Sweden), crops (UK) and integrated monitoring (Sweden).

The EMEP monitoring programme warrants some specific, introductory comments. It was initiated by the ECE in co-operation with the UNEP and the World Meteorological Organisation (WMO) as a part of UNEP's Global Environment Monitoring System (GEMS). The main objective of EMEP is to provide governments with information on deposition and concentration of pollutants, as well as on the quantity and significance of long-range transmission of pollutants. The programme has three main elements: emission data, measurements of air and precipitation quality, and atmospheric dispersion models. The EMEP sampling network consists of some 100 stations in 33 countries, and the work is co-ordinated by three international centres, two in Oslo and one in Moscow. As mentioned, in 1984, a specific EMEP financing protocol was established. Funding is provided by all Parties to the EMEP Protocol, according to a cost sharing agreement developed by the Parties to the Convention on the basis of the UN assessment scale (based on GNP, population and geographic criteria).[20] For instance, the 1996 EMEP budget was $1,990,415 (*Green Globe Yearbook*, 1996: 98).

Finally, a few words about the Secretariat. As indicated earlier, the ECE Secretariat in Geneva co-ordinates the co-operation. More specifically, the Secretariat work is presently being carried out by five full-time professional posts and two secretaries in the air pollution section of the ECE Environment and Human Settlements Division.

5.3.2 Internal organisation

As indicated in the previous section, we are here talking about
formal bodies. The EB discusses and approves the mandates of
the various groups. However, overall, the Secretariat claims that the
groups' work is very autonomous. Other sources indicate that
the degree of autonomy varies somewhat between the groups, and
also between the issues discussed by the groups. As a general rule it
appears that groups discussing general features of problems enjoy a
high degree of autonomy, while groups discussing effects and issues
with more obvious political implications enjoy less autonomy.[21]

Formally, entry is open to all governmentally appointed experts
in all the groups – 'entirely in the hands of governments', as
expressed by the Secretariat. More informally, the Secretariat sometimes indicates certain desirable qualifications with regard to rank,
education etc. *vis-à-vis* the participating countries. All subsidiary
bodies are comprised of government officials (Levy, 1993: 84).
There is a mix between scientists and administrators in all the working groups, including the EMEP Steering Body. Delegations vary
widely with regard to size. Some countries may choose to appoint
delegations with many experts, each covering one topic, whereas
others rely on fewer persons. The mode of appointment also varies
among the countries. However, there is a certain pattern among the
countries, with some countries consistently closer to the scientific or
the administrative 'pole' than others.[22] In the TFs and ICPs, participation is far closer to the scientific than the administrative pole.
Membership requires that research is conducted at the national
level, and that this research is harmonised and shared with other
participants. However, the regularity in participation should not be
exaggerated, as this varies somewhat between meetings. This is
partly issue related: some people participate only in meetings where
certain issues are discussed. This also gives the Secretariat the possibility of influencing participation indirectly: by framing issues in
certain ways, well aware that certain people get tempted to show
up. However, the Secretariat can also formally invite persons/
organisations, but only those with ECOSOC credentials.[23] Given the
multitude of bodies, disciplinary background is obviously heterogeneous. Regarding funding, this is generally in the hands of the
participating governments. However, there are some nuances to this
picture. The EMEP is, as already mentioned, funded according to a
specific protocol and cost-sharing agreement. The co-ordinating

expenses for the ICPs are provided by the lead countries in each of the ICPs, and participating governments pay their own research costs (Levy, 1993: 89).

The groups vary with regard to main functions. The WGE is responsible for assessing effects of air pollution on ecosystems, crops and materials. It addresses dose–response relationships, critical levels and loads and the ecological effects of reduction of air pollution, emissions, concentrations and depositions (*Annual Report*, LRTAP Executive Body, 1991). On the whole, the WGE first and foremost synthesises and 'translates' existing knowledge. It supplies important background material for revised and new protocols, by supplying information relevant for 'critical loads'. Actual research is mainly carried out in the various sub-groups.

The EMEP Steering body has been described as 'the backbone of the Convention'.[24] The Steering Body has first and foremost has a co-ordinating function. It directs scientific work for the improvement of data and information on air pollution, and advises the international EMEP centres on appropriate development of routine measures and research projects. (*Annual Report*, LRTAP Executive Body, 1991). But it also has a 'translatory' function, for instance in cases where the Working Group on Strategies needs certain data as inputs to ongoing negotiation processes. The Steering Body has increasingly been called upon to provide reliable data on pollution levels and loads as a basis for calculating exceedances in relation to 'critical loads'.

The WGT came into operation in June 1992. It took over responsibility for the former WPAP and the earlier Task Force on Exchange of Technology. The WGT has first and foremost a co-ordinating role, supervising the substantive work on technologies for air pollution abatement.

The principal task of the WGS is to prepare protocols on specific air pollutants, or group of air pollutants. Thus, the WGS is the main negotiating body within the LRTAP organisational structure. The body has a co-ordinating and 'translatory' role, as it cannot fulfil its negotiating role without inputs from all the other bodies. Regarding the economic dimension, it should be noted that there is a specific Task Force on Economic Aspects of Abatement Strategies under the WGS. Another interesting body under the WGS is the Task Force on Integrated Assessment Modelling. In connection with the development of the critical loads approach, this group has co-operated closely with the IIASA to evaluate the cost-effectiveness of different abatement strategies. As mentioned, IIASA has developed a system model, the RAINS model, that combines information on emission generation with emission control technologies and abatement costs, also taking into account the long-range transport of pollutants and the environmental effects of acid deposition in different areas of Europe. On that basis, scenarios of different abatement strategies can be analysed (Wuster, 1992: 235).

5.3.3 Communication between scientific and regulatory bodies

All bodies produce annual reports to the EB. In addition to those reports, the Secretariat provides the EB annually with a document on policies and strategies as reported by parties, a document on progress in selected areas, a draft work plan for the forthcoming year, and a note on financial issues. According to the Secretariat, the EB reviews and responds to these reports, but the extent of this response varies a good deal. The standard response formulation in the EB report is that the EB has 'taken note of' the reports produced. This may be regarded as a deliberately ambiguous formulation. 'Take note of' is normally interpreted as an approval, but it may also be interpreted as expressing only that the EB has seen the reports.[25] Conclusions and recommendations for action, expressed in the reports submitted to the EB, have to be endorsed by the EB in order to be implemented. This is normally a very smooth procedure since the relevant subsidiary body has reviewed and approved all draft recommendations beforehand. The main formal response element lies in review of policies and strategies, and adoption of work plan and EMEP budget. In addition, there are the discussions on and formulation of new or revised mandates for the subsidiary bodies, and, if necessary, the TFs. The most far-reaching decisions by the EB concern the adoption of international agreements, i.e. protocols and their amendments.

The question regarding the organisational distance between research and policy-making is also in this context a complex one. However, some broad features may be indicated: first, all research is reported to the WGs and the EMEP Steering Body before reaching the EB. Reports from the WGs are presented to the EB, but this is more of a formality than a thorough advisory process. Second, given the central role of the WGS *vis-à-vis* the EB, it may be assumed that the work carried out in the three TFs directly under the WGS, providing basic information for the negotiations, stand an especially good chance of being communicated to the EB. Besides, given the weight given to the establishment of 'critical loads' in revised protocols, the Task Force on Mapping is quite closely connected to the policy process. This is also explicitly indicated in the organisation map.

5.3.4 How far from the 'optimal' combination?

If the 'ideal combination' is to combine scientific integrity/autonomy on the one hand, and involvement in the political process and responsiveness to decision-makers' questions and needs on the other, how does the complex system described in the preceding questions 'score'? A couple of features stand out at this stage: first, much in common with other environmental scientific–political complexes such as for example the PARCON system, integrity/autonomy is highest in the sub-groups (i.e. in the ICPs and TFs). Autonomy is lower in the working groups, however with variations among the groups and even with regard to issues within the groups. Second, the prominent place of the EMEP monitoring system within this organisational structure ensures a certain core of independent scientists. Third, having a permanent negotiating working group – the WGS – 'computing' inputs from the other groups, provides a continuous formal forum for discussions on science–politics interface issues. Fourth, the gradual rise of the critical loads approach in the late 1980s and up through the 1990s means that various types of scientists are drawn into the LRTAP decision-making process in a perhaps hitherto unprecedented manner within the realm of international environmental co-operation. In general, this can of course be a mixed blessing. On the one hand, it represents additional funding opportunities, and researchers experience an interest in their work and results that they sometimes yearn for. On the other hand, more direct political relevance and implications automatically increase the temptation of political pressure being brought to bear on scientists.

Overall, the impression is that the LRTAP system has achieved a well-functioning combination of scientific integrity and responsiveness to decision-makers' need for usable inputs.

5.4 Institutional impact – 'real' or 'spurious'?

5.4.1 Did institutional design matter for the weight of scientific evidence in the sulphur protocol?

As will be recalled, the assessment was that the acceptance of scientific evidence was increasing considerably over time – although the more specific protocol design had little to do with science. Is it likely that the increasing acceptance of scientific evidence was related to the functioning of the LRTAP 'scientific–political complex', with the EMEP system as a driving force? To some extent, yes. Regarding EMEP, the high priority given to co-ordination of national research programmes and standardisation of data collection strengthened the international and general credibility of national research programmes.[26] This in turn contributed to increased scientific consensus on transport mechanisms and patterns of transboundary air pollution. With regard to specific national developments, Levy (1993: 121) indicates that countries like Finland, Switzerland and Austria were clearly influenced by LRTAP's knowledge-creating activities: 'All of the governments were active participants in [LRTAP] collaborative programs, even though their official positions, initially, were that acidification was not a problem. Once these governments became aware of the extent of damage their countries suffered, they adopted positions favouring reductions in emissions'. Hence, several factors indicate that institutional features connected to the LRTAP system contributed somewhat to the acceptance and weight of scientific evidence. The question then becomes: how about other potential important factors like 'political malignancy' and 'public saliency'? How did they contribute to the degree of acceptance of scientific evidence?

Regarding degree of 'political malignancy', the acid rain issue was of course a quite malign issue when the co-operation started in 1979:[27] emissions stemmed from important economic and societal sectors like power stations, industrial plants and transport, hence abatement efforts would affect 'core' national economic activities, and potentially give rise to malign competitive effects between the countries. Moreover, although several countries were probably both emitters/exporters and receivers/importers of transboundary polluting substances, there was also an important asymmetrical dimension to the matter: major emitters like the UK were seemingly able to export significant portions of their emissions to small

Scandinavian emitters with vulnerable soil characteristics. Last, but not least, it was only the Scandinavians who had experienced visible 'acid' damages. It has been maintained that when LRTAP was created, only two of its 30 members thought acid rain was a serious environmental problem (Levy 1993: 75). Moreover, although the East–West dimension was an important contributing force in the regime-creation process, ideological differences and Western suspicions of Eastern data 'massaging' complicated open and constructive problem-solving in the first decade of the regime's functioning.

But the initial low responsiveness to scientific evidence began to change somewhat from 1982 on. Although most of the fundamental malign features were still there, the pattern of perceived environmental vulnerability and related damages started changing. Things started happening both at the national and international level. At the national level, the most important development was of course the sudden political about-turn of Germany (FRG) in 1982. Like most others, Germany had been a reluctant and passive actor in the early LRTAP days. In 1982, extensive acid rain-related domestic 'Waldsterben' made big headlines, contributed to a stepped-up domestic abatement programme, and for obvious competitive reasons, a new entrepreneurial role for Germany on the international stage – be it LRTAP or the EC. There is little doubt that the changed role of Germany markedly influenced the neighbouring countries' perceptions of the acid rain problem and hence probably also their acceptance of scientific evidence.

At the international level, attention-raising meetings were held from 1982 on. First, there was the arrangement of the aforementioned 1982 Stockholm Conference on Acidification of the Environment. This conference has been hailed as a success model in shepherding an international consensus on scientific information concerning transboundary sulphur pollution: 'At the expert meetings, over one hundred of the leading scientists, engineers and pollution control officials from 20 nations gathered to produce a detailed summary of the current state-of-the-art knowledge of the scientific, technical, and policy issues surrounding the acidification problem' (Wetstone, 1987: 185–6). Second, international political meetings like the 1984 Ottawa Ministerial Conference and Munich Multilateral Conference on the Environment also contributed to a generally heightened public saliency of the transboundary air pollution issue.

Now, to sum up, where does all this leave us with regard to the impact of institutional design? The overall assessment is still that the LRTAP institutional design, and especially the EMEP programme, contributed to the acceptance of scientific evidence. However, a decrease of initially high political malignancy, and a related increased public saliency of the acid rain issue in the first part of the 1980s are probably more important causal factors in this picture. Although perspectives and concepts vary, such an assessment seems to be in line with other authors who have written on the science-politics relationship within the acid rain context. According to Wetstone (1987: 192), 'the level of media interest, the extent of public concern, and external factors, such as economics and international politics, played a key role in determining how governments responded to research data'. Levy (1993: 94) observes that in June 1983 nine government were in favour of 30 per cent cuts; the number had grown to 11 in March 1984, 18 in June, and 20 by year end 1984. He then maintains: 'In effect, the eleven governments that did not consider sulphur dioxide reductions to be in their interest in 1983 changed their minds once the question became highly public and connected to normative principles' (Levy, 1993: 94).

5.4.2 Did institutional factors matter for the role of scientific evidence in the NOx and VOC protocols?

In the cases of NOx and VOCs, although acceptance of scientific evidence increased over time, it was indicated that the role of scientific evidence was at least different from what it was in the sulphur process, and that acceptance possibly also was somewhat lower. Does this mean that the scientific-political institutional apparatus functioned less effectively in these processes than in the sulphur process? As far as one can see, the answer here is negative. In the following, most weight will be given to the better researched NOx case.[28] Moreover, there seem to be several scientific and political similarities between the NOx and VOC processes.

Turning then to the NOx story, in order to establish the necessary scientific basis for negotiations, the Working Group on NOx (WGN) was established in July 1985. Soon it became clear that both scientific uncertainty was high and consensus was quite low. In this situation, a successful knowledge gathering process was organised.[29] This process included, first, the systematic incorporation of existing knowledge in bodies like the EMEP, the ECE, the World Health

Organisation (WHO) and the OECD. Second, the establishment of several sub-groups (Task Forces, Working Groups, Working Parties) helped make a complex problem more manageable. Third, the use of specific 'Governmentally Designated Expert Groups', comprising governmental and independent experts, was an institutional innovation which has been characterised as 'a very effective organisational tool which speeded up the process'.[30] According to Stenstadvold (1991), this organisational approach involved the Parties in a manner which stimulated a common problem understanding, and paved the way for more constructive negotiations than would otherwise have been the case.[31] In this case, however, compared to the growing support for the 30 per cent target within the sulphur process, scientific evidence overall had more of a sobering effect, helping parties to realise the complex relationships as well as the abatement costs involved.[32]

Hence, the question then arises: was the different role of scientific evidence in this process caused by a politically (more) malignant problem? First, like in the case of SO_2, NOx emissions also stem from 'vital' societal activities, especially related to power plants and transport emissions. However, the transport emissions part in both NOx and VOC make these problems in many ways more *complex* than the more stationary point sources sulphur issue. Moreover, in the sulphur process, a strong coalition supporting international regulations emerged over time, including prominent continental states like Germany and France, in addition to the Scandinavians. This coalition broke down in the NOx negotiations, as countries like France and Italy joined forces with the initial LRTAP 'laggard', the UK. Furthermore, countries like Norway and Finland became much more passive, as they during the negotiations became aware of costly transport emissions (Stenstadvold, 1991: 112). Hence, the drive to forge a scientific and political consensus was weakened compared to the sulphur process. Moreover, an important additional aspect which is highly relevant both for the NOx and VOC context is the question of *scientific and regulatory history*. Overall, the NOx and VOC issues must be seen as much less 'mature' than the sulphur issue when negotiations started. The scientific and regulatory history of the sulphur issue dated back to the late 1960s/early 1970s, while the NOx and VOC parts of the acidification story were much more problems really catching general attention in the early 1980s.

Were the differing political malignancy aspects accompanied by a lower public saliency of the related acidification problems than in the sulphur process? Possibly, but the question is difficult to assess. On the one hand, the sulphur process and growing, visible evidence of forest damages in an increasing number of European countries up through the 1980s ensured a certain public saliency related to air pollution problems that benefited later negotiation processes like NOx and VOCs. On the other hand, the NOx process period, i.e. 1985–88, lacked both the occurrence of national 'acid dramas' comparable to the German 'Waldsterben' events in early 1980s, *and* the frequent and high-level meetings of the sulphur process. Hence, on the whole, the impression is that the public saliency related to the NOx problem was somewhat lower than was the case in the sulphur process.

To sum up: first, the LRTAP regime was important for knowledge building in the NOx and VOC processes; and more important than in the preceding sulphur process, much due to the fact that the NOx and VOC problems were much less scientifically and politically 'mature' when the international negotiation processes began. However, the acceptance of scientific evidence was hampered by economically and politically malignant problems, and also by a somewhat lower public saliency of the related acidification and air pollution problems than was the case in the earlier 'Waldsterben' days in the first sulphur process. Hence, although the role of the regime was more important in the NOx and VOC processes than in the sulphur process, less scientifically mature issues, high problem malignancy and lower public saliency weakened the position of scientific evidence as a premise in policy development in the NOx and VOC processes.

5.4.3 The 1994 sulphur protocol: institutional design and the critical loads approach

With regard to the 'adoption' of scientific evidence, the assessment was here that this process comes close to our third and highest level. A widely shared view is to hail this protocol as something special with regard to the relationship between science and politics in international acid rain politics. So how come?

Turning first to the institutional design perspective, as indicated earlier, the negotiations on the second sulphur protocol witnessed a very interesting close collaboration between various types of scientists and administrators. Not least the economic input was considerably stronger and more systematic than in most international environmental co-operation so far. The systematic preparatory work in various LRTAP sub-groups was a pivotal factor in the development of the critical loads approach. Here, the Task Force on Mapping must be mentioned on the methodological side. Moreover, the Task Force on Integrated Assessment Modelling, with its close collaboration with the IIASA, was also very important. This collaboration has been generally successful, as IIASA's suggested reduction targets seem to have been accepted by most of the negotiating parties, even though several of them face considerably tougher targets than under the previous regime. Here, the international and independent dimensions of IIASA's work are probably of crucial importance in increasing the legitimacy of its work, compared with the other more 'national' models referred to in the negotiations.

A less important, but still relevant LRTAP institutional design feature which comes into this picture, is the verification capability represented by the EMEP monitoring system. It has, for instance, been maintained that 'few other international agreements can be said to come equipped with verification instruments of this calibre' (Sand, 1990: 259); however little actively utilised so far. A differentiated and complex agreement based on critical loads will need as much independent verification as it can get. With the establishment of a specific Implementation Committee, the Parties have signalled an increased weight on critical follow-up work, and the EMEP system can be a good backbone in such work.

On the whole, then, the development of a well-functioning scientific–political complex bore applicable 'fruits' in this negotiation process, and undoubtedly contributed to the so to speak 'advanced' form and outcome of this process. But are there other, more basic policy and saliency factors which contributed to the outcome of this process?

With regard to problem characteristics, the basic competitive effects related to emissions reductions remained; and so did the asymmetrical transboundary pollution flows and effects. Still, *some important aspects had changed*. First, over time, most of the countries involved in the LRTAP context had become much more aware of the potential domestic environmental and health damages related to air pollution and acid rain. The negotiations on the NOx and

VOC protocols contributed to this overall learning and awareness-raising process. Second, the changing, more constructive role of the UK – the most important laggard in the previous sulphur process – must especially be mentioned. This is related to several factors: a fundamental energy supply switch from coal to gas; a growing recognition of potential domestic acidification damages; and a general, more constructive re-orientation in British international environmental politics in the late 1980s.[33] In addition, it should not be forgotten that the scientific critical loads approach was generally in line with a more fundamental British preference for science-based environmental politics. Third, the fundamental political changes in Russia and Eastern Europe did away with ideological barriers to open and science-based policy-making. Overall, all these changes contributed to a better climate for constructive and science-based policy-making.

With regard to public saliency, overall, it was probably somewhat lower than in the first part of the 1980s – partly due to the fact that acid rain from the mid-1980s on got competition from other environmental problems like depletion of the ozone layer and global warming. However, the other problem changes described above were much more important in this particular science–politics context.

5.5 Concluding comments

Judged on its own, the LRTAP scientific–political complex has seemingly achieved a nice combination of a quite high (and increasing!) involvement in the political process and a lower, but still significant scientific autonomy/integrity. This does not mean that the institutional design is in any way 'perfect'. As indicated by the organisational simplification in the early 1990s, the system had probably grown a trifle too complicated, with overlap of work and lacking communication between some bodies.

Moreover, the role of the Secretariat warrants some specific comments. Both observers and insiders seem to agree that funding is far from adequate, considering the workload. In fact, personnel resources have remained virtually unchanged in the period after 1985 – a period in which among other things five new protocols have been concluded and an additional negotiation process got underway. This situation obviously constrains the Secretariat's possibilities for fulfilling its co-ordinating and synthesising function in the internal communication chain.

Moving on to the crucial impact question, the LRTAP case is a good example of the complex relationship between institutional design and the role of scientific evidence. Although the institutional machinery has been functioning quite well on its own premises, its impact with regard to the acceptance and 'adoption' of scientific evidence has been variable. In the first sulphur process, the assessment was that most of the decision-makers accepted the substantive conclusions from the scientific community, although the specific regulation adopted was very loosely related to the scientific evidence available. The LRTAP institutional design, and especially the EMEP programme, contributed somewhat to the acceptance of scientific evidence. However, problem characteristics influenced the process in a dual manner. On the one hand, malign competitive aspects and asymmetrical transboundary emission flows and effects hampered the initial acceptance of scientific evidence – as witnessed in the Convention negotiations. On the other hand, important problem changes like the political conversion of West Germany into an 'acid activist' contributed to a wider process of awareness-raising and reappraisal of the improving scientific evidence at hand. A related increased public saliency of the acid rain issue in the first part of the 1980s also contributed in the same direction.

In the NOx and VOC processes, acceptance of scientific evidence was basically at the same level, although the role of this evidence was somewhat different and more politically 'sobering'. The LRTAP institutions played a more important role for knowledge-building in these processes, much due to the less mature character of these issues. Compared to the sulphur power-station issue with a quite long scientific and political maturing period, the NOx and VOC issues were both more complex and had much shorter scientific and political histories. Hence, most of the knowledge improvement processes developed in parallel with the negotiations and, for instance, in the NOx context led to the moderation of initial ambitions of, similar to the sulphur process, agreeing upon a basic 30 per cent reduction target.

In the final process analysed in this connection, i.e. negotiations on revised sulphur commitments, with regard to the 'adoption' of scientific evidence, the assessment was that this process comes close to our third and highest level. In accounting for this, the systematic preparatory work in various LRTAP sub-groups was an important factor. For instance, the Task Force on Mapping must be mentioned on the methodological side. Moreover, the Task Force on Integrated Assessment Modelling, with its close collaboration with IIASA has been very important. However, changing problem characteristics must also be brought into the picture. Over time, most of the countries involved in the LRTAP context had become much more aware of the potential domestic environmental and health damages related to air pollution and acid rain; moreover, a changing, more constructive role of the UK – the most important laggard in the previous sulphur process – must be mentioned; in addition, the fundamental political changes in Russia and Eastern Europe did away with ideological barriers to open and science-based policy-making. Overall, all these changes contributed to a better climate for constructive and science-based policy-making. Hence, a more prominent role for scientific evidence in policy-making can be accounted for by a combination of further institutional development and a certain decrease in basic political malignancy.

As a final reflection, the possibly most important challenge this system is facing, is that with the rise of the critical loads approach, direct scientific involvement in the decision-making process is increasing considerably. The 'administrative' participation model, with scientific working groups composed of government officials, has seemingly not spurred complaints about 'politicisation' so far. Whether an even higher involvement by scientific experts in the political process can be accomplished without seriously threatening the fundamental scientific legitimacy of the system remains to be seen.[34]

Notes

1 This is a revised version of Wettestad (1994a) and (1995). I would like to express special thanks to Per Bakken, The Norwegian Ministry of Environment, and Lars Nordberg, The LRTAP Secretariat, for providing me with background information for this chapter (see also footnote 10). Thanks also to Ann Skarstad and Snorre Fjeldstad, FNI, for language and editorial assistance.

2 For more information on these 'formative' years, see for instance Chossudovsky (1989) and Gehring (1994).

3 These 12 countries were Austria, Belgium, Denmark, Finland, France,

West Germany, Italy, Liechtenstein, The Netherlands, Norway, Sweden and Switzerland.

4 Among the signatories, 15 countries and the EC committed themselves to the regular 30 per cent reduction; four chose the freeze option; and three chose the TOMA option. See Gehring (1994: 180).

5 For an analysis of the negotiations and content of the 1994 sulphur protocol, see for instance Gehring (1994: 185–93); and Churchill, Kutting and Warren (1995).

6 Several interviews with Per M. Bakken, the Norwegian Ministry of Environment (1991 and 1995); Harald Dovland, formerly with the Norwegian Institute of Air Research (1991 and 1995); and Erik Lykke, the Norwegian Ministry of Environment (1991); have been conducted. Moreover, I have had talks with Anton Eliassen, the Norwegian Institute of Meteorology (1991), Jan Thompson, the Norwegian Ministry of Environment (1991), and Lars Nordberg, LRTAP Secretariat in Geneva (1995). In addition, I draw on information gathered through a questionnaire on the effectiveness of LRTAP, carried out in the Spring of 1991. The questionnaire was initially sent out to all the LRTAP countries, and to a selected group of eight more independent observers. I received eight answers from the Contracting Parties group, among them important countries like the UK, the FRG and the Scandinavian countries; and four answers from the observer group.

7 Interview with Harald Dovland, Norwegian Institute for Air Research, 1991.

8 Cited in Wetstone (1987: 186).

9 See for instance Boehmer-Christiansen and Skea (1991: ch. 10).

10 See for instance Hajer (1995) on the shift in Dutch perceptions.

11 This is first and foremost based on Morten Stenstadvold's (1991) account of the negotiation process in his thesis 'The evolution of cooperation. A case study of the NOx-protocol'.

12 See for instance Gehring (1994: 164–6).

13 Germany, who supported a NOx reductions protocol, had a fleet of cars which, first, were already required under 1983 legislation to instal catalytic converters. Second, the cars had a large average engine size, which could accommodate catalytic converters with lower increases in marginal costs than cars with smaller engines. The UK, France and Italy, who opposed such a protocol, had no catalytic converters legislation in place, and an automobile industry producing cars with smaller engines. See Levy (1993: 95).

14 A good example here is Norway. The Norwegian initial 'pusher' position for a reduction protocol changed during the protocol negotiations into a more moderate, middle-ground position, aiming for a stabilisation target (Stenstadvold, 1991). This change was due to a recognition

of a more complicated domestic emissions situation than initially assumed, with among other things higher shipping emissions than initially realised.

15 This section is mainly based upon Gehring (1994) and Levy (1993).

16 For a discursive and institutional discussion of the development of the critical loads approach, see Bäckstrand (1997).

17 For instance, Gehring (1994: 192) states that 'For the first time the basis of negotiations of reduction targets was formed by scientifically founded environmental standards rather than arbitrarily chosen proposals'. Moreover, Levy (1995: 61, 63) states: 'The most dramatic way in which the acid rain problem in Europe has changed is the use of critical loads as a management tool ... The most fundamental effect that critical loads had was to shift the nature of the public debate, both internationally and in many domestic settings, away from determining who the bad guys were, and towards determining how vulnerable each party was to acid rain'.

18 For instance, a model developed by the Stockholm Environment Institute indicated at some point that the UK would need to cut its SO_2 emissions by 88 per cent (if the 60 per cent 'gap closure' was to be achieved). The IIASA RAINS model suggested a target of 79 per cent. In comparison, the UK's own ASAM model indicated that a reduction of 'only' 76 per cent would be necessary (See *ENDS Report* 224, 1993b: 39).

19 For a more comprehensive overview and discussion of LRTAP institutional design, see Wettestad (1999b).

20 Dovland (1987); personal communication with Lars Nordberg, the LRTAP Secretariat.

21 Interviews with Per Bakken, the Norwegian Ministry of Environment.

22 Interview with Lars Nordberg, the LRTAP Secretariat

23 Interview with Lars Nordberg, the LRTAP secretariat.

24 Interview with Lars Nordberg, the LRTAP Secretariat.

25 Interview with Lars Nordberg, the LRTAP Secretariat, May 1995.

26 See Levy (1993: 12): 'Swedish and Norwegian research is better received in Britain today, for example, than it was before LRTAP.'

27 For a further description of the acid rain problem, see Wettestad (1999b).

28 It is here, *inter alia*, possible to base the reasoning on a quite detailed study of the NOx negotiation process, covering among other things the structure and impact of the institutional apparatus, i.e. Stenstadvold (1991).

29 See also Gehring (1994) for a detailed account of the negotiation processes and related organisational aspects.

30 Interviews with Per Bakken, Norwegian Ministry of Environment, and Anton Eliassen, Norwegian Meteorological Institute, cited in Stenstad-

vold (1991: 92).

31 Stenstadvold maintains: 'The information gathering and diffusion process, and the way this was organised, included several institutional innovations regarded as very successful. This organisational approach involved the Parties in a manner which stimulated a common problem-understanding, and paved the way for more constructive negotiations than would otherwise have been the case' (Stenstadvold, 1991: 102, my translation).

32 This is further discussed in Wettestad (1998).

33 See for instance Levy (1995: 63–4); Wettestad (1996).

34 For some further notes on the relationship between 'usability' and 'credibility' in relation to the role of science in international environmental regimes, see Andresen, Skjærseth and Wettestad (1993).

The ozone regime

6.1 Introduction

6.1.1 The scientific background

In 1974 Richard Stolarski and Ralph Cicerone, two Michigan University scientists, published a study indicating that chlorine released in the stratosphere could destroy ozone. At the same time, but independent of the Michigan findings, Mario Molina and Sherwood Rowland discovered that chlorofluorocarbons (CFCs) are not broken down in the lower atmosphere like most other gases, but persist and migrate slowly up to the stratosphere where they are eventually broken down by solar radiation. During this process, large quantities of chlorine are released in the stratosphere. The combination of the two theories, therefore, implied a link between CFCs and ozone depletion. The Rowland–Molina hypothesis set off a major research programmeme conducted jointly by the National Academy of Science (NAS), the National Aeronautics and Space Administration (NASA), the National Oceanic and Atmospheric Administration (NOAA) and leading universities. In the following years the validity of the chlorine–ozone linkage was confirmed, but the hypothesis could not be definitively proved.

The first international initiative on the ozone issue was the UNEP-sponsored Washington Meeting held in March 1977 that included representatives of 33 nations and the EC commission. The meeting drafted the 'World Plan of Action on the Ozone Layer' and recommended the establishment of a 'Co-ordinating Committee on the Ozone Layer' (CCOL). In May 1977, UNEP's Governing Council created the CCOL and adopted the Plan of Action. Until 1982, the CCOL was the only formal international body concerned with the ozone issue. The main task of the CCOL was to co-ordinate research undertaken by national and international agencies (see, for instance, Parson, 1991; 1993).

In an effort to provide scientific information to governments concerning the potential threat of ozone depletion, a major co-operative venture was launched in 1984. The project was co-sponsored by three US scientific agencies (NASA, NOAA, FAA), three international organisations (WMO, UNEP, EC), and a West German scientific agency (The German Federal Ministry for Research and Technology) and resulted in a scientific assessment report published by WMO and UNEP in 1986. The assessment was generated through a series of workshops held in 1984 and 1985, with the participation of approximately 150 scientists from 11 countries (Benedick, 1991; Litfin, 1991; 1994).

In 1988, the Ozone Trends Panel (OTP), initiated by NASA in 1986, presented its report. With this report, the scientific consensus on the ozone issue was confirmed. In October 1988 scientific input to the political process was institutionalised in four Assessment Panels (scientific, environmental, technological and economic). Three scientific assessments, published under the auspices of UNEP and WMO within the framework of the WMO 'Global Ozone Research and Monitoring Project', have been provided; in 1989 (including the 'Synthesis Report'), 1991 and 1994. Furthermore, an 'Assessment Supplement on Methyl Bromide' was provided in 1992 (WMO, 1994).

6.1.2 *The political background*

In 1981 UNEP's Governing Council approved a Swedish initiative to establish a working group to start negotiations on an international convention on the ozone layer. The first meeting of the group took place in Stockholm in January 1982. The CCOL was designated to be its scientific and technical advisory body. The Working Group met seven times in the following three years, at which time the Vienna Convention was adopted in 1985. The signatories of the convention agreed to take 'appropriate measures' to protect the ozone layer, although no effort was made to define such measures in the convention text. The convention did, however, empower UNEP to immediately convene Working Group negotiations for a 'follow-up' protocol. Under the leadership of UNEP's Executive Director Mustafa Tolba (from 1986), these meetings eventually led

to agreement on the Montreal Protocol on Substances that Deplete
the Ozone Layer in September 1987. In the Montreal Protocol the
Parties agreed to a 20 per cent cut, from 1986 levels, of production
and consumption of the five major CFCs by the end of 1994, and a
50 per cent cut by the end of 1999 (WMO, 1992). It was further
agreed to freeze, at 1986 levels, production and consumption of
halons by 1992. The special situation of developing countries was
acknowledged in the ten-year delay in compliance entitled to developing countries in the Protocol (Article 5). By December 1988, 29
countries plus the European Commission had ratified the treaty, and
the Protocol entered into force 1 January 1989. The First Meeting
of the Parties took place in Helsinki in May 1989. The meeting
resulted in the Helsinki Declaration approved by consensus. This
was a non-binding document, calling for a phase-out of CFCs no
later than the year 2000. It also called for a phase-out of halons and
'other ozone depleting substances' not covered by the Montreal
Protocol 'as soon as feasible' (Benedick, 1991). At the Second Meeting of the Parties in London, in June 1990, the London Amendment
was adopted. The parties agreed to increase the scope of the Montreal Protocol by including several gases not covered by the 1987
agreement (several CFCs, carbon tetrachloride and methyl chloro-
form), accelerate the CFC phase-out (a 20 per cent cut of 1989
levels by 1993, an 85 per cent cut by 1997 and 100 per cent phase-
out by 2000), and to phase out halons by the year 2000 (with a 50
per cent cut of 1986 levels by 1995). (Benedick, 1991; WMO,
1992). The parties also agreed to a 'financial mechanism', including
a multilateral fund, for providing financial and technical assistance
to enable developing countries to comply with the Protocol. In
November 1992, the parties of the Montreal agreement met in
Copenhagen. At this meeting it was agreed to accelerate phase-
out further; a 100 per cent phase-out by 1996 for CFCs, and by
1994 for halons. In the Copenhagen adjustment the parties
also agreed to regulate HCFCs (a consumption cap beginning in
1996, and gradual phase-out between 1996 and 2020) and that a
0.5 per cent production 'tail' would extend for ten years (Global
Environmental Change Report [GECR], 4 December 1992). In the
Vienna amendments of 1995, the parties agreed to phase-out
and reduction measures directed towards methyl bromide and
HCFCs. Moreover, for the first time, developing nations also
agreed to controls on methyl bromide and HCFCs, contingent

upon additional funding from industrialised nations (GECR, 1995b).

6.2 Did scientific evidence count?

The ozone treaty has been highly praised as one of the most successful efforts of international environmental co-operation to date (see, for instance, Benedick, 1991; Parson, 1991). One explanation of this, it has been claimed, rests in the co-operation and dialogue that prevailed between scientists concerned with the ozone issue and decision-makers concerned with negotiations on a convention to protect the ozone layer (see, for instance, Benedick, 1991; Haas, 1992b).

The political process on ozone depletion is characterised by a sequential approach: first, adoption of a framework convention (1985) with few obligations in terms of specific control measures, then agreement on a protocol (1987), and eventually protocol amendments gradually increasing the parties' commitment to freeze, reduce and phase out major ozone depleting substances (1990, 1992, 1995). Furthermore, each step of this process seems to be correlated with the gradually increased scientific understanding of the ozone problem. Three events in particular are illustrative in this respect:

First, the Würzburg Meeting in April 1987 concluded that the chemical CFC113 and halons 1211 and 1301 could cause significant ozone depletion even if the other CFCs were controlled. In September negotiators succeeded in including these controversial chemicals in the protocol, although a freeze on halons was successfully delayed by the EC Commission: 'After the Würzburg findings were thoroughly aired, there was no support at Montreal outside the European Community for narrow chemical coverage' (Benedick, 1991: 79).

Second, the OTP Report of March 1988 seems to have been the major catalyst behind the altered positions of the UK in 1988. During the summer of 1988 the UK 'was transformed from a reluctant follower to a world leader in the drive to protect the ozone layer' (Benedick, 1991: 114). The role of DuPont in this transformation may also have been significant, a point to which we will return below. This development also had significant impact on the speed of ratification of the Montreal Protocol. With the EC ratification in December 1988, a delay in the protocol's entry into force was prevented at the last moment.

Third, the Synthesis Report of the four expert panels (institutionalised in October 1988) presented in November 1989, and especially the 'chlorine-loading' approach[1] adopted by the Science Panel, became the basis for negotiations on the Protocol Amendments finally agreed upon in London 1990.

This 'symmetry' between the presentation of new scientific findings and policy response indicates that scientific input did have impact on the outcome of the decision-making process, at least in the sense that the scientific findings were accepted as scientifically authoritative and factually valid by policy-makers. In order to substantiate this proposition further, however, we will briefly look into the extent to which the scientific advice was also acted upon, i.e., the extent to which scientific advice is reflected in the agreements actually made.

Parson claims that, 'it was not science, but bargaining, that determined the decisions adopted in Montreal. The 50 per cent cut that was agreed had no particular scientific prominence' (Parson, 1991: 25). The scientific community was at that time divided between those favouring much weaker control measures (CFC freeze only) and those favouring much stronger control measures. The 50 per cent cut agreement, therefore, was a bargained outcome between the EC's proposed freeze and the US proposition of 95 per cent cuts (Parson, 1991).

Furthermore, it seems as if the scientific community did not really formulate explicit advice beyond a general 'controls-are-necessary' statement. On the other hand, this 'advice' became more and more substantiated as knowledge accumulated, uncertainty was reduced, and the urgency of acting was emphasised by the scientific community. Moreover, at the pre-negotiating Workshops in Rome and Leesburg in 1986 (arranged by UNEP), Environmental Protection Agency (EPA) scientists formulated indirect advice by focusing on the *implications* of negotiating positions (primarily the EC position) in terms of predicted ozone depletion (see, for instance, Litfin, 1994; 1995). Similar examples are found at the Würzburg Meeting, where the implications of not including CFC113 and halons were emphasised, and later in the Synthesis Report's adoption of the chlorine-loading approach. By focusing on chlorine-loading instead of ozone depletion, the scenario modelling field was opened up 'to anyone with a powerful desktop computer' (Parson, 1991: 27). Thus, it seems as if scientists, rather than formulating explicit advice, provided decision-makers with *decision-making tools.*

On this basis, it seems reasonable to conclude that the scientific input into the political process did serve as a decision premise, although the exact control measures adopted were largely determined by negotiations, not explicit scientific advice. To this extent, therefore, the scientific knowledge presented by the scientific community seems to have been accepted and acted upon by decision-makers. This conclusion is substantiated also in the sense that the incremental development of the policy response corresponds well to the incremental development of the scientific knowledge base. To what extent may this outcome be explained by the institutional arrangements of the science–policy dialogue?

6.3 Institutional arrangements

In Chapter 1 we suggested that one key to a constructive science –policy relationship would be to *combine* scientific autonomy on the one hand, and involvement in the political process on the other. Each dimension is conceived of as a function of multiple variables. In this section we will discuss each dimension in terms of the indicators listed in Chapter 1 with regard to the case of the ozone regime.

6.3.1 Degree of autonomy: The process of producing knowledge
A general characteristic of the ozone process is that before 1988, when the four Assessment Panels were established, the science–policy relationship was only to a very little extent formally institutionalised. Illustrative in this respect is the fact that until the Ad Hoc Working Group started negotiations on preparations for an international convention on ozone in 1982, CCOL was the only formal international body concerned with ozone. The assessment process on ozone science was largely initiated, conducted and controlled by scientific institutions themselves. The group of scientists involved in the process enjoyed high autonomy, and their work was to a very little extent directed or controlled by a political body.

The group of scientists involved in the process before 1988 constituted a network rather than a formal body (see Haas, 1992b; 1993a). This network, however, seems to have been quite firmly connected; throughout the process, the same scientific institutions (to some extent the same scientists) were mainly responsible for initiating and co-ordinating research. Furthermore, one country, the USA, dominated the field, although important contributions also came from other countries.

The process was thus dominated by US scientific agencies. Most of the research was initiated, conducted and carried out by US scientific institutions, with NASA serving as a driving force. Research funding was primarily provided by US national institutions – governmental, industrial as well as scientific. Illustrative in this respect is the incident where the British Antarctic Survey, after having discovered the Antarctic ozone hole in 1985, was denied necessary additional funding from the British government because of budgetary constraints. Ultimately the funding was provided by a US industry association (Benedick, 1991). Although carried out by US institutions (particularly NASA and NOAA), research findings were published under the auspices of WMO and UNEP.

Research was primarily conducted by US scientific agencies, but scientists from all over the world were invited to participate in scientific assessments. Thus, entry was restricted, but the criteria for participation in these assessments were both scientific and political. With regard to this aspect, two tendencies seem to be significant: Separate research projects conducted by one, or a small number of scientific institutions were primarily carried out by the institutions' regular staff of scientists, or 'specially invited' scientists from other institutions (both national and international). For this category of research activity, entry was primarily based on scientific criteria such as scholarly merit. In joint venture projects and workshops, on the other hand, the criteria for participation were both scientific and political. In the scientific assessment co-ordinated by Robert Watson (NASA) and published by WMO/UNEP in 1986, the political motivation behind broad participation to mitigate nationalistic biases is evident in the fact that Watson is reported as saying: 'Let's go ahead and have a person from a certain country, even if that person has nothing to contribute. We might be able to get something started there, or at the very least that person might be able to take the message home' (Cicerone in interview with Litfin, 1991: 6). Thus, it seems as if the 'politically nominated' participants to some extent served as intermediaries between the scientists and each individual representative's respective government in order to 'take the message home'. In this manner, the political necessity of broad (and to some extent 'politically' motivated) participation was accommodated, while scientists at the same time maintained a firm control of the process and so prevented these actors from gaining any significant influence on actual research and scientific conclusions.

The main function of the scientific institutions involved in the process was to produce new knowledge (regular research activities) and co-ordinate and supervise research activities. There are several examples of institutions serving both these functions, for instance, NASA. The main co-ordinating body, however, was the CCOL, whose main function was to 'bring together scientists from governments, industry, universities, and international agencies to assess the risks of ozone layer depletion' (Benedick, 1991: 40). The CCOL assessments were published in periodic reports that served as important references for policy-makers. The character of CCOL is usually described as being primarily scientific. However, Parson notes that before the working group was established in 1982, CCOL reports had 'moved from science summaries toward cautious calls for international regulatory action' (Parson, 1993: 37, fn. 27). Thus, before the establishment of a political body at the international level, the CCOL also to some extent formulated policy advice. With the working group establishment, however, the CCOL 'returned' to its primarily scientific function (Parson, 1993).

The chemical industry participated actively in the provision of scientific assessments, represented by the Chemical Manufacturing Association (CMA) in CCOL. This involvement 'led to their substantial support of ozone research, and to their final support for the Montreal agreement' (Isaksen, 1992: 4). By involving governmental representatives in CCOL, a continuous update on the science to governments was also achieved. Thus, the CCOL seems to have played an important role – in addition to the co-ordinating function – by providing an arena for science–policy dialogue. Furthermore, it seems as if it was mainly at this level, more or less as an outcome of the dialogue, that scientific findings were transformed into decision premises and policy recommendations were formulated.

In October 1988, as an implication of Article 6 in the Montreal Protocol but before the protocol formally entered into force, the scientific process was institutionalised and made formally subordinate to the political body with the establishment of four expert panels: a scientific, an environmental, a technological and an economic panel. The main task of the panels was to provide the necessary knowledge base for the assessment and review of the adopted control measures every four years beginning in 1990. The science panel assessed the science of ozone depletion. The environment panel assessed the state of knowledge of health and environmental effects of altered ozone concentrations and increased ultraviolet radiation. The technology panel assessed technical options for reducing ozone-depleting substances, and the economy panel assessed the costs and benefits of reduced use of ozone depleting substances, the costs of technical solutions, and the implications for technology transfer to developing countries (Benedick, 1991: 128). The panels were meant to replace the CCOL although it still formally exists. No meetings in the CCOL have been arranged, however, since the panels were established (personal communication with Per Bakken).

The most important implication of the institutional change in 1988 was that of broader participation. Before 1988 the scientific process was heavily dominated by industrial nations (the US in particular) more or less as a consequence of the existing structure of scientific networks. Other representatives participated only to the extent that they were invited by leading scientists and scientific institutions, and usually only in connection with isolated projects or conferences. The institutional change therefore served to increase the geopolitical representativity of the process. Furthermore, before 1988 the process had mainly been concerned with the science of ozone depletion and to a lesser extent focused on other aspects related to the problem, such as environmental effects, technological options for substitution of ozone depleting substances and economic calculations on costs. Thus, the establishment of the four expert panels also served to broaden the area of research by including issue areas that had not been covered in a systematic manner earlier.

Although the scientific body now became directly subordinate to the political body of the regime (the Meeting of the Parties to the Montreal Protocol), scientists still seem to have enjoyed high autonomy. In all panels recruitment was mainly based on scholarly merit; the participants were active in research, and all reports were peer reviewed according to the standard procedures of science at large.[2] In the terms of reference for the panels, it is pointed out that they 'shall consist of selected experts who are qualified in the field ... and internationally recognised as such.' It is, however, also pointed out that 'the experts who are best qualified in the subject matter of the various chapters [of each report] shall be selected ensuring the widest possible geographical balance' (UNEP/OzL.Pro. 1/L. 1/Add. May 1989).

The funding mechanism remained largely unchanged; that is, research was mainly funded by national governments and by the traditional mechanisms for research funding at the national level. The technology panel, however, was organised into sectoral sub-panels that mostly consisted of user-industry experts who were financed by their companies (Parson, 1991).

The formal subordination of the scientific body did imply some restrictions in the panels' operational autonomy since their mandate was now given by the regulatory body of the regime. The meeting of the parties to the protocol determined the chairpersons of the panels as well as the chapters the reports should include. The subdivision of the issue area into chapters, however, seems to follow areas of specialisation within the research field at large, and does therefore not seem to represent a substantial restriction in the panels' operational autonomy. The chairs of the panels were responsible for selecting chapter chairs, and the panels were free to include whomever they found competent to contribute to the assessments in accordance with the terms of reference set up by the meeting of the parties. Substantially, therefore, the panels' operational autonomy seems to have been relatively high, despite the restrictions implicit in the subordination.

The panels were generally regarded as forums 'with the stamp of international objectivity and authoritativeness' (Parson, 1993: 61).With regard to the report of the economic panel, however, some criticism was expressed about the objectivity of the assessment. In this panel only two representatives from developing countries participated, and at the second session of the first meeting of the parties to the protocol several delegations found that some of the parts of the Synthesis Report concerning this matter 'did not fully reflect some of the points that these delegations regarded as fundamental to an objective economic analysis, so that they felt bound to express a reservation in regard to those conclusions' (UNEP/OzL.Pro.WG.I (2)/4 Final Report, September 1989). The criticism was met by adopting the report Ad Referendum, implying an opportunity to comment and modify the report at subsequent meetings, and by establishing a drafting group in order to integrate proposals for amendments of the report. It was, however, agreed that any amendment 'had to stem from the Panel Reports', and that 'additional technical information' not included in the panel reports could be included in the meeting report rather than in the Synthesis Report (UNEP/OzL.Pro.WG.I (2)/4 Final Report, September 1989).

6.3.2 *Level of involvement: communication between scientific and regulatory bodies*

Before 1988 the formulation of advice and research activities were separated. Scientists primarily performed the research, while the outcome of CCOL activities constituted the formulation of advice.[3] The CCOL, on the other hand, was designated to serve as a technical and advisory body to the Ad Hoc Working Group established in 1982 and thus served as the main link between the scientific and the political segment. Throughout the process several workshops were arranged with a more or less explicit 'political' function (for instance, the workshops held in Rome and Leesburg in 1986); they were political in the sense that decision-makers were invited and that (tacit) negotiations took place, but the main (official) function of these workshops was the dialogue between scientists and decision-makers (see, for instance, Litfin, 1991). Through these workshops a feedback mechanism was established. Atmospheric scientists participating in the provision of scientific assessments were therefore indirectly involved in the political process, mainly through their participation in the advisory body, CCOL, which also served as the main arena for communication and discussions between scientists and policy-makers.

With the establishment of the four expert panels in 1988, the scientific segment became formally subordinate to the political body of the regime, and thus more directly involved in the process. The indirect and implicit character of the formulation of advice seems, however, to have remained unchanged. The mandate of the panels was to assess the control measures adopted in the Montreal Protocol in terms of their effectiveness with regard to the recovery of the ozone layer and in terms of preventing possible damage from ozone depletion. Thus, they provided implicit policy advice through their conclusions. The Synthesis Report concluded that 'even if the control measures of the Montreal Protocol were to be implemented by all nations, today's atmospheric abundance of chlorine ... will at least double to triple during the next century' (UNEP/OzL.Pro.WG. I(2)/L.1/Add.1, Draft Report, September 1989: 6). With the shift of focus in the science panel from ozone depletion to stratospheric chlorine concentrations ('chlorine loading') they were able to assess at what point, in terms of parts per billion by volume (ppbv), damage to the ozone layer had occurred, and accordingly at which levels of chlorine concentrations the ozone layer would recover. They concluded that 'the Antarctic ozone hole will not disappear until the atmospheric abundance of chlorine is reduced to the levels of the early 1970s: 1.5 – 2 ppbv assuming present climate' (as compared to the 1989 levels of 3 ppbv) (UNEP/OzL.Pro.WG. I(2)/L.1/Add.1, Draft Report, September 1989 15). By studying four scenarios with different regulatory measures ranging from freeze to full phase-outs, they found that 'even with a global phase out, chlorine will continue increasing to about 4.5 ppb around 2010, and will not return to 2 ppb until 2060.' (Parson, 1991:16). With these scenarios and the conclusion from the technology panel that phase-outs were technically feasible, the report certainly implied recommendations to phase out ozone depleting substances, although the recommendations were not stated explicitly. The Executive Director of UNEP, Mustafa Tolba, emphasised, however, that a strengthening of the protocol was required to 'protect our planet's ozone layer'(UNEP/OzL.Pro.WG.I(2)/4, Final Report, September. 1989). On the basis of the reports, he made several 'specific recommendations for adjustments and amendments to the Montreal Protocol for consideration by the participants' (UNEP/OzL.Pro.WG.I(2)/4, Final Report, September 1989).

In 1988, the Meeting of the Parties to the Montreal Protocol also established an 'Open-Ended Working Group' for the consideration of reports of the four expert panels, and their integration into one 'Synthesis Report'. This group was open to all parties to the protocol, as well as to governmental and non-governmental observers. In this manner, the reports developed by experts and scientists in their personal capacities were reviewed and synthesised by an intergovernmental body (Gehring, 1994: 270).

Throughout the process, therefore, the functions of research, policy advice and policy-making were formally differentiated – at least in the sense that different segments of the process served different functions. Before 1988, the CCOL seems to have performed an important function as a link between the scientific and the political segment, while the open-ended working group seems to have performed the same function after 1988. The formulation of advice also seems to have taken place at this level, and not by the scientists themselves. Moreover, in his professional capacity as the Executive Director of UNEP, under which the process was organised, Dr Tolba also seems to have played an important role in terms of communicating the findings and conclusions of the expert panels to policy-makers.

This does, however, add up to a quite complicated picture of the level of involvement between the scientific and the political processes. Before 1988, the scientific and the political segments were separated, but both processes (the CCOL, with regard to the scientific process) were formally organised by UNEP. Between the CCOL and the political process, therefore, the organisational distance was relatively 'short'. For instance, Dr Tolba participated actively at both levels. The scientists in the process were, however, only indirectly involved in the political process (although some of the front figures of the scientific process also constituted a 'link' between the segments, and were, to some extent, more directly involved in the political process). Formally, the organisational distance between research, formulation of advice and policy-making was therefore present and clearly greater than after the subordination of the scientific process in 1988. After 1988 a separation was no longer provided by institutional means as it was before 1988, when CCOL seems to have served as a 'buffer' between the bodies. The open-ended Working Group established in 1988 may, however, have served a similar function. In practice, therefore, the functions were still separated.

Throughout the process, communication channels between the segments were provided. However, before 1988, although both processes (the CCOL and the negotiations) were organised under UNEP, no *formal* channels of communication existed. Communication took place informally – through the CCOL and the various workshops that were arranged. Parson thus argues that one implication of the institutionalisation was that it 'provided a formal channel for science to feed directly into the negotiation process' and that this served to increase scientists' influence on the negotiations (Parson 1993: 61). The establishment of the open-ended Working Group also provided a channel for scientific input to the negotiation process. Even with this formal channel between the scientific and the regulatory bodies, however, the level of involvement within the formal framework of the assessment process seems to have been relatively low. This is certainly the case as compared, for instance, with the corresponding scientific assessment process on climate change (see Chapter 7 in this volume). In the ozone process, scientists were to some extent involved in the policy making process, but largely at other arenas than those provided through the institutional framework. Scientific findings were also 'brought into' the policy making process by other actors than the scientists. Litfin's study indicates, for instance, that one major explanatory factor of the outcome of the ozone process was the operation of 'knowledge brokers' who were instrumental in bringing scientists and policy-makers together in workshops and conferences outside the *formal* framework of the science–policy dialogue, and in interpreting and framing the knowledge base (provided in the scientific assessment process) (Litfin, 1994). Thus, there was 'involvement' in the sense of a link between the scientific and the policy making processes, but it was not mainly provided as a function of the institutional arrangements of the science–policy dialogue.

6.4 The impact of institutional arrangements

When the potential link between CFC gases and ozone depletion was discovered in 1974, 'the international scientific community was well organised and the foundation for large scale research on stratospheric ozone was in place' (Isaksen, 1992: 1). This appears to have had significant implications for the manner in which the scientific process functioned and the science–policy dialogue evolved. The process of knowledge accumulation seems largely to have worked according to the existing scientific networks and the norms and standards of the scientific community. Thus, the institutional design of the scientific process on ozone seems to a larger extent to be a function of the existing structure of the scientific community, rather than the other way around. If anything, this probably also constitutes the main feature of the institutional design in this case; the institutional design to a large extent permitted the science on stratospheric ozone to work according to its own traditions, rather than 'forcing' a structure, dictated by the enlarged political context of the issue upon the scientific community that was already there.

From our point of view, it is interesting that it remains unclear whether this institutional framework was the result of deliberate design. It seems rather to have been the result of the scientific community's ability to retain control over the scientific process. It could be argued that before 1988 the relationship between the scientific and the political segment was characterised by informal *collaboration* rather than formal *institutionalisation*. The scientific input into the political process was provided by an already existing scientific network with the will and ability to communicate their findings to decision-makers. Thus, at least before 1988, the scientific 'body' seems to a very little extent to represent an institution with *formalised* rules and procedures. Moreover, while the 1988 restructuring implied a formal link to the decision-making body, it does not seem to have implied a formalisation of the rules and procedures governing the scientific assessment process. In this regard, the scientific body operated according to informal, rather than formal, rules and procedures even after the 1988 restructuring.

The authority of the scientific findings also seems to stem from the fact that the scientific process, directly or indirectly linked to the political process, was perceived as representative for, and working according to, the norms of the scientific community at large. One important aspect in this regard seems to have been participation. Both before and after the institutional change in 1988 it was emphasised that recruitment should be based on scholarly merits: before 1988 as a more or less implicit function of the network structure of the process, after 1988 explicitly stated in the terms of reference for the expert panels. Moreover, it was largely left to the scientists themselves to determine who were best qualified to contribute to or review the reports – with due consideration, however, of ensuring the widest possible geographical balance. The provision of knowledge, therefore, seems to have been recognised as 'objective and authoritative', despite the fact that scientists from industrialised countries (particularly the USA) – also after 1988 – dominated the scene (see also Parson, 1991; 1993).

Thus, the extent to which scientific findings were accepted by the political body as a legitimate basis for decisions seems to have resulted more from leaving the scientific bodies to themselves than from deliberate institutional design. The lack of formal and explicit rules and procedures 'guiding' the scientific assessment process permitted the scientific bodies to perform their task in accordance with the informal norms and standards governing scientific inquiry at large. Thus, the process worked according to its own (informal) rules and norms, and the major institutional device was *not* to enforce detailed rules and procedures upon the scientific bodies in their provision of assessments. This feature also seems to be the source of the widely acknowledged scientific authority of the assessments.

To the extent that permitting the scientific bodies to operate according to the norms and standards of science at large qualifies as an 'institutional arrangement', the institutional framework of the science–policy dialogue in this case served to maintain scientific autonomy to a larger extent than it served to increase scientists' involvement in the policy-making process. That is, the 'balance' between scientific autonomy and involvement in this case is 'biased' towards scientific autonomy. During the initial phases of the process, however, the CCOL served an important function as a link between the political and the scientific segments. Although all actual research took place outside the CCOL, the CCOL served as a co-ordinating instrument, and not least as a channel for communication in both directions. After 1988, the open-ended Working Group may have served similar functions. Moreover, it is also worth noting that the co-ordination of scientific assessments under the joint sponsorship of WMO and UNEP has been important. The beginning of the 1980s was characterised by fragmentation in the assessment of ozone science. During a two-year period, at least five major assessments were carried out by different agencies (Kerr, 1997). As a result, 'both the scientists and the policy-makers were looking at the differences between the reports rather than the similarities. Policy-making was already complicated enough; we realised we needed an international umbrella' (Robert Watson in interview with Kerr, 1997).

Generally speaking, therefore, the institutional arrangements do not seem to explain the policy response very well in this case – at least not in terms of achieving an 'optimal' balance between scientific autonomy and involvement in policy-making. Institutional arrangements seem to be biased towards scientific autonomy while 'involvement' was achieved elsewhere and by other mechanisms. This conclusion is substantiated further when we look at other likely candidates for explaining the policy response. We have chosen to focus on three factors: the status of scientific knowledge, the political setting of the issue and its public saliency.

6.5 Control variables

6.5.1 *The science background on ozone depletion*

Initially the ozone depletion theory was characterised by a significant amount of scientific uncertainty. This uncertainty was gradually reduced, however, and with the 1988 report of the OTP, 'Ozone
layer depletion was no longer a theory; at last it had been substantiated by hard evidence ... The panel concluded that the evidence
"strongly indicates that man-made chlorine species are primarily
responsible for the observed decrease in ozone"' (Benedick, 1991:
110). Thus, policy-makers were (increasingly) confronted by scientific findings that were very hard to disregard or question and an
issue area in which a strong scientific consensus prevailed. Parson
points out that 'particularly given the strong results they had to
report, scientists' influence over the negotiations has advanced
beyond the prior agenda setting role, to exercising substantial influence over certain aspects of the negotiated decisions' (Parsons,
1991: 26). In addition to strong results and scientific consensus, the
scientific findings became more and more alarming: in the Synthesis Report scientists concluded that 'the scientific basis for the 1987
Montreal Protocol on Substances that Deplete the Ozone layer was
the theoretical prediction that, should CFC and halon abundances
continue to grow for the next few decades, there would eventually
be substantial ozone layer depletion. The research of the last few
years has demonstrated that actual ozone loss due to human-made
chlorine (i.e., CFCs) and bromine has already occurred, i.e., the
Antarctic ozone hole' (2nd draft, Synthesis Report, Sept. 1989). In
London too, as negotiators were considering the proposed revisions
of control measures, they were confronted by new and alarming
data presented to them by the Norwegian scientist Ivar S. A. Isaksen
and G. O. P. Obasi, the secretary-general of the WMO:

> Although the new data were still provisional, ground-based measure-
> ments from northern Europe and Canada appeared to indicate a 'very
> pronounced decline' in ozone concentrations of nearly 0.5 percent
> annually over a 20-year period, while satellite measurements showed
> a 2 to 3 percent drop during the last decade over equatorial regions.
> Such rates of decline far exceeded the model predictions (Benedick,
> 1991: 170).

This tendency thus indicated that the scientific uncertainty, that
after all is associated with model predictions, in this case went in the

direction of *underestimations* of anticipated ozone depletion, rather than overestimations.

While it may be argued that in this case scientific findings to some extent have spoken for themselves, several scholars have also emphasised the skill and power of individual agents in bringing scientific findings to the attention of policy-makers:

> It could be argued that, if Bob Watson had been hit by a bus in 1980, we would not now have a treaty to save the ozone layer ... Watson did not discover the hole in the Antarctic ozone, calculate how chlorofluorocarbons (CFCs) reach the stratosphere, or write models that predict the damage. What he did do, however, was bring the scientists who did that work together to reach a consensus on what was happening. He then helped to translate what they said into a language that politicians could not obfuscate or ignore. The result was the ozone treaty (McKenzie, 1989).

The work of Karen Litfin is important in terms of drawing attention to the role of individual agents, 'knowledge brokers', in the communication of scientific findings. She defines knowledge brokers as 'intermediaries between the original researchers, or the producers of knowledge, and the policymakers who consume that knowledge but lack the time and training necessary to absorb the original research' (Litfin, 1994: 4). The influence or power potential of knowledge brokers lies in their ability 'to frame and interpret scientific knowledge', and they are especially influential 'under the conditions of scientific uncertainty that characterise most environmental problems' (Litfin, 1994: 4). In the case of the ozone treaty, knowledge brokers were particularly important with regard to the development of the 'chlorine loading' methodology, which had a significant impact on the political proceedings. Litfin's study indicates that the development of the chlorine loading concept merely represented a shift in the *framing* of the issue, from a focus on *ozone depletion* (and calculations of the 'ozone depleting potential' of various gases), to *atmospheric concentrations*; a change made possible by the discovery of the Antarctic ozone hole: 'The decision to shift the debate from ozone depletion to concentrations was a "strategic one," according to Michael Gibbs. He recalls the decision as follows: "There was no new information here, just *a different way of framing it*. We thought: since the hole may be linked to concentrations, *let's shift the debate ... It only worked because of the Antarctic hole*'" (Litfin, 1994: 100, original emphases).

During the course of the negotiation process, therefore, scientific uncertainty was reduced and the scientific findings became increasingly alarming. Moreover, the scientific uncertainty that was associated with model predictions was increasingly perceived as going in the direction of underestimation, rather than overestimation, of anticipated ozone depletion. This induced policy-makers to adopt a precautionary approach to the problem. This is well illustrated in the fact that the discovery of the Antarctic ozone hole came as much as a surprise to the scientific community as it did to everyone else, and that its detection served to shift the debate towards precautionary action. Thus, 'strong' scientific evidence, cleverly communicated by individuals and knowledge brokers, seems to have had an independent impact.

6.5.2 The political setting of ozone depletion

The political setting of this process was to a large extent characterised by a two-dimensional conflict structure: The USA, Canada, the Nordic countries, Austria and Switzerland (who 'joined forces' in the Toronto group in 1984) constituted one side, which favoured strong regulations, and the EC (primarily) constituted the other, which opposed strong regulations.[4] At least before 1989, there was no major conflict between developed and developing countries. This implied that complicated and often ideological North–South issues were largely avoided. With this bi-polar conflict structure, negotiations became a question of convincing the opposing parties to join the regime, and the major tool was that of science (Litfin, 1994). After 1989 the USA took on a leadership role in the drive for CFC regulations. Scientific research on ozone depletion was heavily influenced by US scientific institutions. The institutionalised political setting with iterative decision-making provided the necessary framework for gradual persuasion. Thus, it seems correct to characterise the political problem structure as relatively benign, at least as compared to the related problem of climate change. Furthermore, the problem itself has features that serve to demonstrate this point.

First, production of CFCs was concentrated: In 1986, 35 per cent of the global production was in the USA, 36 per cent in Western Europe, 8 per cent in the Soviet Union and Eastern Europe, 18 per cent in Asia and the Pacific, and 3 per cent in Latin America (Haas, 1992b: 197). Second, at the time of the negotiations CFCs were being produced by only 17 companies in 16 countries, and in this market DuPont was the world leader. DuPont held 50 per cent of the US market, and over 25 per cent of the global market, as well as being the only company that produced for the three major markets, North America, Europe and Japan (Haas, 1992b). As Haas points out: 'Given the size of DuPont's market and the fact that the United States was the largest CFC-producing and CFC-consuming country, it is not surprising that the United States became the most powerful actor involved in ozone research and negotiations' (Haas, 1992b: 197).

DuPont's leading role was not merely limited to its part as the world's largest producer of CFCs; one of the first reactions to the OTP Report of March 1988 came from DuPont. DuPont announced that they would stop manufacturing all CFCs and halons by the end of the century and accelerate research into substitutes (Benedick, 1991). This development also probably served as the catalyst for the actions of ICI, the major producer in the UK, which also 'coincided' with the change in the position of the British government (see also Skjærseth, 1992). Thus, the impact of science should be seen in relation to this development in the chemical industry and its implications for the structure of the CFC market. When the chemical industry accepted the risks to human health associated with CFCs and, even more important, anticipated international regulations and realised their potential competitive advantage in being in the forefront of the development of substitutes, substitutes were soon developed and the costs of a phase out for the industry significantly reduced, or turned into a potential profit. Maxwell and Weiner point out that 'long-term interests were one of the primary reasons that DuPont sought, and ICI would ultimately accept, international regulation that helped create the market for substitution chemicals' (Maxwell and Weiner, 1993: 28). This development in the chemical industry may, however, also have been induced by its participation in the process of knowledge accumulation. Industry experts took part in the process from the beginning, both in CCOL and the technology panel. This involvement implied both a continuous updating on, and an active part in, the scientific progress on the issue area and is likely to have served to increase their willingness to accept the findings and their implications.

Politically, therefore, this was a relatively benign problem. Ideo-logical North–South confrontations did not dominate the negotia-tion process, and technical options for a solution were developing rapidly. This political situation is likely to have significant explana-tory power for the policy response to this issue.

6.5.3 *Public saliency*

The US position on ozone was to a large extent formed by strong domestic pressure towards CFC regulation. From the beginning, the public concern about the ozone depletion theory was much stronger in the USA than in Europe. As a response to the public reaction to the ozone depletion theories, Congress passed in 1977 a stratos-pheric ozone protection amendment to the US Clean Air Act, which authorised the administrator of the EPA to regulate 'any substance … which in his judgement may be reasonably anticipated to affect the stratosphere, especially ozone in the stratosphere, if such effect may reasonably be anticipated to endanger public health or welfare' (cited in Benedick, 1991: 23). The critical element in this legislation was the adoption of a precautionary approach. In 1978, further-more, the USA banned all nonessential use of CFCs as aerosol pro-pellants. The discovery of the Antarctic ozone hole also served to arouse public concern. To the lay public the ozone hole may have been regarded as the 'proof' of the ozone depletion theory.

In Europe, on the other hand, national governments were under heavy pressure from domestic chemical and user industries, but without counter-pressure from the public or environmental groups. Indeed, industry representatives sat on the delegations of some EC countries (Litfin, 1994). The impact of this situation is reflected in, for instance, that the pre-Montreal European national legislation on CFC emissions was underdeveloped as compared to that of the USA.

The negotiation process profited substantially from the leader-ship provided by the USA. It is likely that the leadership role the USA took on can be at least partly explained by the public pressure in the USA to regulate ozone-depleting substances. In this regard the public saliency of the issue provides some explanation to its out-come.

6.6 Conclusion

The study of this process demonstrates that science played a major role in the formation and functioning of the ozone regime. It seems reasonable to argue that the institutional design contributed to this effect, at least with regard to the extent to which scientific findings were accepted by the political body as a valid and scientifically sound basis for decisions. The manner in which the scientific assessment process was organised contributed to a general perception (in the political bodies) of the scientific process as being authoritative and their findings impartial. The institutional setting, however, only to a very little extent provided arenas for science–policy dialogue and communication. Such arenas were largely established outside the formal framework of the science–policy interaction process of the ozone regime, notably in the many workshops arranged by UNEP, the EPA and other actors performing in the interface between science and politics. These events were probably more important than the institutional arrangements of the interaction in terms of facilitating the dialogue and providing arenas for mutual discussion and negotiation. They constituted an important supplement to the work taking place within the formal bodies of the interaction process. Thus, the impact of the institutional arrangements in this case is not, as anticipated, a function of a balance between scientific autonomy and involvement. While scientific autonomy was maintained within the formal institutional framework, involvement was largely a function of other factors.

We have pointed to a set of factors that seem better suited for explaining the extent to which scientific findings were acted upon than the institutional arrangements of the science–policy dialogue. First, the ozone issue turned out to be a relatively benign political issue increasingly characterised by win-win opportunities for negotiating parties. This is especially the case after technological options for CFC substitution were in the pipeline and the industry became aware of the profit potential of being in the lead in this regard. Moreover, there was substantial public pressure, especially in the USA, for political action on this issue. Public attention and awareness was galvanised by the discovery of the Antarctic ozone hole in 1985, which the scientific models had not been able to predict. The Antarctic ozone hole, moreover, seems to have induced a change in policy-makers' thinking about the issue in the direction of precautionary action. Finally, the effective communication of scientific findings seems, during the course of the process, to have been as much the result of individuals performing as knowledge brokers as the institutional framework of the science–policy dialogue. The scientific research on ozone also to a large extent spoke for itself in the sense that, during the course of the process, it became increasingly consensual and uncontroversial as well as alarming.

In conclusion, while the institutional arrangements were important during the initial phases of the process for bringing the issue on to the political agenda, this factor seems less important during the course of the process. The political process seems increasingly to have built up its own momentum towards regulatory action. The process was to some extent science driven, but science seems to have had an impact in combination with factors other than institutional design. In this case a balance between scientific autonomy and involvement in the political process was achieved, but not mainly as a result of institutional design. Scientist involvement was accomplished mainly in arenas outside the formal framework of the ozone process.

The novelty of this mode of conducting a science–policy dialogue should not, however, be underestimated. In particular, the broad collaboration between scientists and policy-makers, as well as the development of arenas for simultaneous negotiations and information exchange have had significant precedence implications. As we shall see in the next chapter, the institutional design of the IPCC builds on the experiences made in the ozone process, although with the important distinction that, with regard to the IPCC, the broad collaboration and high level of involvement between science and politics was the result of a deliberate institutional design. While indications of a direct effect of institutional arrangements in terms of policy acceptance and especially policy response to scientific findings are weak in the case of ozone depletion, this way of conducting the science–policy dialogue introduced new modes of organising science–policy interaction with significant implications for subsequent processes of this kind – notably the case of climate change.

Notes

Acknowledgements: I am grateful for the assistance provided by Per Bakken and Ivar S. A. Isaksen in personal communications and in terms of access to documentation, as well as in helping me understand the course of events of the ozone process. The full responsibility for any shortcomings and misinterpretations rest with the author.

1 Already in 1985, Harvard scientists were working with a theory of 'threshold levels' of chlorine concentrations: that a sudden collapse of ozone concentrations might occur once the amount of chlorine passed a certain level (Benedick, 1991). By the shift of focus, from measurements of the 'ozone-depleting potential' (ODP) of different gases, to chlorine loading, scientists were able to assess at which levels of chlorine concentration damage to the ozone layer had occurred, and accordingly, at which levels the ozone layer would recover.

2 A total of 136 scientists from 25 countries contribted to the report of the science panel (87 scientists from 15 countries prepared the report, while 78 scientists from 23 countries participated in the peer review process). Forty-eight scientists from 17 countries contributed to the report on environmental effects (20 scientists from eight countries prepared the report, while 28 scientists from 12 countries peer reviewed it). One hundred and ten experts from 22 countries prepared the report of the technology panel. Twenty-four experts from 12 countries prepared the report of the economy panel, while it was peer reviewed by 25 experts from 18 countries (UNEP/OzL.Pro.WG.I (2)/L.1/Add.1, 2nd Draft Synthesis Report, September 1989).

3 A too rigid dichotomisation of this aspect, however, may prove artificial in this case: when scientific research discovers that human-made emissions of pollutants can lead to ozone depletion, the conclusion, by implication, holds a recommendation to reduce emissions.

4 The EC was split on this issue, with Denmark, The Netherlands and Belgium favouring regulations (FRG adopted this position in 1987). However, the Council had accepted a proposal from the Commission implying that all member states and the Commission should ratify the Montreal Protocol *unanimously* (Benedick, 1991; see also Litfin, 1994; 1995).

The Intergovernmental Panel on Climate Change

7.1 Introduction

Throughout the nineteenth century, studies on the relationship between the Earth's surface temperature and the chemical composition of the atmosphere appeared at regular intervals. The impetus for international efforts to better understand climate variations and the possible problem of a human-induced climate change, however, is generally regarded to be the UN Conference on Human Development in Stockholm in 1972. In 1979, the World Climate Conference was held in Geneva, and the World Climate programme (WCP) was launched. The creation of the WCP set forth a series of workshops organised under the auspices of the World Meteorological Organization (WMO), the United Nations Environment programme (UNEP) and the International Council of Scientific Unions (ICSU), held in Villach, Austria, in 1980, 1983 and 1985 (Agrawala, 1998a). At the 1985 Villach meeting, an international group of scientists reached a consensus that, as a result of the increasing concentrations of greenhouse gases in the atmosphere, a rise in the global mean temperature 'greater than any in man's history' could occur in the first half of the next century (WMO, 1985: 1). This group of experts also stated that 'the understanding of the greenhouse question is sufficiently developed that scientists and policy-makers should begin active collaboration to explore the effectiveness of alternative policies and adjustments' (WMO, 1985: 3).

In combination with a set of other factors, especially anomalous weather conditions in Europe and America, the 1985 Villach meeting was instrumental in bringing the climate issue on to the international political agenda. In 1986 the Advisory Group on Greenhouse Gases (AGGG) was set up under the joint sponsorship of WMO, UNEP and ICSU. Each of these bodies nominated two experts. The panel comprised a total of seven members: Gordon Goodman, Bert Bolin, Ken Hare, G. Golitsyn, Sukiyoro Manabe, M. Kassas and G. White (Agrawala, 1998a).

During the latter half of the 1980s the climate issue increasingly gained saliency among the public, scientists and policy-makers. At the Toronto Conference of the Atmosphere – where more than 300 scientists and policy-makers from UN organisations, IGOs, NGOs and 48 different countries participated – an explicit policy recommendation calling upon national governments to reduce carbon dioxide (CO_2) emissions by 20 per cent from 1988 levels by 2005 was agreed upon.

Meanwhile, the WMO and UNEP, in close co-operation with various US agencies, agreed that an *intergovernmental* mechanism was needed to undertake further internationally co-ordinated scientific assessments of climate change, and invitations to governments to the first session of the Intergovernmental Panel on Climate Change (IPCC) were sent out early in 1988 (personal communication with Bert Bolin; for a detailed account of the history behind the establishment of the IPCC see Agrawala, 1998a). The AGGG, set up in 1986, was gradually replaced by the IPCC and has not met since 1990.

The first session of the IPCC took place in November 1988. Its objective, formulated by the governing bodies of WMO and UNEP, was twofold: 1) to assess the scientific information related to the various components of the climate change issue and the information needed to evaluate the environmental and socio-economic consequences of climate change, and 2) to formulate 'realistic response strategies for the management of the climate change issue' (report of the first session of the IPCC). Three WGs were set up to attain this objective: WGI to assess available scientific information on climate change; WGII to assess environmental and socio-economic impacts of climate change; and WGIII to formulate response strategies (report of the first session of the IPCC). In 1990 the First IPCC Assessment Report was presented to the Second World Climate Conference, where it was accepted as an adequate basis for negotiations on regulations of greenhouse gases. In 1992, the IPCC was reorganised: WGIII merged into the old WGII, while a new WGIII was set up to deal with socio-economic and other cross-cutting issues related to climate change.[1] The IPCC Plenary accepted the Second IPCC Assessment Report in December 1995. In the period between the first and the second assessment reports, the IPCC provided two interim reports: one in 1992, and one in 1994. Work on a third assessment is underway (current time frames suggest finalisation in 2001). (See list below for a rough overview of the IPCC's chronological history from 1988 to 1995.)

1988 The IPCC is established. First Plenary session held in November.
1989 The Special Committee for Developing Countries is established.
1990 The First Assessment Report is finalised.
1991 Formal rules of procedure are adopted.
1992 The IPCC is restructured: WGII and WGIII are merged. New WGIII to assess information on socio-economic and other cross-cutting issues. The Special Committee on Developing Countries is dissolved. The Supplementary Report is finalised.
1993 The rules of procedure for the acceptance and adoption of reports are made explicit. Reports accepted and approved by WGs cannot be amended by the full Panel Plenary. The Panel Plenary is made responsible for adopting 'Synthesis Reports'.
1994 The Interim Report is finalised.
1995 The Second Assessment Report is finalised.

In December 1990 the Intergovernmental Negotiating Committee for a Framework Convention on Climate Change (INC/FCCC) was formally established by UN General Assembly (UNGA) Resolution 45/212. Thus, the political process was put under the direct control of the General Assembly, while the IPCC is organised under the auspices of WMO and UNEP. In February 1991 the first session of the INC took place. From February 1991 to April 1992, five sessions were held. The fifth session resulted in a Climate Convention ready for signing at the UNCED in Rio de Janeiro, June 1992. The

Climate Convention entered into force in March 1994. In December 1997, the Conference of the Parties to the Climate Convention (CoP) agreed upon the Kyoto Protocol.

7.2 The policy response

The stated ultimate objective of the 1992 UN Framework Convention on Climate Change (UNFCCC) is 'to achieve ... stabilisation of greenhouse gas concentrations in the atmosphere at a level that would prevent dangerous anthropogenic interference with the climate system' (Article 2). Each of the Parties to the Convention have committed themselves to 'adopt national policies and take corresponding measures on the mitigation of climate change, by limiting its anthropogenic emissions of greenhouse gases and protecting and enhancing its greenhouse gas sinks and reservoirs' (Art. 4.2.(a)). Moreover, Parties are committed to communicate to the CoP 'detailed information' on such policies and measures and the resulting projected emissions of greenhouse gases, 'with the aim of returning individually or jointly to their 1990 levels these anthropogenic emissions of carbon dioxide and other greenhouse gases not controlled by the Montreal Protocol' (Art. 4.2.(b)). Finally, the Parties agreed to review the 'adequacy' of these commitments at the first session of the CoP (Art. 4.2.(c)). The outcome of the first session of the CoP, held in Berlin in March/April 1995, was the Berlin Mandate, in which the parties acknowledged the inadequacy of the commitments made in the Climate Convention and agreed to begin the process of strengthening them in an additional protocol or another legal instrument which was to be signed at the third session of the CoP in December 1997. The Ad Hoc Group on the Berlin Mandate (AGBM) was set up to address this task.

The Kyoto Protocol to the climate convention was agreed upon at the third session of CoP in December 1997. In the Kyoto Protocol, Annex B parties agree to a set of differentiated reduction targets amounting to a total reduction of greenhouse gases (GHGs), measured in CO_2 equivalents, of 5.2 per cent by 2012 as compared to 1990.

To what extent has science influenced the making of this climate regime? What is the 'score' on our dependent variable in this case? We have defined our dependent variable according to three levels (see Chapter 1): At the first level, policy-makers turn to the scientific community for advice; at the second level policy-makers accept, at least conceptually, the findings presented by the scientific community; and at the third level the scientific findings are acted upon by policy-makers.

Seven years after the adoption of the first IPCC Assessment Report (Houghton, Jenkins and Ephraums, 1990a; MacTegart, Sheldon and Griffiths, 1990; *The IPCC Response Strategies*, 1990), governments have committed themselves only to very limited reduction targets for emissions of GHGs.[2] The scientific knowledge base provided by the IPCC, therefore, has only to a very limited extent been followed by a policy response in terms of actions by governments to restrict the accumulation of GHGs in the atmosphere. The commitments to reduce emissions of GHGs agreed upon in the Kyoto Protocol will only have a marginal to negligible effect in this regard (Bolin, 1998). Therefore, this agreement does not qualify as an 'adoption' of the scientific knowledge base in the sense that knowledge has served as a premise for the policy decisions made. However, while the score in this case is considered low in terms of the extent to which scientific knowledge has been acted upon, it is relatively high with regard to the first and second levels. First, the IPCC was established on the initiative, and under the auspices, of UNEP and WMO – two intergovernmental bodies of the UN. Moreover, funding for carrying out the IPCC's mandate has been made available by participating governments. Second, the 1992 Climate Convention indicates that the problem of a human-induced climate change has been accepted by governments as constituting a political problem that needs to be resolved through co-ordinated action at the international level. Borione and Ripert, for instance, maintain that 'the IPCC, under the wise chairmanship of Professor B. Bolin, gave the diplomats a firm scientific foundation that was never once seriously challenged during the negotiations' (Borione and Ripert, 1994: 84). The agreement on the 1997 Kyoto Protocol confirms this impression of a relatively high level of acceptance among policy-makers of the factual validity and scientific authority of the knowledge base provided by the IPCC. An additional indicator of policy-makers' acceptance of the knowledge base is the extensive political institution building at the national, and especially, at the international level that has taken place since the beginning of the 1990s. The major international institution is the CoP to the 1992 Climate Convention and its subsidiary bodies (the

AGBM; the Subsidiary Body for Implementation [SBI]; and the Subsidiary Body for Scientific and Technological Advice [SBSTA]).

The extent of acceptance of the IPCC conclusions is also well illustrated by the increasing support from the industrial lobby. In 1996 two major companies, British Petroleum America and the Arizona Public Service Company, a Phoenix-based electric power utility, withdrew from the Global Climate Coalition, the US-based energy lobbying group to the IPCC and CoP meetings. According to Nature (Masood, 1996b), Mark De Michele, chief executive of the Arizona Public Service Company, said that 'global climate change is a serious problem and we need to take steps to deal with it'. Similarly, in May 1997, British Petroleum Chief Executive Officer John Browne stated that 'there is now an effective consensus among the world's leading scientists and serious and well-informed people outside the scientific community that there is a discernible human influence on the climate'. He further stated that 'we need to go beyond analysis to seek solutions and take action,' calling it 'a moment for change and rethinking of corporate responsibility' to the environment (GECR, 1997). On the other hand, the US energy industry launched a major campaign against climate measures during the summer and autumn of 1997, prior to the third CoP meeting in Kyoto in December 1997. The campaign was not directed against IPCC's credibility, however. Rather, it was a campaign designed to persuade the US government not to commit themselves to CO_2 emissions reductions, at least not without developing countries such as India and China making similar commitments.

Taken together, these indicators suggest a mediate score for our dependent variable. Scientific findings seem to have been adopted in terms of the first two levels on our cumulative scale: Policy-makers have turned to the scientific community for information and advice, and, as parties to the Climate Convention, policy-makers have accepted the findings presented by the scientific community. To what extent can the institutional arrangements of the science–policy dialogue explain this outcome?

7.3 Institutional design

7.3.1 *The science–policy distinction within the IPCC*
The political nature of the IPCC process has been evident since its beginning: the Executive Council of WMO and the Governing

Council of UNEP established the IPCC as an *intergovernmental* organisation under UN auspices. These bodies also initially determined the IPCC's mandate. Being a UN body, the IPCC is submitted to the traditional UN procedures governing most UN bodies. Thus, the main characteristic feature of the IPCC is that it has a scientific mandate, while it is organised within a *political* institutional framework. This is reflected in a distinction *within* the IPCC itself, between the bodies largely serving 'administrative/political' functions and the bodies constituting the 'scientific/technical core' (Figure 7.1).

Until 1992, the main bodies of the IPCC were the Plenary, the Bureau, three WGs (some with *ad hoc* task force establishments on specific issues) and, from 1989 to 1992, a Special Committee for

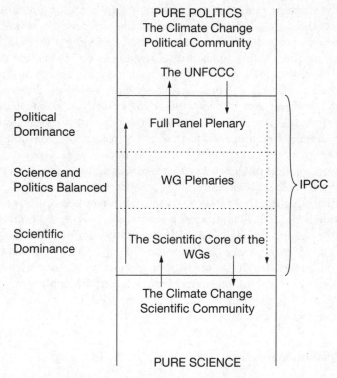

Figure 7.1   *The institutional set-up of the IPCC*

Note: The arrows are rough illustrations of formal and informal channels of communcation (see also Lunde, 1991).

Developing Countries. The science–policy distinction seems to run through the WG level, between WG-Plenary (as distinguished from Panel Plenary) and task force establishments. The bodies constituting the scientific core are principally responsible for providing the knowledge base, while the administrative/political bodies (the WG Plenary and the full Panel Plenary) are responsible for accepting and approving the outcome of the work taking place in the scientific core. At the ninth Plenary session of the IPCC (June 1993), the procedures guiding the Panel's acceptance and approval of reports were made explicit. An 'approved' report has been subject to detailed, line-by-line discussions in a Plenary session of the relevant WG. The full assessment reports are 'accepted' *en bloc*.

At the 1993 session it was also decided that the status of the reports published by the IPCC should be explicitly stated on its front page. Four categories were identified: 'supporting material' (contributions), 'Reports accepted by WGs' (assessment reports), 'Reports approved by WGs and accepted by the Panel' (summaries for policy-makers) and finally, 'Reports approved by the Panel' (synthesis reports). This categorisation also signals the extent to which the reports have been submitted to negotiations. While neither contributions nor assessment reports are negotiated at all, the summaries for policy-makers are negotiated at WG Plenaries, and Synthesis reports are negotiated at Panel Plenaries. Since the same governmental actors are represented in both forums, a report that has been approved and accepted by the WG Plenary may not be amended by the Panel Plenary. This institutional device is important for ensuring that the summaries actually reflect the reports upon which they are based, since the lead authors are present in the WG Plenary while they usually do not participate in the Panel Plenary.

7.3.2 Administrative bodies

The IPCC Plenary constitutes the main decision-making body of the IPCC; all subsidiary bodies (WGs and task forces) are constituted, and their mandates established and approved, by the Plenary. Furthermore, scientific assessments provided by the WGs have to be discussed and accepted by the Plenary before they are considered to represent the official IPCC view. The Plenary also elects the leadership of each WG (chairs and vice-chairs). The leadership of the respective WG (the Bureau of the WG) appoints lead authors on separate issues of each WG. In the preparatory work for the second

assessment report, fairly detailed rules of procedure for preparation, review, acceptance, approval and publication of IPCC reports
were adopted by the Plenary. Furthermore, although the actual election of lead authors still lies with the leadership of each WG, the
Plenary has to a larger extent become involved in this election in
that the geopolitical representativity of the groups of lead authors
has been given more emphasis. Thus, the geographical balance of
the groups has become an issue for discussion and approval in the
Plenary. Before 1992, the election of lead authors was left entirely
to the leadership of each WG.

Since 1989, entry to the IPCC Plenary and Working Group (Plenary) sessions are in principle open; invitations are extended by the
Chairman of the IPCC to governments 'and other bodies' (WMO,
UNEP, scientific IGOs and NGOs). Thus, any expert nominated by
governments can participate. Experts can also be invited to contribute in their personal capacities, but their respective governments
'should be informed in advance'. In the administrative bodies, government officials, rather than scientists active in research, largely
dominate the composition of participants.

It is interesting to note, however, that the IPCC initially was
designed on the basis of 'core membership' in the WGs. In the
report of the first session it is noted that, 'while participation by all
countries interested in the activity of a Working Group would be
essential to achieve a comprehensive and balanced outcome of its
work, there is a need to provide for a manageable and effective
group composition. Therefore, it was agreed that a core membership would be established for each Working Group' (agenda item
3.6). Thus, the WGs initially consisted of thirteen to seventeen 'core
members'. The inconsistency between this participation procedure
and the intergovernmental status of the body was recognised, however, even in the first session, where it was noted that,

> this would not imply that other interested countries would not be wel-
> come to join in a Group's activity. The Panel suggested that, on the
> contrary, each Working Group should strive to obtain the best possible
> expertise, on a world-wide basis ... The Panel further suggested that
> any country interested in the work of a particular Working Group
> should be invited to designate a focal point for purposes of communi-
> cation and to attend sessions of the Working Group, if desired'. (IPCC,
> report of the first session, agenda item 3.7)

At the second Plenary session in 1989, the principle of core membership was abandoned altogether (IPCC report of the second session, agenda item 6.1).

In all IPCC bodies, participation is intended to reflect a balanced geographic representation. With regard to WGs and task forces, the modification 'with due consideration for scientific and technical requirements' has been added. In the Plenary report from the eighth session (after the restructuring), this point is further emphasised: 'it is highly desirable that governments ensure the scientific-technical integrity and credibility of the IPCC by nominating relevant experts for participation in the work of the Panel. Thus, the Chairman will request that a government indicate the relevant expertise of the candidate it nominates' (IPCC, item 6.16).

Nevertheless, the aspect of geographic representativity is important. In the initial phases of the process, Western industrialised countries heavily dominated the IPCC. Lunde points out that 'this bias was early recognised … as an important challenge to the success of the IPCC effort.' (Lunde, 1991: 84). Thus, a Special Committee on Developing Countries was set up early in 1989. Its main function was to 'promote, as rapidly as possible, full participation of developing countries in IPCC activities' (WMO/UNEP IPCC, 1990a). Developing–country participation has increased substantially since 1988 from 14 non-OECD participants at the first Plenary session, to 48 in 1990 (the First Assessment), and 98 in 1995 (the Second Assessment) (Agrawala, 1998b).

With the restructuring in 1992, it was agreed that instead of a Special Committee on developing country participation, 'the special situation of the developing countries should … be given attention as part and parcel of all the work carried out by the Panel and its groups (working groups/subgroups/task forces)' ('Chairman's Revised Proposal on IPCC Structure', 1992). Thus this issue is now integrated at all levels of IPCC activities, and the Special Committee on Developing Countries has been dissolved. The organisational change implied, first, a restructured bureau in order to achieve a better geographical balance, and second, increased impact of the recruitment principle of geopolitical representativity in all IPCC bodies and at all levels.

The IPCC's activities are funded by voluntary donations from national governments administered by the IPCC Trust Fund. The Trust Fund covers financial support to developing-country participants, meeting expenditures (such as translation costs, printing, etc.) and IPCC Secretariat functions. Research activities are mainly funded separately by national governments and the traditional funding mechanisms of scientific institutions at the national and international level.

7.3.3 The assessment process
During the initial phases of the IPCC process there were few formally stipulated rules of procedure for the development of assessments. Until 1991 (the fifth Plenary session), the work was guided only by the rather sketchy 'Terms of Reference' adopted at the first session. This implied that the WGs and their task forces, sub-groups and lead author meetings, in which the actual development of the assessments took place, enjoyed a relatively high operational autonomy in their work. Within their mandate, they could organise their own agendas, decide upon the division of labour within the group as well as the allocation of specific roles such as lead authors, contributors and reviewers (personal communication). It was not until the fifth Plenary session in 1991 that the IPCC adopted a set of formal rules of procedure. These were also rather sketchy, however, occupying no more than one page. The most important point in these rules of procedure is perhaps that it formally establishes that 'the IPCC Plenary and Working Groups shall use all best endeavours to reach consensus' (Principles Governing IPCC Work, item 6, cited under agenda item 2.1.2. of the IPCC report to the fifth Plenary session). It further stipulates that if consensus is not reached, the IPCC must follow the General Regulations of the WMO in procedural issues, and explain and, upon request, record differing views with regard to conclusions and the adoption of reports. The 1991 rules of procedure guided the IPCC until the completion of the Second Assessment in 1995, but they have been supplemented and expanded in 1992 and 1993 to gradually cover more areas of IPCC activities[3].

Until 1992 the IPCC served three main functions: scientific assessment, assessment of impacts, and formulation of response strategies, carried out by WGs I, II and III, respectively. The nature of these tasks implied that the results of the work carried out in WGI and II would be the basis for the work to be carried out in WGIII. In the first session of the IPCC 'it was specifically pointed out that the activity of the Working Group on response strategies would heavily depend on the results obtained by the other Working Groups. Nevertheless, the three Working Groups should start their work immediately' (IPCC report of the first session, 1988). Throughout the period from 1988 to 1990, WGI seems to have dominated the work of the IPCC as a whole. Moreover, the scientific knowledge base (developed by WGs I and II) upon which the policy recommendations (the old WGIII) were supposed to rest were developed simultaneously. A much criticised aspect of the IPCC also refers to the co-ordination problems between the WGs during this initial phase. Sonja Boehmer-Christiansen has, for instance, found that, 'communications between the groups was poor to non-existent. Some scientists interviewed [in WGI] were unaware of WG II and III' (Sonja Boehmer-Christiansen, 1993c: 390).

Before 1992 the tasks of WGs I, II and III had an increasingly political nature. In WGI the line between science and politics was more clear-cut than in WGII and, especially, in the old WGIII. This also had significant implications for the manner in which the WGs carried out their tasks, and the extent to which the political nature of the institutional framework of the Panel served to politicise their work accordingly. Since WGI and the old WGIII represent opposite poles in this regard, we will concentrate our discussion on these two WGs.

In WGI[4] research activities are primarily carried out by the task forces established on separate issues under the mandate of the WG and their individually appointed contributors. Input to the assessments is generated through a series of workshops and lead- and contributing-author meetings, and lead authors are appointed to write the respective assessments following each issue. The assessments are then peer reviewed by scientists who have not taken part in the preceding process. These two stages of the process seem to be well shielded against political pressures (Lunde, 1991; personal observation and personal communication with participants). The work seems, to a large extent, to accommodate the rules, norms and procedures that govern science at large. Due to the scientific nature of the task and the mechanisms applied to provide the assessments, there thus seems to be little room for purely political considerations to gain any significant influence on the outcome: The level of scientific complexity in itself serves to exclude non-experts from influencing the discussions (personal communication with participants).

The result of this process is then discussed in the WG Plenary, where non-scientists and government-appointed experts also participate.

At this level, the debate takes on a character we believe to be quite distinctive to the IPCC process. The discussion that takes place in the WG Plenary constitutes the first stage in the process whereby a political acceptance of the knowledge base put forward by the scientists is acquired. It takes the form of a debate (very often straightforward negotiations) between the lead authors of the scientific report and government experts (often indistinguishable from low-level policy-makers) concerning the formulations of the 'Summary for Policy-makers' (SPM), which is based on the full assessment report. At this level, the SPM is submitted to paragraph-by-paragraph, line-by-line and often word-by-word negotiations between these two groups of actors. The nature of the debate provides an excellent illustration of how a piece of scientific knowledge can be expressed and formulated in a number of ways. An essential aspect of the science–policy dialogue is to develop agreement between scientists and policy-makers on how scientific findings should be expressed. It goes without saying that the scientific knowledge base, at this stage of the IPCC process, is exposed to massive attack and efforts to influence its content also on non-scientific grounds – not only from governments, but also from environmental and industry NGOs. Still, lead authors have acquired a special status as authorities in the debate, and substantive changes to the text are never made without consent from the lead authors of the chapter under discussion. Moreover, the WGI Plenary serves a very important function as an arena for an interactive dialogue between scientists and policy-makers concerning the appropriate interpretation of the scientific findings and their potential policy implications.

It seems inevitable, however, that the summaries be criticised for containing discrepancies from the full assessment reports. There will necessarily always be some discrepancies since the conclusions always are subject to interpretations and the summaries are not blueprints of passages from the full reports. With regard to the First Assessment some reviewers felt 'that their comments had not been considered adequately and hence objected to being listed as this implied concurrence … ' (IPCC, report of the eighth session, item 5.2.). The leadership of the Panel maintains that this incident was largely due to the tight deadlines for the development of the assessment, where, first, reviewers were permitted very little time to review the documents, and, second, the lead authors were given insufficient time to consider the comments properly (personal communication). Similarly, with regard to the Second Assessment, modifications made to the assessment report after the material had been accepted by the WGI Plenary Session in Madrid 1995 aroused a lot of debate. In this case, the Global Climate Coalition accused the IPCC of 'scientific cleansing' (Masood, 1996a: 546; Weiss, 1996). The accusations were addressed by the convening lead author of the chapter in question, the Chairmen of WGI as well as the Chairman of the IPCC, who claimed that the criticism was based on a misconception of the rules of procedure of the IPCC. The modifications were made to the *draft* report of the WG, which was accepted by the WG Plenary on *condition* that these modifications were made. The modifications were therefore not a violation of IPCC's rules of procedure, as claimed by the critics. On the contrary, the rules of procedure would have been violated had these modifications not been made since they represented the final incorporation of comments put forward in the extended review process the IPCC adheres to (Bolin, Houghton and Filho, 1996). Moreover, in an interview with *Nature*, Ben Santer, the convening lead author of the chapter, emphasised that the report's key argument 'was approved by all 100 participating governments' (Masood, 1996a: 546).

The extended peer review procedure is the backbone of the IPCC's scientific credibility. It is therefore considered essential that it functions well. The IPCC leadership admits, however, that the incorporation of comments, especially 'diverging views', put forth in the review has not always been satisfactory (personal communication with Bert Bolin). Under the rules of procedure governing IPCC bodies until 1995, the incorporation of review comments is left entirely to the discretion of the lead authors. That is, there has been no external supervision over the actions of lead authors on review comments (Agrawala, 1998b). In an effort to abate this short-coming, the IPCC is currently discussing the establishment of 'editorial boards' with independent expertise to supervise the review process (IPCC Decision Paper from the thirteenth Plenary session of the panel, item 7; see also Agrawala, 1998b; Kerr, 1997).

The 1993 rules of procedure imply that a report adopted in the WG Plenaries cannot be amended by the full Panel Plenary. This institutional device is important for ensuring consistency between the summaries and the scientific assessments upon which the summaries are based. In WGI the lead authors' scientific authority is used to prevent changes in the summaries that would distort the relationship between the summaries and the underlying report. Thus suggestions of substantial changes are not adopted without the approval of the respective lead authors. This means that the rules of procedure, at least when employed with a certain 'diplomatic finesse', provide the lead authors with the power to veto changes they regard to be scientifically unsubstantiated.

This institutional device also prevents the reopening of controversial issues in the full Panel Plenary that were already settled in the WG Plenaries. A situation like the one that arose in the 1990 Plenary session with the adoption of the summary may thus be avoided. In 1990, negotiations in the Panel Plenary almost went into deadlock and threatened to overthrow the whole process (see, for instance, *New Scientist*, 1990). At the time, explicit rules of procedure on the Panel's adoption of summaries had not been adopted. A summary based on the three reports, developed by Bert Bolin himself, was met by massive criticism and brought latent conflicts into the open (Agrawala, 1998b; Brenton, 1994). Agreement was achieved in this situation by using text already agreed upon in the WGs. While Bert Bolin maintains that his own inexperience and naïvety may account for how this situation developed (personal communication), new, and most important explicit rules of procedure have also contributed to a smoother decision-making process.

The scientific nature of the task ascribed to WGI also has impact on recruitment and participation patterns in the WG. At task force and peer review levels, members are largely scientists recruited on the basis of scientific criteria and scholarly merits. In WGI individual scientists are invited to contribute in their personal capacity either as contributors or as reviewers, thereby also counteracting the immanent potential for politicisation following from the recruitment principles adopted by IPCC Plenary. WGI can therefore draw upon a relatively well-organised and easily identifiable community of scientists in the development of the scientific assessments on climate change, and their work is peer reviewed according to traditional scientific standards.[5]

There is a significant difference between the functioning of WGI and the old WGIII. With the political nature of the task ascribed to this WG and the complexity implied in terms of drawing a definite line between science and politics, it should come as no surprise that

WGIII experienced an increased substantive politicisation of their work as compared to the other WGs (Boehmer-Christiansen, 1993a; Lunde, 1991). The WG was dominated by low-level policy-makers and negotiators with only a few legal and environmental experts, and the standard scientific review procedures did not apply. Thus, the work of the old WGIII was not submitted to a scientific peer review process, although the summary for policy-makers went through a government review as did the reports of the other WGs. Boehmer-Christiansen claims that 'the third WG became a forum mainly for government people and lobbyists' (Boehmer-Christiansen, 1993a: 19), and 'the main forum for pre-negotiations and conflicts' (Boehmer-Christiansen, 1993a: 22). The political intricacies of the task assigned to the old WGIII are also reflected in their relatively greater difficulty in reaching consensus and the diplomatic formulations that resulted from their discussions.

In some respects, the establishment of WGIII may seem premature: In order to fulfil the task of formulating response strategies, a *pre-established* scientific knowledge base was required. At the time, however, the required knowledge base was under development. Thus, the basis and the condition for fulfilling the task were lacking. Furthermore, there did not exist a political forum for discussion of interpretations of the science in terms of response strategies at the time the WGs were set up (negotiations on a climate convention started in 1991). There was therefore no forum through which the political aspects of the issues to be dealt with in WGIII could be channelled. Under these circumstances the old WGIII became the 'cockpit' for much of the climate change politics of the pre-1990 period (Brenton, 1994: 179). Still, the old WGIII produced 'a wordy but carefully hedged document whose one important recommendation was that the world should start to negotiate a global framework convention on climate change' (Brenton, 1994: 182).

The tasks assigned to the old WGIII are also included in the restructured IPCC, although in a significantly modified form.[6] In its restructured form (the old) WGs II and III are merged. The task of the new WGIII is mainly to provide 'technical assessments of the socio-economics of impacts, adaptation and mitigation of climate change over both the short and the long term and the regional and global levels' (IPCC report of the eighth Plenary session, item 6.10). Thus, the new WGII is now responsible for assessing information on possible impacts of climate change and response options. The wording of the task is therefore modified, from *formulations* of response strategies (the old WGIII) to *assessments of information* on response options. In contrast to the period before 1992, all WGs are now doing *assessments* of published accounts within their various fields. Thus, as of 1992, the IPCC does not formulate policy recommendations. It is furthermore explicitly pointed out, with regard to all WGs that 'a peer-review process should be incorporated in the preparation' of the reports of the Working Group' (IPCC report of the eighth Plenary session, agenda item 6.10.2).

The mandate of the new WGIII falls within the sphere of socioeconomics. Hence, in contrast to its pre-1992 period, the research field now addresses itself to a clearly defined scientific community or research network. This has modified the most apparent problems of politicisation characterising this WG before 1992, although not resolved them altogether. The problems of politicisation still troubling this WG are very much linked to the nature of this field of inquiry, and it is questionable whether they ever can be removed altogether (personal communication with Cutajar). This is, for instance, illustrated in the controversy regarding the value of a 'statistical life' which took place in relation to the development of the Second Assessment Report in 1995 and which developed into a heated debate between (some) lead authors and developing-country delegates (see *inter alia* GECR, 1995a; Grubb, 1996; Meyer, 1995). Although it is emphasised in the report of WGIII that what is valued is a *statistical* life, 'a change in the risk of death', not human life itself (Pearce *et al.*, 1995: 196), the significant difference between the values assigned a statistical life in OECD countries as compared to developing countries is controversial.[7] Giving a monetary value to statistical lives is controversial even among economists and is obviously problematic within the framework of a process so heavily marked by a potentially paralysing North–South controversy. The strength of this controversy may, however, also have been a result of an inadequate incorporation of review comments. It is possible that this controversy could have been avoided, or at least minimised, had the issue been dealt with a bit more cautiously in the first place. Moreover, an external agent supervising the incorporation of review comments might have been instrumental in avoiding the situation that arose in WGIII, or at least in resolving the controversy in a more amicable manner (see also Agrawala, 1998b).

7.3.4 *The scientific autonomy of the IPCC*

As the preceding discussion illustrates, the IPCC's score on the autonomy dimension cannot be evaluated solely by studying its relationship to the regulatory body (CoP). Scientific autonomy, in this case, is to a larger extent a function of the relationship between the bodies of the IPCC itself.

Both the formal and the operational autonomy of the IPCC in relation to the CoP is high. The two bodies are organised under different UN bodies, and the CoP is in no position to place either restrictions or prescriptions on the manner in which the IPCC chooses to organise its work. The CoP may specify which questions they wish the IPCC to address, but the IPCC is free to choose whether and when to respond to the inquiry. On the other hand, it is governments that provide the funding for all IPCC activities on a voluntary basis – a very unfortunate situation according to one member of the Saudi Arabian delegation, due to its possible consequences for the IPCC's independence (personal communication).

When we turn to the relationship of the bodies within the IPCC, however, the autonomy of its various bodies seems to have varied a great deal, both 'vertically', between decision-making levels (between Plenary, WG and scientific core), and 'horizontally', between the scientific cores of the three WGs. As the discussion shows, the main distinction between the bodies runs between the more politicised WG and Panel Plenaries and the scientific core constituted by task forces, sub-groups and the lead author meetings. Although the decision-making authority of the IPCC lies in the Panel Plenary, where the intergovernmental status of the institution has significant impact on the composition of participants, this does not seem to have severely restricted the operational autonomy of the scientific core. They still have decision-making power on such aspects as the division of labour within the group, lead authors on the respective areas, contributors and scientific reviewers.

The extent to which this *potential* operational autonomy has been *realised* seems, however, to have been dependent upon, *inter alia*, the individual capabilities of the most central actors in the process, notably the scientific qualifications and independence of the WG chair, as well as the capability of scientific agents to exercise 'diplomatic finesse'. Appointing the head of the US delegation to the INC also as chair of the old WGIII may have served to restrict the operational autonomy of the scientific core of this group. Similarly, the controversy that arose in 1995 regarding the value of a 'statistical life' might have been avoided if a little bit more sophisticated 'diplomacy' on the part of the scientists (lead authors) had been exercised. It should also be recalled, however, that the scientific 'safety net' of the process, the extended peer review procedure, was not capable of preventing the situation from arising.

The most important explanation of the observed variation in autonomy between the scientific cores of the WGs seems, however, to be found in the nature of the *task* assigned to the WG. The task assigned to WGIII before 1992 lies very close to the political domain and it is not encompassed in any clearly identifiable scientific discipline or group of experts with pre-established scientific networks. Because of these circumstances the responsibility for providing the knowledge base was shifted from the bodies constituting the scientific core to the more politicised decision-making levels of the IPCC, and the group's autonomy was reduced accordingly. Even after 1992, the nature of the task assigned to WGIII has been such that the distinction between science and politics is blurred. On the other hand, in their balancing between science and politics, the entire IPCC is 'walking on eggs' (expressed by Michael Zammit Cutajar in personal communication).

The autonomy of the IPCC has been questioned also by individual scientists and scholars who to a varying extent have participated in the process. The two most central critics of the IPCC are Fred Singer and Richard Lindzen (see also Pearce, 1997). Singer has been instrumental in bringing together the work of IPCC sceptics in periodic reports following the publication of the IPCC reports, mobilising some 13–15 contributors (see, for instance, Singer, 1992). Lindzen has been concerned that the IPCC's assumption of a positive feedback from water vapour, the most significant GHG in the atmosphere, is wrong and that the feedback really is negative (Lindzen, 1990). A negative feedback from water vapour would have significant implications for projections of future warming resulting from increased concentrations of GHGs in the atmosphere. Especially in relation to the writing of the 1992 supplement report, extensive efforts were made by the leadership of WGI to get Lindzen to participate in the lead author meeting in which this subject was to be discussed – without any success. Despite numerous phone calls and faxes urging him to come, he did not show up (personal communication with leadership of WGI). 'I wouldn't touch the IPCC because it is an illegitimate process', Lindzen said in personal communication with this author. According to Lindzen, the IPCC consists of mediocre scientists. Among the scientists that in his view are the best, the 'IPCC greenhouse theory' has no support (personal communication).

While this controversy has received quite a lot of attention in the media, the sceptics have not been very successful in mobilising support for their views within the scientific community. For instance, there are few published accounts in the scientific peer-reviewed literature of their propositions. To the extent that their propositions have been published, they have largely appeared in 'grey' journals without peer-review procedures. Thus, IPCC sceptics have not succeeded in deconstructing the IPCC's scientific platform, upon which governments of all sorts of opposing positions now increasingly base their policies.

While many of the lead authors in WGI maintain that the arguments put forward by 'IPCC sceptics' are not sufficiently scientifically documented to be included and discussed in IPCC reports (personal communication), Bert Bolin admits that they should have been dealt with more explicitly by the IPCC (personal communication).[8] As it is, these viewpoints have been widely communicated in the mass media and to the general public. Cutajar maintains that the IPCC's inadequate handling of this criticism has implied that it has received much more media attention than it deserves (personal communication).

Despite these attacks against the IPCC, however, we would argue that, especially where WGI is concerned, the scientific autonomy and integrity of the IPCC has been relatively high. In WGI, there is a scientific core within the IPCC comprising scientists with high personal integrity, and their conclusions have to a very little extent been distorted by politics at the higher decision making levels of the IPCC.[9] While WGIII, both the old and the new, has experienced somewhat more turbulence, we would still argue that this conclusion is valid also for the new WGIII.

7.3.5 *The level of involvement characterising the IPCC*
The IPCC is under the auspices of UNEP and WMO, while negotiations, by implication of UN Resolution 45/212, are under the control of the UN General Assembly. The resolution acknowledges 'the important work accomplished by the [IPCC]' and the *ad hoc* secre-

tariat of the Intergovernmental Negotiating Committee (INC) is requested 'to co-operate closely with the [IPCC] to ensure that the Panel can respond to the needs and requests for objective scientific and technical advice made during the negotiation process'. The dialogue between the two bodies seems to take place by representation: the Chairman of the IPCC is invited to speak at INC/CoP sessions, and the Chairman of the INC/CoP is invited, in an *ex officio* capacity, to attend the IPCC (Plenary), the Bureau and the Working Group sessions. Overlapping participation seems, moreover, to play an important role in strengthening the relationship between the bodies since very many of the participants of IPCC Plenary sessions are also delegates at INC/CoP sessions, especially the delegation heads attending IPCC Plenaries.

While there are both formal and informal channels of communication and dialogue between the IPCC and the INC/CoP, a dissatisfaction with the IPCC's ability to provide reports in accordance with the time schedules of the Convention has, however, been voiced (New Scientist, June, 1994). In March 1993, Bert Bolin initiated the establishment of the IPCC–INC Joint Working Party to improve the dialogue between the two institutions. This group has met since November 1993, after 1995 under the name of the 'Joint Working Group', and consists of the senior officials of the two institutions[10] (Agrawala, 1998b; personal communication with Bert Bolin). Furthermore, at the 11th Plenary Session of the IPCC it was decided that the Panel should provide more targeted Special Reports and Technical Papers on specific issues as requested by the CoP (via SBSTA). These reports are to be based on the existing assessment reports and need not be subjected to the extensive review procedures of assessment reports. Such reports can, therefore, be provided within shorter time frames. The first Special Report was presented at the SBSTA meeting in Bonn in October, 1997. Thus, formal links between the scientific and regulatory bodies have been established, as well as both formal and informal channels for dialogue and communication.

Before 1992, WGIII was assigned the task of formulating policy recommendations. During this period, the provision of a scientific knowledge base (scientific assessments by WG I and WGII) and the provision of policy recommendations (the 1990 report of WGIII) took place within the framework of the IPCC, although the tasks were handled by different WGs. In this regard, the organisational distance between the bodies providing knowledge and advice was relatively short. (On the other hand, the IPCC has been criticised for a lack of co-ordination between these WGs.) However, because of the circumstances discussed above, the *status* of the outcome of WGIII proceedings (before 1992) is somewhat problematic. With the scientific uncertainties characterising the issue area, the political potency of the problem, and no pre-existing research networks, it proved difficult to keep the control of the old WGIII in the hands of its environmental and legal experts. The old WGIII, therefore, may be regarded as a largely political forum for pre-negotiations, and the texts drafted by this group held general, compromise formulations bearing clear signs of being reached through negotiations. Thus, the 'advice' was as much based on purely political evaluations as scientific. On the other hand, the work of the old WGIII has been argued to have made an important substantial contribution to the early negotiations in the INC (Agrawala, 1998b; Borione and Ripert, 1994).

The political dimension of the old WGIII did become problematic, however, especially in the development of the much criticised emissions scenarios depicting hypothetical future patterns of greenhouse gas emissions. In an effort to place it more firmly within the scientific realm, the task of developing scenarios was moved to WGI. Working Group I updated the scenarios in their 1992 Supplementary Report. Some of the scientists in WGI, however, also felt that the scenarios were 'too political', and did not feel comfortable with not being able to rely on published material in their development (personal communication). These scenarios were then evaluated by the new WGIII in the 1994 Interim Report (Skodvin, 1999).

After the restructuring of 1992, IPCC's advisory function has dwindled. Still, given the main purpose of the IPCC being to inform policy-makers, their work does imply some sort of implicit advice, and over the years they have developed more sophisticated methods for separating science and politics in this regard. This is perhaps best illustrated in the 1995 Synthesis Report in which alternative paths to achieving a stabilisation of CO_2 concentrations in the atmosphere at various levels (450, 550, 750 and 1000 parts per million by volume) are illustrated. In this case the CO_2 emissions reductions needed to stabilise concentrations at these various levels are illustrated without having to rely on arbitrary speculations of future energy use, population growth etc., as was the case with regard to the development of scenarios.

Already in 1990, *New Scientist* reported that the scientists of the IPCC have learned 'how to talk science to politicians' while at the same time 'not to play at being politicians' (*New Scientist*, 1990). While this proposition may have been somewhat premature in 1990, it certainly seems to have gained validity in the period since. There are examples where the formulations of the WGI reports have been carefully worded with due consideration of the distinction between science and politics. This seems to have been the case in the 1992 Supplementary Report, where WGI discussed the question of how their findings on the negative warming potential of SO_2 should be presented due to their possible policy implications (personal communication with participants). A similar discussion on the borders between science and politics also took place at the WGI Plenary in Maastricht in 1994 in the context of a discussion of the new Global Warming Potential (GWP) for methane. In this case the appropriate borders between science and politics were not at all obvious and were subject to discussions between the lead authors of the WG and scientists with close links to policy making (see Shackley and Skodvin, 1995).

As the preceding discussion demonstrates, one main characteristic feature of the IPCC is the progressively increasing level of procedural politicisation as we move from the lower to the higher decision-making levels of the institution (see also Figure 7.1). The distinction between science and politics becomes, in this case, a *zone* rather than a clear-cut line. In this respect the IPCC operates in the *interface* of science and politics in the most literal sense of the term. This progressive movement from science to politics within the IPCC indicates a high level of involvement in the political process of the climate change issue. It should be noted that while the high level of involvement characterising the IPCC to some extent is a function of the formal and informal links between the IPCC and the INC/CoP (regulatory bodies), it is to a larger extent a function of the close links between scientists and policy-makers within the IPCC itself.

7.4 Balancing scientific autonomy and involvement

Our discussion suggests that scientific autonomy and involvement in the policy-making process is fairly well balanced in the IPCC. After the 1992 restructuring, a balance *within each* WG has been achieved, from the relatively scientifically autonomous scientific core to the more politicised WG and full Panel Plenaries. Before the 1992 restructuring, a balance *within the IPCC as a whole* was achieved, with WGI firmly placed within the scientific domain and WGIII closely associated with the policy domain.

The intergovernmental status of the IPCC implies a vulnerability to politicisation. This vulnerability, exacerbated by the lack of explicit rules of procedure is particularly pronounced during the initial phases of the process, before the process has found its 'track' and developed its own dynamics. While the lack of formal rules of procedure did provide the scientific core of WGI with a significant formal and operational autonomy, it proved problematic in the adoption of the reports particularly at the Panel Plenary level (personal communication). The problems at the 1990 Plenary in Sundsvall when the First Assessment was adopted is an illustrative case in point. In the case of the old WGIII the lack of formal rules implied that there were no guiding principles for how the work was to be carried out and no instruments by which to handle the very strong political pressures directed towards this WG. Hence, the intergovernmental mechanism of the IPCC implies a disposition towards involvement rather than scientific autonomy. In this regard, the outcome of the IPCC process – especially in terms of its acknowledged scientific authority – may be regarded as an outcome achieved *in spite of* rather than *because of* its institutional design.

On the other hand, the establishment of the old WGIII, which they had to know would become a more or less purely political forum, may have served as a 'lightning rod' to direct political attention away from the other WGs. It is likely that, at least partly because of WGIII's establishment, WGI and WGII were less exposed to political pressures during this period than they might have been had political discussions not been pooled in WGIII as they actually were (personal communication). Thus, while the WGIII establishment of 1988 was premature in terms of its own mandate (it is difficult to make policy recommendations on the basis of a knowledge base that is not yet there), it seems to have served a very important function as a 'buffer' for WGI and WGII. In this respect, the institutional design of the IPCC contributed to the balance between scientific autonomy and involvement in the political process that actually was achieved. It is difficult to judge, however, whether this effect was calculated, and hence the result of a conscious design, or whether it was an 'accidental' result of the course of events. The latter interpretation is perhaps the most likely.

Since IPCC's establishment in 1988, IPCC participants and especially the IPCC leadership have undergone a learning process. The incremental development of explicit rules of procedure gradually governing more and more IPCC activities reflect their increasing experience with this kind of scientific assessment process and have carefully been accommodated to the needs of the IPCC in terms of maintaining scientific autonomy while also aiding a policy-making process. Thus, the balance between scientific autonomy and involvement in policy-making achieved within the WGs after the 1992 restructuring (and the 1993 rules of procedure supplement) may to a larger extent be regarded as the result of a conscious design. The most important institutional devices for achieving this balance are first and foremost the extended review procedures and the decision that reports adopted in WG Plenaries may not be amended in the panel. The former device is extremely important for ensuring the scientific authority of the reports, while the latter device is extremely important for ensuring the reports a 'safe journey' through the decision-making system of the IPCC. All efforts to ensure scientific autonomy at the lower decision-making levels of the institution are wasted if they are not accompanied by efforts to prevent scientifically unsubstantiated changes to be made at higher decision-making levels. The procedures and institutional arrangements whereby the report, and particularly their summaries, are submitted to close investigation and critical review by parties representing different and potentially conflicting interests in the policy area seems equally important for policy-makers' acceptance of the knowledge base. In the IPCC this is ensured through the extended review procedures (which include a government review) and the institutional mechanisms to ensure a geographic balance in participation.

Finally, the competence of the leadership of the IPCC is also an important element for understanding the extent to which the IPCC has succeeded in maintaining its scientific authority within this highly politicised institutional environment. First, the scientific leadership of WGI, in close co-operation with the leadership of the IPCC as a whole (Bert Bolin in particular), have managed to maintain control over important scientific decisions: the Plenary can, for instance, only suggest *candidates* for lead authors and contributors, while the actual choice is made by the scientific leadership of the WG. Before 1992, the scientific leadership of the WGs made these decisions quite freely. With the restructuring in 1992, the increased emphasis on the geopolitical balance in the group of lead authors implied some restrictions in their scientific autonomy in this regard, but the decision remains in the hands of the scientific leadership of the WGs (personal communication). Keeping these decisions, and their like, outside the control of the Plenary has most probably prevented endless discussions on who should hold the various positions in the WGs. More importantly, however, political nominations to positions *in the scientific core* of the WGs have been restricted, thereby also increasing the operational autonomy of the WGs and the scientific authority of the outcome. Second, the leadership of the IPCC have been instrumental in the incremental development of rules of procedure and their accommodation to the special requirements of this kind of process in terms of balancing science and politics. The adoption of rules of procedure is a matter for the full panel Plenary to decide. This body is heavily dominated by government officials and bureaucrats. At this decision-making level the scientists are represented only by the leadership of each WG. In this regard, policy-makers have a certain 'control' over the rules of procedure of the institution. In most cases proposed changes in the rules of procedure have been met by scepticism and opposition by some members of the full Plenary, especially if the proposed changes imply restrictions in the Plenary's 'control' over the process (as was the case with regard to the proposal that the IPCC should make Technical Papers not submitted to the adoption procedures of the Plenary). The leadership's competent handling of such issues in the Plenary has been important in the development of the current rules of procedure. Without it, this political 'control potential' is likely to have had more significant implications in terms of substantive politicisation. Third, the leadership of the IPCC (WG Chairs and vice-chairs and Panel Chair and vice-chairs) have served as an important link between the decision making levels of the institution. While IPCC scientists operate within a highly politicised environment, the regular scientist seldom meets policy-makers 'face to face'. The regular scientist, therefore, has relatively limited knowledge and experience with what is going on at the other decision-making levels. The lead authors have an important function in the

WG Plenaries in ensuring consistency between the assessments and their summaries and in 'fighting off' scientifically unsubstantiated proposals for changes in the texts, but it is only the WG and Panel leadership that participate at all levels. The leadership thus serves an important function as a communicative link between the decision making levels – in terms of communicating results and future plans to policy-makers at the higher decision-making levels and inquiries and needs of policy-makers to the scientists at the lower decision-making levels (personal communication). In this regard a relatively high level of involvement in the policy-making process has been achieved in combination with a separation of science and politics.

'The proof of the pudding is in the eating', and the 'eating' in this case is the adoption of scientific findings as a decision premise in policy-making: To what extent has all of this mattered for the policy response?

7.5 The impact of institutional design on policy response

To what extent can the institutional arrangements of the science–policy dialogue explain the extent to which the scientific knowledge base was accepted and acted upon by policy-makers?

The climate change issue touches upon vital national interests and thus involves a high potential for serious political conflict. Furthermore, the issue is scientifically complex and associated with profound scientific uncertainty. Scientific findings are to a large extent open to interpretation, with a corresponding risk of information distortion. The combination of these features seems to have implied a desire by decision-makers to ensure scientific objectivity. This is, paradoxical as it may seem, achieved by submitting the scientific process to political control through the rules of procedure. Rules of procedure are determined in the full Panel Plenary, where government officials dominate the composition of participants. In this case, therefore, it seems as if an important condition for policy-makers' acceptance of the knowledge base as well as the policy response was the achievement of an optimal balance not only between autonomy and involvement, but also even more paradoxically, between 'political control' (involvement in the 'opposite direction') and scientific autonomy. This need also seems to be the origin of the distinctive manner of organising the assessment process.

The key factor in this regard is the intergovernmental status of the IPCC, which permits governmental participation at the main decision making levels. Through this institutional device policymakers are permitted to participate in the development of the knowledge base. They thus have access to very detailed information, not only concerning the nature of the problem at hand, but also concerning the *manner* in which this knowledge has been generated. Especially the latter aspect constitutes very important information in a conflictual negotiation setting because negotiating parties are then provided with a basis for evaluating the reliability of the information they receive regarding the nature of the problem at hand. In this case, moreover, the intergovernmental status of the IPCC implies that policy-makers have significant influence over the manner in which the knowledge base is provided – the rules and procedures according to which the IPCC operates. They can therefore contribute to the establishment of rules and procedures that, in their view, serve to increase the reliability of the knowledge base. This, however, can also be used as an instrument to undermine the IPCC's credibility. That is, delegations deprived of scientifically based arguments to support their political positions can accuse the IPCC of violations of their own rules of procedure in the development of the knowledge base and hence demand that conclusions and findings be deleted. The argument would then go something along the lines that, 'these scientific findings may well be true, but they have not come about in the correct manner. We can therefore not be *certain* that they are true, and they should therefore be deleted'. There are several examples in IPCC's history that illustrate that delegations, especially from the largest oil-producing countries such as Saudi Arabia and Kuwait, have adopted this strategy (see Skodvin, 1999). The above-mentioned debate, which took place after the finalisation of the Second Assessment, is but one example. The political control over the rules of procedure was thus utilised by some governments as a tool for delaying the process, and posed a difficult challenge for the IPCC leadership.

This design could have been devastating for the development of a scientific knowledge base on global warming because it left the process particularly vulnerable to undue political influence on the substantive content of the knowledge base. When such an influence cannot be traced, the WGIII establishment during the initial stages of the process may provide some explanation. Another, perhaps even more important factor seems to be the ability of the IPCC leadership to retain control over the scientific process and serve as an authoritative guide in the incremental development of the rules of procedure. Their success in this endeavour has meant that the institutional design of the IPCC, especially the functioning of the WGI Plenary, serves the very important function of providing an arena for a broad science–policy dialogue. WGI Plenary meetings do not only constitute an opportunity for sceptics and opponents to employ delaying tactics and attempt to modify aspects of the reports that do not correspond to their political positions, they also serve as for where scientists and policy-makers can discuss various interpretations of the findings, seek clarification in cases where it is necessary, exchange opinions concerning potential policy implications, and discuss which future tasks the IPCC should embark upon. In this regard, the institutional design of the IPCC seems to constitute a crucial factor in explaining the high level of acceptance among policy-makers of the scientific knowledge base provided by the IPCC. While it is methodologically impossible to control this effect, it seems unlikely that the knowledge base could have gained the level of acceptance that it actually has in this case if the knowledge base were provided, for instance, by an 'independent' body in complete isolation from the political process on climate change.

This proposition is supported by the leadership of the IPCC in personal communication with this author. The intergovernmental status of the IPCC is emphasised by the leadership as its most important institutional device. Without it, it is maintained, policy-makers would not have had to listen and the potential for influencing policy would have been significantly reduced (personal communication). This point has also been made by Bob Watson, chairman of WGII until 1997 and the new Chairman of the IPCC as of September 1997: 'I believe the IPCC process is much, much more powerful than the single-agency approach. The most important thing when you have an assessment process is that it has to be credible to all stakeholders. They may not all agree with the outcome, but if they're all part of designing the process in the beginning, they'll be more willing to let the chips fall where they may' (Bob Watson interviewed in Kerr, 1997).

The level of involvement of governments in the provision of a knowledge base on climate change has been subject to a continuous debate. In the context of the controversy that arose after the Second

Assessment, Bill Hare, climate policy adviser for Greenpeace, said to Nature that 'he is not against government involvement. "But I feel that at present, the balance of influence is too much in their favour"' (Masood, 1996aa: 455). Sir John Houghton, Chairman of WGI, on the other hand, stated on this occasion that, 'any move to reduce political involvement in the IPCC would weaken the panel and deprive it of its political clout. "The presence of government scientists is vital to the IPCC," he says. "They own the findings. If governments were not involved, then the documents would be treated like any old scientific report. They would end up on the shelf or in the waste bin."' (Masood, 1996).

On this basis it is our judgement that the institutional arrangements of the IPCC – and especially the extent to which one has succeeded in combining scientific autonomy and political involvement – constitute a key explanatory factor of policy-makers' acceptance of the scientific knowledge base and the extent to which this knowledge base has served as a decision premise for the policy decisions made. A crucial condition for this effect, however, is the leadership functions served by the WG and Panel Chairmen. As it seems, this effect is entirely dependent upon their capacities in this regard. Our judgement of the explanatory power of institutional design in this case is, however, also based on the fact that a set of other factors that may be assumed also to influence the policy response largely pull in the opposite direction – that is, in the direction of no Climate Convention at all.

7.6 Control variables

7.6.1 Political malignancy

As emphasised above, the political setting of the issue is extremely complicated and conflictual, not least because of the North–South conflict. Moreover, there are severe conflicts within the 'blocs' of North and South, implying rigid positions in the negotiations because the positions from the outset are compromises. This is particularly true for the South, as they to a larger extent than the North have tried to act as one bloc. It is obvious that a coalition consisting of both the oil-producing Saudi Arabia and the poorest countries in Africa is bound to have problems in co-ordinating its positions. The Northern 'bloc' countries, or the industrialised countries, have generally accepted that the main responsibility for bearing the burdens of regulatory measures to mitigate global warming is theirs, although the USA signalled that their co-operation could be conditional on stronger commitments also from developing countries.[11] There are, moreover, severe conflicts over what constitutes a 'fair' burden-sharing even among industrialised countries due to large variations in energy structures, energy-efficiency etc. Thus, the opportunities and risks that greenhouse gas emissions reductions may present are not at all shared equally among the industrialised countries. A general impression with regard to the political process on climate change, therefore, is that the level of conflict does not correspond at all to the extent to which the scientific knowledge base has been accepted by policy-makers.

This level of political conflict first serves to strengthen our conclusion in the sense that we can at least rule out the possibility that the level of acceptance witnessed in the case of the IPCC knowledge base simply mirrors a political consensus on this issue. Even if we restrict our focus to industrialised countries only, most of them face high costs in a greenhouse gas control regime. Second, taking this level of political conflict into account, we could tentatively suggest that the linkage to science may have served to strengthen the policy response to date. That is, the policy response might have been even weaker without the strong linkage to science (for example, no Climate Convention at all, and, especially, no Kyoto Protocol). While this amounts to no more than mere speculation, the possibility cannot be ruled out either. What can be said, however, is that this level of political conflict amply demonstrates that scientific consensus by no means implies political consensus, although scientific consensus may constitute a necessary but not sufficient condition for the *development* of political consensus.

7.6.2 *Public saliency*

The public saliency of the global warming issue was quite high when INC negotiations started in 1991. During the late 1980s, anomalous weather conditions in various parts of the world aroused public awareness and speculations about whether we were already experiencing a rapid increase in the global mean temperature. Furthermore, the issue of climate change was probably linked, in people's minds, with the threat of ozone depletion, which had already aroused public concern. However, despite extreme weather conditions, there has been no 'crisis' in the global warming issue comparable to the discovery of the Antarctic ozone hole. Moreover, because of the complexities of the science on this issue, it has been easy for politicians to pay lip-service to the problem instead of implementing effective policies towards solving it – thus signalling to the public an *intention* of solving the problem and thereby reducing public pressure. The CO_2 reduction and stabilisation plans of OECD countries during the early 1990s could be described as symbol politics, since very few of the countries that made this commitment have implemented strategies to enforce it. In terms of developing agreement on the Climate Convention, public pressure may therefore have had some impact during the initial stages of the process. Generally, however, we judge the impact of public pressure to have been limited.

7.6.3 *Status of knowledge*
The knowledge base on climate change is characterised by a significant scientific uncertainty. Despite conclusions from the IPCC such as 'the balance of evidence suggests a discernible human influence on global climate' (SPM to the Second Assessment of WGI, 1995), scientific uncertainties are discussed at length in the reports. While more is known about the functioning of the climate system now than when the IPCC process started in 1988, the amount of scientific uncertainty has not really been reduced. New knowledge and increased understanding has a tendency to be also accompanied with an increased understanding of what one does not know. There is no parallel, for instance, to the sense of reduced uncertainty characterising the assessment process on ozone depletion.

One consequence of high levels of scientific uncertainty and poor knowledge is that the scientific knowledge base cannot be employed to develop tools for decision-making. In comparison, the development of tools for decision making seems to have played an important role both in the ozone process, with the development of the 'chlorine-loading methodology', and in the acid rain process, with the development of the 'critical loads' methodology (see Chapter 5 and 6 in this volume). The science on climate change seems to be too much associated with uncertainty to have had an independent impact on policy response.

7.7 In conclusion

While the IPCC has experienced problems with politicisation, especially during its initial phase, a balance between scientific autonomy
and involvement seems nevertheless to have been achieved. During
the initial phase of the IPCC process (before 1992), a balance was
achieved within the IPCC as a whole – with WGI firmly placed
within the scientific domain, and WGIII closely associated with the
political domain. The old WGIII also seems to have served as a
'buffer' for WG I and WGII, (re-)directing political attention and
pressure away from these WGs. It is likely, however, that this effect
was an 'accidental' result of the course of events rather than a calculated design. After 1992, a balance is achieved within each WG
between the relatively scientifically autonomous scientific core and
the more politicised WG and Panel Plenaries.

The institutional arrangements of the IPCC seem to have contributed to this balance between science and politics. The most
important institutional features for maintaining the scientific autonomy and credibility of the IPCC is the extended review procedures
and the decision that documents accepted at the WG Plenary level
may not be amended by the full Panel Plenary. Involvement, in this
case, goes in both directions; scientists' involvement in the policy
making process, and policy-makers' involvement in the scientific
process. The main institutional device contributing to this level of
involvement is the functioning of the WG Plenary as an arena for an
interactive dialogue between scientists (represented by lead authors)
and policy-makers (represented by government officials and government scientists). An important condition for this effect of the
institutional design is, however, the competence of the leadership of
the IPCC. The institutional design of the IPCC, and especially the
involvement of policy-makers in the assessment process, left the
IPCC vulnerable to politicisation and loss of scientific authority.
The apparent lack of this effect seems to be very much due to the
competence of the leadership of the IPCC (see Skodvin, 1999).
Moreover, the success in maintaining the IPCC's scientific authority and credibility, and the manner in which the assessment process
conducted by the IPCC is organised (particularly its intergovernmental mechanism), seem to have played a crucial role for the
extent to which policy-makers have accepted the knowledge base.

Notes

Acknowledgements: I gratefully acknowledge comments on earlier drafts of this chapter from Bert Bolin, Bruce Callander, Simon Shackley, Sonja Boehmer-Christiansen and Kalle Hesstvedt. Thanks are also due to Sonja Boehmer-Christiansen and Leiv Lunde for generously giving me access to their data on the IPCC, and Simon Shackley and Nils Roll-Hansen for stimulating discussions. Important sources of information have been interviews with Bert Bolin, Robert Watson, Sir John Houghton, Bruce Callander, Ivar S. A. Isaksen, Susan Solomon, Richard Derwent, Cath Senior, John Mitchell, A. Al-Gain, Richard Lindzen and Michael Zammit Cutajar, conducted during the period from 1993 to 1997, and personal observation at Panel Plenaries 1993–95, WGI Plenaries 1994–95, a WGII Plenary in 1994 and a lead author meeting in WGI in Brighton, 1995. My attendance at IPCC meetings was made possible by the Norwegian Ministry of the Environment and the Technical Support Unit (TSU) for WGI in Bracknell, for which I am grateful. I am particularly grateful for the assistance of Øyvind Christophersen and Håvard Thoresen (Ministry of the Environment) and Judy Lakeman (WGI TSU in Bracknell) in this regard. The analysis presented in this chapter is based on a PhD thesis in political science at the University of Oslo (Skodvin, forthcoming), financed by the Norwegian Research Council and the CICERO.

1 The IPCC is currently undergoing a restructuring in preparation for the Third Assessment Report.

2 It should be noted that this time span is not unusual, however. In comparison, it took 13 years before the first protocol with legally binding commitments to reduce SO_2 emissions was agreed upon from when the acid rain issue first surfaced on the international political agenda (1972–85) (see Chapter 5 in this volume).

3 The IPCC is currently revising its rules of procedure in preparation for its Third Assessment Report.

4 WGI has not been subject to restructuring during the course of the process.

5 Illustrative in this regard is that the science component (provided by WGI) of the 1992 Supplementary Report involved 115 lead authors/contributors from 21 countries, and 341 reviewers from 60 countries and 19 non-governmental organisations (IPCC report of the Eighth IPCC Plenary Session, appendix B).

6 Initially it was suggested that the IPCC be reduced to two technical working groups, leaving the complicated political issues with ad hoc task forces, thus signalling a desire to return to a less politicised environment (Boehmer-Christiansen, 1993a; 'Draft Report of the Second Session of the IPCC Task Force on IPCC Structure).

7 While a cash value of $1.5 million was assigned to a statistical life in the

OECD countries, the similar measure for developing countries was a mere $150,000 (Agrawala, 1998b).

8 Lindzen's proposition that the feedback effect of water vapour is negative, is, as a matter of fact, mentioned and discussed both in the 1992 Supplementary Report (Gates *et al.*, 1992: 115) and the 1995 Second Assessment Report (Dickinson *et al.*, 1995: 200).

9 A modification of this proposition should be mentioned, however. The close relationship between science and politics may have influenced scientists' thinking *indirectly*. Shackley and Wynne discuss an example of this with regard to the development of GWPs. They suggest that scientists' preoccupation with the *development* of GWPs prevented them from conducting proper *validation* tests. 'If a correct interpretation, this is a vivid illustration of how perceived policy pressures and needs come to construct scientific tools in a way which closes down reflexive debate and thorough validation' (Wynne and Shackley, 1997: 105).

10 See also Discussion Paper prepared by Bert Bolin for the tenth Plenary Session in 1994, 'The Future of the IPCC', IPCC-X/Doc.5 (20.X.1994), ITEMS 4.2/4.3.

11 The Kyoto agreement does not impose regulatory commitments on developing countries. Its ratification by the US Senate is, therefore, far from ensured.

Comparative conclusions

8.1 A note on method

The time has come to try to integrate some of the main observations and findings that we have made in the five cases analysed in Chapters 3–7. In this comparative analysis we shift gears and use a different methodological strategy. More specifically, we shift to a kind of analysis that can be characterised as simple pattern-tracing, meaning that we ask to what extent the patterns of variance that emerge across as well as within regimes is consistent with our expectations as summarised in Chapter 1 (Table 1.4, p. 17). For this purpose we use distinct *components* (such as the various protocols under LRTAP) and/or *phases* (for, *inter alia*, the IWC) as units of analysis, rather than the regimes themselves. The five regimes in our study have been split into 19 components or phases, and these units constitute the observations to be compared. Clearly, the low number of units gives us a very weak basis for any multivariate analysis, all the more so since these components and phases make up connected *chains* of events rather than mutually independent observations. Moreover, because of the small number of observations available we can deal only with the *main* factors, which means, for example, that we have constructed aggregate indexes for 'autonomy' and 'involvement' rather than explored the impact of more specific institutional factors.

For these and other reasons, we use the pattern-tracing strategy with great caution, and mainly as a supplement to the kind of qualitative judgements and inferences that each of the case study authors have already made about factors that facilitate or impede the transformation of research-based knowledge into policy premises in their particular case(s). This qualitative approach enables the authors to consider a wider range of potentially important factors – including each of the institutional factors identified in Chapter 1 – and above all to go beyond simple correlation in search of causal *mechanisms* at work. The problem is, of course, that such judgements necessarily will have to build upon counter-factual assumptions about what would have happened under different, hypothetical circumstances, and also rely on somewhat impressionistic techniques of measurement. The reliance on counter-factual reasoning renders these conclusions somewhat weak and speculative, when considered one by one. Thus, this chapter concentrates only on differences and similarities actually observed in our case-studies. By combining the two approaches we will at least to some extent to be able to check (a) that judgements made on the basis of in-depth analysis of single cases are consistent with the overall patterns of variance that we discern through more rigorous comparative analysis of a larger set of cases, and (b) that patterns emerging from the comparative analysis can be given a substantively plausible interpretation, i.e. reflect causal mechanisms which seem to be at work.

8.2 Is science really a major source of inputs?

To reiterate, our dependent variable is the extent to which conclusions from scientific research are utilised or adopted (undistorted) as (consensual) premises for policy decisions. We conceive of 'level of adoption' in terms of a cumulative scale with three levels. At the first and lowest level, decision-makers recognise the relevance of knowledge produced through scientific research and look to the scientific community for information. At the second level they accept as factually valid the substantive conclusions reached by general consensus within the community of competent scientists. At the third level, decision-makers also respond positively to policy 'implications' or more explicit advice from scientists; not only are conclusions accepted as factually valid, explicit advice and implicit suggestions are also acted upon in a positive manner.

The general impression, based on the limited set of cases that we have studied, may be summarised as follows:

1 Scientific research seems generally to be recognised as a major supplier of relevant knowledge. In all five regimes decision-makers have turned to science for problem identification and

diagnosis, and in some cases also for explicit policy advice. In all five regimes research-based knowledge has been generally perceived as an important basis for making informed or rational policy decisions.[1] Interestingly, this applies even in cases where the state of scientific knowledge was recognised to be relatively poor. One indication is the fact that some kind of scientific body or bodies have been established as more or less integral parts of the decision-making system in all these regimes. Moreover, we find a tendency towards increasing formalisation of links between decision-making bodies and the scientific community as regimes 'mature'. Even though the pattern is not very robust, we can also see a tendency towards higher level utilisation of research-based knowledge over time. Arguably, there may also be a tendency towards broadening the *range* of scientific inputs requested, notably to include not only natural sciences but also to some extent economics. In our sample, the climate change negotiations and the more recent LRTAP protocols are the most salient examples.

2 Governments rarely explicitly dispute what the scientific community considers to be 'consensual knowledge'. This is not to say that uncertainty and knowledge gaps are not exploited for tactical purposes in international negotiations. On the contrary, particularly in the early phases we see that progress is often hampered by one or more parties demanding more conclusive evidence or by competing interpretations of available information. Yet, the evidence we have suggests that most governments are reluctant to dispute openly the factual conclusions that a clear majority of competent scientists consider 'state-of-the-art' knowledge. The recent climate change negotiations indicate that this applies even where a substantial amount of uncertainty persists. Moves to exploit uncertainty or favour biased interpretations are common, but open and explicit challenges seem to be rare.

3 Faced with broad consensus among competent experts on the description and diagnosis of a (severe) environmental problem, governments do in fact most often take some kind of collective action. In all five problem-areas analysed in this book some substantive targets were set or regulatory measures introduced. Moreover, it seems that these steps were taken at least in part as a response to scientific evidence. This is by no means to suggest

that scientific evidence is a *sufficient* condition for collective action. Nor do we suggest that policy responses are typically *derived* from research-based knowledge. Only in a couple of instances – the later phases of the stratospheric ozone negotiations, an interim phase of the IWC, and the second LRTAP sulphur protocol – can the regulations adopted be seen as explicitly designed and 'dosed' to match criteria or cures prescribed by scientific advisory bodies. And even in those cases it would be an exaggeration to say that regulations were in any strict sense derived from scientific inputs. The typical pattern seems to be one where new evidence about environmental damage or resource depletion leads, first, to increased attention and requests for further study, and – perhaps at a later stage – to some substantive measures designed to alleviate the problem. In other words, scientific evidence often plays a major role in agenda-setting, and often serves to precipitate *some* kind of policy response. The *substance* of that response, however, is determined essentially by politics rather than science. The first LRTAP protocols, IWC regulations, and the agreements pertaining to pollution in the North Sea are good illustrations.

4 Even though broad consensus among competent experts about the nature and ramifications of a problem tends to facilitate international negotiations, conclusive evidence is *not* a necessary condition for collective action. The North Sea Conference system agreed on substantive measures in the absence of conclusive evidence about (the amount of) environmental damage. So did the third Conference of Parties of the climate change regime. In the mid-1980s the IWC even moved substantially *beyond* the recommendations made by its scientific advisory body. The increasing support for decision rules such as the precautionary principle might suggest that we can expect to see more instances of proactive environmental regulation in the future. As pointed out by Wettestad (p. 79), this will not necessarily change the overall level of attention paid to research-based knowledge, but it may well change the *way* in which inputs from science are used and conceivably also the kinds of inputs requested by policy-makers. For a truly proactive environmental policy, science seems to be useful particularly to the extent that it can serve as a kind of early warning system, identifying future risks.[2]

5 In thinking about the role of science in international environ-

mental regimes we probably see science primarily as a supplier of warnings serving as spurs for protective measures. This image has considerable merit, but our case studies indicate that scientific evidence can sometimes have the opposite effect. As Wettestad points out in his study of LRTAP, a better understanding of the NOx problem had a 'sobering' effect upon some of the initial 'pushers'. Similarly, in the case of IWC the improved knowledge about whale stock populations achieved in recent years tends to undermine rather than support the blank moratorium on commercial whaling. These examples should remind us that better knowledge about the environment will not necessarily serve to support the most radical demands for regulatory intervention.

6 Normally, we would also expect to find a positive relationship between the demand for and the supply of scientific inputs. Thus, we would expect the demand for inputs from science to increase as the state of knowledge improves, and supply to be cut back when demand declines. Andresen's analysis of the IWC case suggests, however, that the two may not at all move in tandem. The scientists working to strengthen the knowledge base for IWC regulations found themselves sidelined just as they were able to report substantial progress. Then, as the ruling coalition of the IWC showed less interest in their findings, they seem to have intensified their research efforts. The causal mechanisms behind this odd pattern are complex, and I am certainly not suggesting that demand slackened *as a consequence of* improvement in supply![3] The interesting point is that supply and demand are driven in large part by *different* mechanisms, and that the dynamics of interplay seems to be more complex than recognised by 'conventional wisdom'.

8.3 Patterns of variance

In Chapter 1 we hypothesised that the extent to which propositions and findings from research are adopted as premises for policy decisions depends, first and foremost, on the state of relevant research-based knowledge and the political malignancy of the issue in question (perhaps reinforced by public saliency). We furthermore suggested that within the constraints determined by these background factors, institutional arrangements – more specifically those determining the autonomy and involvement of the relevant scientific community – would make a difference, and that this impact would be sufficiently large to warrant attention to these dimensions as potential tools for the design of international environmental regimes.

To test these hypotheses we now proceed in two main steps. First, we will examine the impact of our two main control variables – state of knowledge and problem malignancy – on the level of adoption. We will then examine the impact of institutional arrangements, controlling – as far as our limited range of observations permits – for state of knowledge and problem malignancy.

8.3.1 State of knowledge and problem malignancy

A first cut is simply to compare the level of adoption scores actually observed to the expectations summarised in Table 1.4. The results are reported in Table 8.1.

Table 8.1   *Adoption of inputs as a function of state of knowledge and type of problem (actual v. hypothesised mean scores)*

Type of problem ↓	State of knowledge						N
	Poor		*Intermediate*		*Good*		
Malign	1.1	0	2	1(0)	1.5	1(2)	16
Mixed	†	0(1)	1.5	1(2)	3	2–3	3
Benign	†	0–1	†	2(3)	†	3(2)	0
N	7		9		3		19

Notes: Actual mean scores to the left, hypothesised scores to the right.
        † = missing data.

The first thing that strikes us about Table 8.1 is that the range of variance in our sample is too small to enable us to examine the full matrix. Particularly important is the fact that we lack cases that can be considered truly benign. We are inclined to view this not as a sampling error but rather as an implication of the very nature of environmental issues. International environmental policy usually deals with issues characterised by externalities and hence by some degree of political malignancy. Within the limited range we can cover, we may first of all observe that scores in the two least favourable categories are somewhat higher than we expected. This can be interpreted as good news, indicating that science is at least considered relevant even under the least favourable circumstances. Looking at the differences across cells, we can see that the level of adoption is lowest under the least favourable circumstances (poor knowledge, malign problem) and highest in the most favourable context (good knowledge, mixed problem). This is, of course, consistent with our expectations. Within the set of intermediate categories, however, we find no consistent pattern. At a later point we will explore more in depth whether our institutional variables can help account for the deviance, but a quick look inside the categories concerned immediately makes apparent one interesting observation:

One case, the third phase of the IWC regime, stands out as a conspicuous 'outlier' in that it combines the *lowest* score with regard to use of research-based knowledge with one of the *highest* scores in terms of state of knowledge and conducive institutional arrangements. The explanation for this paradox seems to be straightforward: this is the only case in our study characterised by a stark conflict over *basic values*. When basic values collide, the main issue will be the overall purpose of management (in this case, conservation to increase sustainable yield v. preservation). Research can produce information on the state of a stock or an ecosystem and provide factual inputs for determining sustainable levels of harvest, but there is no way it can resolve the issue of whether it is morally right or wrong to utilise a particular species for consumptive purposes. As Andresen points out, introducing 'bargaining over values has proven even more difficult than the bargaining over numbers that took place in the first phase of the IWC' (p. 59). Whenever conflict focuses on basic values, (natural) science is likely to be sidelined – however sophisticated its models and however accurate and reliable its conclusions may be.

The latter proposition is not fundamentally at odds with the general line of reasoning we developed in Chapter 1; what we have just done is, after all, to explain a low score on our dependent variable in terms of one of our background variables (problem malignancy).[4] It does, however, suggest that our conceptualisation of 'political malignancy' needs to be refined; the particular conceptualisation that we have adopted here does not distinguish between conflict of *interests* and conflict of *values*. The case of the IWC clearly indicates that this can be a very important distinction for understanding the role of science as a supplier of input for environmental policy and resource management.

Whenever we face one or a few outliers for whom we have a straightforward substantive explanation, a case can be made for reporting also the results obtained when the deviant case(s) are left out. In Tables 8.2 and 8.3, results obtained when IWC_3 (the third phase if the IWC) is deleted are reported in brackets.

In Tables 8.2 and 8.3 we report two measures of statistical association between the two background variables and level of adoption. One, referred to simply as 'difference', measures the change in mean scores on the dependent variable that we get as we move from one category to the next along each of the background variables.[5] The other reports beta coefficients from a trivariate MCA analysis. In Table 8.3 we have substituted the variable of problem malignancy with an additive index measuring the combined impact of malignancy and saliency, the underlying argument being that saliency tends to reinforce the impact of malignancy.

Table 8.2   *Adoption of inputs as a function of state of knowledge and problem malignancy (MCA beta coefficients and bivariate differences in mean values. N=19 [18])*

Variable	Beta (MCA)		Difference	
State of knowledge	.49	(.97**)	.52	(.85)
Problem malignancy	.05	(–.22)	.44	(.33)
R^2	.26	(.81)		

Notes: ** = significant at .01 level.
Figures in brackets are results when IWC_3 is left out.
– indicates that the *direction* of impact is contrary to expectations.

Table 8.3 *Adoption of inputs as a function of state of knowledge and a combined measure of problem malignancy and saliency (MCA beta coefficients and bivariate differences in mean values. N=19 [18])*

Variable	Beta (MCA)		Difference	
State of knowledge	.84**	(.87**)	.52	(.85)
Malignancy + saliency	.90**	(−.03)	.01	(−.40)
R²	.83	(.77)		

Notes: See Table 8.2.

The fact that we have a limited range of variance with regard to type of problem and a small number of observations calls for a cautious interpretation of these figures, in particular in comparing coefficients reported for state of knowledge and problem malignancy. As far as they go, however, Tables 8.2 and 8.3 suggest the following conclusions.

First, taken together, the background variables account for a substantial proportion of the variance observed in terms of the use of research-based inputs. The bivariate correlation between level of adoption and a combined measure of state of knowledge and problem benignity is .45. This general pattern is clearly consistent with the thrust of the arguments made in our case studies. Second, so far the critical factor determining the extent to which inputs from research are adopted as premises for policy decisions seems to be the *quality of the products that science has to offer* (i.e. state of knowledge).[6] This observation can be interpreted as good news for those who would like to see policies based on the best knowledge available. We may also take heart by the indication that, although important, a good state of knowledge seems *not* to be a *necessary* condition for policy-makers to respond to explicit recommendations or policy 'implications'. The first IWC total allowable catch limit was based on a quite arbitrary figure suggested by the scientific advisory committee. It was generally recognised that only very crude and uncertain stock estimates were available at that time. Similarly, the first regulations pertaining to marine pollution in the North Sea were established in the absence of firm knowledge. On the other hand, a pessimist may note that even a good state of knowledge is by no means a *sufficient* condition for collective action.

There are also indications that problem malignancy – particularly when combined with high public saliency – can make an important difference. However, when we control for state of knowledge we find no consistent pattern.[7] At the very least, the results reported above seem to indicate that research-based knowledge can be an important source of inputs for policy-makers also in dealing with what we have coded as 'malign' problems. The case of the IWC strongly indicates, though, that there may be a threshold of malignancy above which even sophisticated models and fairly accurate and reliable knowledge are likely to be neglected or seen as irrelevant. As indicated above, we suggest that this threshold can be found at (stark) conflict over basic values and management goals. But the evidence we have clearly suggests that, *below* that threshold problem malignancy does not constitute an insurmountable obstacle to the use of research-based knowledge. Moreover, it may also be read as indicating that the risk of 'contamination' from politics is not as great as one might have feared. True, political malignancy and state of knowledge are negatively correlated (Spearman's rho = -.35). Yet, our case studies – particularly those dealing with whaling and climate change – suggest that at least when it has acquired its own institutional base the scientific community can run its core business pretty much according to its own rules and standards also in the presence of political conflict over the substantive issue-area in focus.

As indicated above, the fact that we are dealing with connected *chains* of events rather than mutually independent observations makes the kind of comparative analysis that we have reported above vulnerable to charges of 'a-historicism' and neglect of context. This analysis should therefore be supplemented with an approach that enables us to identify correlates of change occurring *within* each regime in utilisation of research-based knowledge as we move from one component, issue-area, or phase to another. This kind of data is summarised in Table 8.4.

Table 8.4 strongly supports the conclusions we have drawn on the basis of our cross-regime analysis. First of all, we can immediately see that changes in the level of utilisation of research-based knowledge within regimes is strongly associated with changes in the state

Table 8.4 *Intra-regime correlates of changes in level of adoption*

Level of adoption ↓	State of knowledge			Problem malignancy			N ↓
	Improving	Constant	Declining	Increasing	Constant	Declining	
Increasing	7	0	0	0	6	1	7
Constant	1	1	0	0	2	0	2
Declining	1	0	4	1	4	0	5
N	9	1	4	1	12	1	14

of knowledge (gamma =.95). In all the seven intra-regime transitions where the level of adoption increased we see improvement in the state of knowledge (and in one of these we also note a decline in malignancy). In four out of the five cases where level of adoption *de*creased we see a shift to a problem that is less well understood. The one exception is the transition from the second to the third main phase of the IWC – a case in which we can note a substantial increase in problem malignancy and to some extent also in saliency. Overall, however, we must conclude that since political malignancy – as measured here – is fairly constant *within* regimes, it obviously cannot account for much of the intra-regime variance that we observe in the utilisation of research-based knowledge in international policy-making processes.[8]

8.3.2 *The impact of institutional arrangements*

The time has come to bring *institutions* into the equation. In Chapter 1 we focused on two main institutional dimensions: the autonomy/integrity of the relevant scientific community or network, and its involvement in a continuous dialogue with policy-makers. More specifically, we suggested (1) that high autonomy would be important to establish and preserve confidence in scientists as impartial experts, and (2) that a moderate to high level of involvement in the negotiations themselves would be important to get findings and conclusions across to decision-makers, and to enhance the sensitivity of the scientists involved to the questions and concerns of the latter. We also suggested, however, that autonomy and involvement can be hard to combine, at least at high levels.

In the analysis below, we first examine the overall pattern, focusing on the dimensions of autonomy and involvement. For this purpose, we measure each of these dimensions in terms of additive, standardised indexes, built on the sets of sub-dimensions introduced in Tables 1.1. and 1.2. Our second step will be to combine these aggregate measures with the interpretations and conclusions provided in our five case-studies to search for important institutional *mechanisms* at work. Before reporting results we should again like to remind the reader that our findings are based on a small set of observations. Accordingly, they should be read primarily as suggesting promising hypotheses for future research, and by no means as conclusive evidence.

The resulting figures are somewhat sensitive to the exact specification of the core model and also to the kind of measures used, but the overall pattern is captured fairly well by Figure 8.1.

Let us try to interpret these results step by step. If we first look at the relationship between our two main institutional dimensions, we see that the bivariate correlation between autonomy and involve-

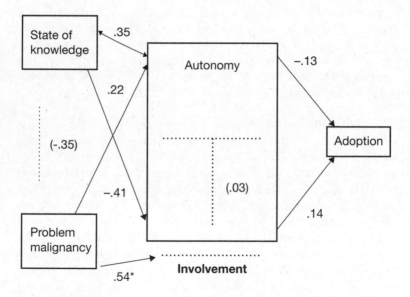

Notes: * = significant at .05 level

Figures in brackets are bivariate Spearman rank order correlations

Figure 8.1 *Pattern of correlation, core model (partial correlations)*

ment is close to zero. This may be interpreted as suggesting that autonomy and involvement is easier to combine than we expected. That being said, we should note that only in the cases of WGI and the new WGIII of IPCC has a high degree of autonomy been combined with high involvement. For the other four regimes taken together, the correlation between autonomy and involvement is − .42.

Moving on to the association between state of knowledge and problem malignancy on the one hand and institutional autonomy and involvement on the other, the immediate impression is that these correlations are in most cases not strong. This can be seen as 'fortunate' in a substantive as well as a purely methodological sense. In substantive terms, strong correlations would have indicated that the leeway for using institutional design as a tool in environmental policy-making would be limited. The methodological implication would have been that we would not be able to separate the impact of institutions from that of our background variables. The important question here, however, is which causal relationships might be behind the coefficients reported. A plausible substantive interpretation of the general pattern could be summarised in four main points:

- Problem malignancy is negatively associated with the autonomy of the scientific networks or bodies concerned. In other words, as political malignancy increases, the autonomy of the relevant scientific network or body tends to decrease. This may suggest that political conflict tends to induce policy-makers to maintain tighter control. One of the conclusions that we could draw from our case studies is that the closer the work of a scientific body comes to the substance of the main political issues, the lesser institutional autonomy it tends to have (see, in particular, the chapters on LRTAP, marine pollution and climate change).
- Malignancy is positively associated with involvement, suggesting that political conflict may enhance the demand for inputs from research – either to support one set of interests against another or to settle competing claims.
- Well-established knowledge is, of course, more useful than poor knowledge. By implication, the better the state of knowledge in a particular issue-area, the stronger the demand for inputs from science is likely to be, and the more inclined policy-makers may

be to develop links to the relevant scientific community in order to tap that knowledge. This pattern is rather weak, though, and not without interesting exceptions (see section 8.2.).

- State of knowledge and autonomy of the scientific networks or bodies involved are positively correlated. In this case we have drawn causal arrows in both directions in order to indicate (a) that autonomy is likely to facilitate high quality research,[9] and (b) that scientific communities with high confidence in their own expertise may be more assertive (cf. Skodvin's account of the ozone case in Chapter 6), and therefore also more successful in persuading policy-makers not to interfere in ways that might upset a well-performing enterprise.

Finally, let us examine the relationship between institutional arrangements on the one hand and the utilisation of inputs from research on the other. A first observation is that we are dealing with very weak correlations.[10] By any reasonable measurement, our background variables – state of knowledge in particular – account for a substantially larger proportion of the variance observed in level of adoption than our two institutional dimensions. This impression is confirmed by comparing the institutional correlates of *intra*-regime transitions (Table 8.5) with the similar data for state of knowledge and problem malignancy (Table 8.4).

Table 8.5   *Institutional correlates of intra-regime changes in level of adoption*

Level of adoption ↓	Autonomy			Involvement			N ↓
	Improving	Constant	Declining	Increasing	Constant	Declining	
Increasing	3	4	0	1	4	2	7
Constant	2	0	0	0	2	0	2
Decreasing	2	2	1	2	2	1	5
N	7	6	1	3	8	3	14

Out of the seven cases where level of adoption *in*creased, autonomy *and* involvement increased in only one (ozone). In two other cases (phases of the IWC and components of the IPCC) autonomy increased, but involvement decreased. Looking at the five transitions where level of adoption *de*creased, we find only one (within the IPCC) where both autonomy and involvement also decreased. On the other hand, we have two cases where both *in*creased (within IWC and IPCC). The gamma coefficients between intra-regime changes in level of adoption and changes in our two institutional dimensions are .09 for autonomy and -.30 for involvement, compared to .95 for state of knowledge.

In Chapter 1 we suggested that organisational arrangements would be most important in 'intermediate' circumstances. In particular, we argued that when confronted with cases characterised by poor knowledge and malign problems there would not be much organisational engineering could do to help. The latter proposition is indeed supported by our data, but contrary to our expectations we can find no consistent correlation between institutional arrangements and level of adoption in the intermediate range.

This can by no means be considered impressive support for the assumption that institutions matter. However, even weak correlations might suggest substantively interesting hypotheses. The fact that all our case-studies attach some importance to institutional arrangements reinforces the case for pursuing the analysis. Our interpretation of the results reported in Figure 8.1 can be summarised as follows:

- Involvement is positively, albeit weakly, associated with level of adoption. This is consistent with our expectations; the better developed the channels and links between science and politics, the easier it will be for the scientific community to call attention to findings and conclusions, and the easier it will be for decision-makers to get their questions and concerns across to the scientific community. This conclusion is strongly supported by our case-studies. In his analysis of the process leading up to the second sulphur protocol Wettestad describes a 'well-functioning scientific-political complex' (p. 115) with important similarities to an epistemic community (Haas, 1990; 1992a; 1992b). The Working Group on Strategies served as an important arena where scientists and decision-makers could meet to develop a common understanding of the problem. Similarly, Skodvin's account of the role of IPCC in the climate change negotiations suggests that close institutional links, including the establishment of arenas where policy-makers and scientists meet regularly to discuss key issues, has contributed substantially to confidence in IPCC reports. Skodvin's quote provides a vivid summary: 'If governments were not involved [in the process of interpreting the implications of scientific findings], then the documents would be treated like any old scientific report. They would end up on the shelf or in the waste bin.' (Houghton in interview with *Nature*, in Masood, 1996aa: 455)

- Autonomy is negatively – though again weakly – correlated with level of adoption. This may appear at odds with the argument we made in Chapter 1. Someone eager to defend this argument could easily find sound reasons for dismissing this particular finding as a measurement error. However, a more fruitful strategy may be to search for a meaningful substantive interpretation. Again, our case studies offer some very interesting clues. Recall that the expert bodies enjoying the highest institutional autonomy tend to be those that are preoccupied with the day-to-day conduct of research, i.e. those that are closest to the 'pole of science'. The bodies whose work come closest to the substance of politics tend to have less institutional autonomy (but also higher involvement); the contrast between the WGI and the former WGIII in the context of the IPCC is a good illustration. Combined with the pattern found in Figure 8.1, this suggests an interesting re-specification of the argument outlined in Chapter 1. A reasonable interpretation would be to suggest that autonomy is good for the *production* of knowledge but not in and of itself for the *utilisation* of research-based knowledge as inputs for policy. This, in turn, implies that the impact of autonomy on level of adoption will have to be traced through at least two different paths – one direct and the other indirect – and that these tend to work in opposite directions. As far as we can determine, the *direct* impact of autonomy on the transformation and adoption of inputs from science, if any, seems to be *negative*. The *indirect* effect goes through state of knowledge and is likely to be *positive*. To the extent that autonomy facilitates the production of knowledge, it will *in*directly have a positive effect also on utilisation since state of knowledge seems to be the principal factor affecting the use of inputs from science in policy-making processes.

The upshot of all this is that autonomy and involvement seem to serve *different* functions; autonomy facilitates the *production* of knowledge, involvement the *transformation* of knowledge into inputs for policy. If this is correct, the two dimensions can be combined (at least) to the extent that *institutional arrangements can be differentiated according to function*. This is exactly what seems to be happening in at least most of our cases, most clearly in LRTAP and the climate change negotiations. What Wettestad and Skodvin describe are, in essence, two- or even multi-tiered systems, where roles are differentiated so that the scientists who are most directly involved in the dialogue with decision-makers serve primarily as co-ordinators of research and as mediating agents ('knowledge brokers'), while most of those who are engaged in the basic scientific activities seem to enjoy a fairly high degree of operational autonomy and be well secluded from the political process. Even in less complex regimes where there is no clear-cut *formal* differentiation of institutions, such as the IWC, we can see an informal differentiation of roles along similar lines.

This interpretation seems consistent with Miles' 'buffer hypothesis' and the argument made by Jasanoff (1990), summarised in chapter 2. To review, Miles suggests that ' indirect rather than direct links to management decisions will facilitate the emergence of scientific consensus' (Miles, 1989: 49). Furthermore, he maintains that ' ... from the scientific perspective, it is preferable that the research being conducted be of sufficient concern to warrant continued government support, but that decision processes be deliberately designed so as to provide a buffer between research results and their utilisation for regulation and – especially – for the distribution of benefits and/or apportionment of costs' (Miles, 1989: 50). While Miles states the argument primarily from the perspective of science itself, our analysis suggests that this kind of functional differentiation can be useful also from the perspective of policy-makers. Interestingly, the reforms made in the procedures of e.g. the PARCON/North Sea Conference system seem to be moves towards this kind of differentiated structure.

Confidence in the kind of inputs that research can provide may, it seems, be drawn from at least two different sources. One is a combination of scholarly competence, integrity and independence. The other is the adversarial scrutiny by people representing conflicting interests. When it comes to dealing with malign problems, the latter may well be the more important. Adversarial scrutiny can be accomplished through different procedures ranging from the well-known scientific quality control mechanism of extensive and open peer review, to deliberate efforts to involve scientists and other experts from countries with conflicting interests in the issue area concerned (in particular from sceptical 'laggards), to the establishment of arenas where governments are in control and where science is subordinate to politics (e.g. the former WGIII in the IPCC). The latter seems to be particularly important for governments finding their countries to be in a position of 'inferiority' within the international research community. In the context of global environmental negotiations, most developing countries often find themselves in a position in which they are asked to accept a problem description and diagnosis developed essentially in North America and Western Europe (see, e.g., Gupta, 1997). Given the distance in perspectives, values and interests between 'North' and 'South', the latter may have sound reasons for scepticism.

We can now see that the argument we outlined in Chapters 1 and 2 needs to be differentiated and refined. The crux of the matter is that autonomy and involvement serves *different functions for different parties*. For the 'centre', autonomy for the scientific enterprise to operate according to its own professional standards seems to be a major source of confidence in its findings. For the 'periphery' things look different. From their perspective, 'autonomous' science means essentially research undertaken by – and probably also *for* – the 'centre'. The more marginal their role in international research and the greater the difference in political values and interests, the less likely are 'periphery' countries to find autonomy for science a reassuring arrangement. Add to this the fact that the notion of scientific research as an independent realm of activities is very much a 'parochial' Western ideal – not necessarily shared by governments and societies with different cultures and ideologies – and we can see that the recipe for a constructive science–politics relationship in international environmental regimes is more complex than we realised at the outset. Paradoxically, autonomy and control can to some extent serve as functional equivalents – the former being a source of confidence for the 'centre', the latter a means of reassurance for the 'periphery'.

Combine all this with the observation that while mechanisms promoting the competence, integrity and independence of science –

supplemented with the familiar quality control procedures of critical peer review – seems to work well at the *production* stage, the demand for political scrutiny and control pertains primarily to the *transformation* stage – particularly to conclusions that are seen as having policy 'implications' for controversial issues. The key to 'success' , then, is to meet difficult *combinations* of requirements. Institutional autonomy and involvement can both serve useful functions, but these functions are *different*, and take on different *meanings* for different actors.

8.4 Concluding remarks

In general, our findings indicate that the two institutional dimensions that we have focused upon in this study do *not* seem to be critical factors in determining the degree to which research-based knowledge is utilised as premises for environmental policies. At least the state of knowledge seems to be a more important determinant than organisation and procedure. It would, however, be a grave mistake to jump from this observation to the conclusion that decision-makers need not worry about institutional arrangements. There can be little doubt that the institutionalisation of science–politics nexuses that we have described in our case studies has made some difference. In cases such as acid rain, ozone, and climate change it is very hard to imagine that international regulation would have reached the level and scope that it has in the absence of (effective) institutional mechanisms for transforming knowledge into decision premises.

One final note: our interest in this project has centred on the role of *institutions*. Yet, one of the by-products of our analysis is the observation that the transformation of research-based knowledge into policy premises hinges not only upon the formal institutional setting in which it occurs, but also upon the *skills* and *behaviour* of individuals occupying important boundary roles (cf. section 2.4). As indicated particularly by the history of the ozone regime and the climate change negotiations, there is sometimes considerable scope for intellectual and entrepreneurial leadership in brokering knowledge to decision-makers. Although we cannot pursue the topic of leadership further in this study,[11] the general observation may serve to remind us that institutional arrangements are themselves political constructs, and that the relationship between institutions and outcomes is *interactive* rather than unidirectional. This means that the demand for input from research provides the scientific community itself with incentives for co-ordinating research activities and establishing some mechanism for translating the multitude of hypotheses and findings into a coherent, authoritative and relevant description and diagnosis of the problem. Thus, the demand from policy-makers for 'policy relevant' outputs may induce reorganisation of the scientific community itself. Conversely, the supply (and also clever marketing) of more or less authoritative conclusions seems to stimulate demand, and also the development of institutional arrangements for utilising the knowledge that the scientific community can offer. At this intersection there seems to be considerable room for boundary role leadership in organising supply, stimulating demand, and 'matching' demand and supply. It is easy to see that the science-politics interface is fraught with pitfalls and very real risks of 'perversion' of incentives and behaviour (cf. Boehmer-Christiansen, 1993a; 1997). But it is equally easy to realise that for the development of informed environmental policies, building on the best knowledge available, it is important that this kind of boundary role leadership is somehow provided.

Notes

1 The latest phase of the IWC is the only exception in our study. We will have more to say about that case in section 8.3.1.
2 Arguably, our discussion of the role of science in Chapter 1 may be 'biased' in the sense that it builds primarily on a more traditional, 'reactive' conception of environmental policy.
3 For the pro-whaling countries, investment in research may, though, have been an attempt to 'prove' their case.
4 In Chapter 1 we furthermore hypothesised that public saliency would tend to reinforce the impact of political malignancy. In this respect, too, the IWC record seems basically consistent with our expectations.
5 This measure can easily be standardised for complete data matrixes. When we are dealing with empty cells, however, there is no straightforward way of standardising these measures.
6 A brief note may be required to explain how this interpretation squares with the observation we made in section 8.2. that policy-makers sometimes act in the *absence* of conclusive scientific evidence. The point is simply that in the latter case policy may have been *precipitated* by inputs from science, but it is not in any strict sense *derived from* a par-

ticular problem diagnosis or policy advice. Only in the latter case is policy directly based upon inputs from science. As indicated by the ozone and LRTAP cases, for policy to be formulated as a direct response to the description and diagnosis provided by scientists it seems that the knowledge base itself will have to meet fairly demanding standards.

7 Recall, though, that we have no data for politically *benign* problems; the results we get give us the difference between *mixed* and predominantly *malign* problems.

8 The methodological implication is important but straightforward. Under the circumstances, we cannot measure adequately the impact of intra-regime variance in problem malignancy. What we can do, however, is to conclude with confidence that the changes that we have observed here in the level of adoption *within* regimes occur mainly for *other* reasons.

9 In this study we do not examine the impact of institutional arrangements upon the *production* of knowledge; our concern is only the transformation of research-based knowledge into premises for environmental policy.

10 These coefficients measure the statistical effect of each of the institutional dimensions upon level of adoption when the other is controlled for. Unfortunately, our small sample size does not permit us to control in a reliable way also for state of knowledge and problem malignancy; as far as we can determine, however, the basic pattern would remain the same (if anything, the positive impact of involvement seems to be strengthened).

11 The role of leadership in the context of IPCC and the climate change negotiations is, however, studied in Skodvin (1998).

Bibliography

Agrawala, S. (1998a). 'Context and Early Origins of the Intergovernmental Panel on Climate Change', *Climatic Change*, 39 (4): 605–20.

—— (1998b). 'Structural and Process History of the Intergovernmental Panel on Climate Change', *Climatic Change*, 39 (4): 621–42.

Allen, K. R. (1980). *Conservation and Management of Whales* (London: Butterworth).

Anderson, R. M., Beverton R. J. H., Semb-Johansson, A. and Walløe, L. (1987). *The State of the Northeast Atlantic Minke Whale Stock – Report of the Group of Scientists Appointed by the Norwegian Government to Review the Basis for Norway's Harvesting of Minke Whales* (Økoforsk AS, Norway).

Andresen, S. (1989). 'Science and Politics in the International Management of Whales', *Marine Policy*, 13, April: 99–117.

—— (1993). 'The Effectiveness of the International Whaling Commission', *Arctic*, 40: 108–15.

—— (1996). 'Effectiveness and Implementation within the North Sea/North East Atlantic Cooperation: Development, Status and Future Perspectives', In *The Effectiveness of Multilateral Environmental Agreements*, Nordic Council of Ministers Report, 18: 60–83.

—— (1998). 'The Making and Implementation of Whaling Policies: Does Participation Make a Difference' in D. G. Victor, K. Raustiala, and E. B. Skolnikoff (eds), *The Implementation and Effectiveness of International Environmental Commitments* (Cambridge, MA: MIT Press).

—— (1999). 'Order for the Whaling Regime at the Turn of the Century?', in D. Vidas and W. Østreng (eds), *Order for the Oceans at the Turn of the Century* (Dordrecht: Kluwer International Law)

—— (forthcoming). 'The International Whaling Commission: More Failure than Success?' in E. L. Miles *et al.* (eds), *Explaining the Effectiveness of International Environmental Agreements: Confronting Theory with Evidence* (Cambridge, MA: MIT Press)

Andresen, S. and Østreng, W. (eds) (1989). *International Resource Management: The Role of Science and Politics* (London: Belhaven Press.)

Andresen, S., Skjærseth J. B. and Wettestad, J. (1993). 'International Efforts to Combat Marine Pollution: Achievements of North Sea Cooperation and Challenges Ahead', *Green Globe Yearbook* (Oxford: Oxford University Press, for the Fridtjof Nansen Institute).

Bäckstrand, K. (1997). 'What Can Nature Withstand? Science, Politics, and the Emergence of Critical Loads', paper prepared for the conference 'Society, Environment and Sustainability – The Nordic Perspective', Oslo, 25–27 August.

Bakken, P. M. (1989). 'Science and Politics in the Protection of the Ozone Layer', in S. Andresen and W. Østreng (eds), *International Resource Management: The Role of Science and Politics* (London: Belhaven Press).

Benedick, R. E. (1991). *Ozone Diplomacy, New Directions in Safeguarding the Planet* (Cambridge, MA: Harvard University Press).

Birnie, P. (1985). *International Regulation of Whaling*, 2 vols, (New York: Oceana Publications).

Boehmer-Christiansen, S. (1984). 'Marine Pollution Control in Europe – Regional Approaches 1972–80', *Marine Policy*, 8: 259–70.

—— (1989). 'The Role of Science in the International Regulation of Pollution', in S. Andresen and W. Østreng (eds), *International Resource Management: The Role of Science and Politics* (London: Belhaven Press).

—— (1990). 'Environmental Quality Objectives versus Uniform Emission Standards', Special North Sea Issue of *International Journal of Coastal and Estuarine Law*, edited by D. Freestone and T. Ijlstra: 139–50.

—— (1993a). 'Scientific Uncertainty and Power Politics: The Framework Convention on Climate Change and the Role of Scientific Advice', paper prepared for the conference 'Geopolitics of the Environment and the New World Order', Chantilly, January.

—— (1993b). 'Precautionary Principle', *Environment*, January/February: 42–4.

—— (1993c). 'Science Policy, the IPCC and the Climate Convention: The Codification of a Global Research Agenda', *Energy & Environment*, 4: 362–407.

—— (1997). 'Uncertainty in the Service of Science. Between Science Politics and the Politics of Power', in G. Fermann (ed.), *International Politics of Climate Change* (Oslo: Scandinavian University Press).

Boehmer-Christiansen, S. and Skea, J. (1991). *Acid Politics: Environmental and Energy Politics in Britain and Germany* (London: Belhaven Press).

Bolin, B. (1998). 'The Kyoto Negotiations on Climate Change: A Science Perspective'. *Science*, 279, 16 January: 330–1.

Bolin, B., Houghton, J. and Filho, L. G. M. (1996). 'Open Letter to Ben Santer', *Bulletin of the American Meteorological Society*, 77: 1965–6.

Borione, D. and Ripert, J. (1994). 'Exercising Common but Differentiated Responsibility', in I. M. Mintzer and A. J. Leonard (eds), *Negotiating Climate Change: The Inside Story of the Rio Convention* (Cambridge: Cambridge University Press).

Brenton, T. (1994). *The Greening of Machiavelli: The Evolution of International Environmental Politics* (London: Earthscan Publications).

Burke, W. T. (1996). 'Memorandum of Opinion on the Legality of the Designation of the Southern Ocean Sanctuary by the IWC', *Ocean Development and International Law*, 27: 315–27.

'Chairman's Revised Proposal on IPCC Structure' (1992). Discussed at the Third Session of IPCC Task Force on IPCC Structure, November, IPCC/TF/3rd/Doc. 2.

Cherfas, J. (1992). 'Key Nations Defy Whaling Commission', *New Scientist*, 4 July: 7–11.

Chossudovsky, E. (1989). *East–West Diplomacy for Environment in the United Nations* (New York: UNITAR).

Churchill, R., Kutting, G. and Warren, L. M. (1995). 'The 1994 UN ECE Sulphur Protocol', *Journal of Environmental Law*, 7: 169–97.

Cole, S. (1992). *Making Science: Between Nature and Society* (Cambridge, MA: Harvard University Press).

Collingridge, D. and Reeve, C. (1986). *Science Speaks to Power: The Role of Experts in Policy Making* (London: Frances Pinter).

Cox, R. W. (1981). 'Social Forces, States and World Orders: Beyond International Relations Theory', *Millenium*, 10: 126–55.

Dickinson, R. E., Meleshko, V., Randall, D., Sarachik, E., Sila-Dias, P. and Slinge, A. (1995). 'Climate Processes', in J. T. Houghton *et al.* (eds), *Climate Change 1995: The Science of Climate Change*, Contribution of Working Group I to the Second Assessment Report of the Intergovernmental Panel on Climate Change (Cambridge: Cambridge University Press).

Dovland, H. (1987). 'Monitoring European Transboundary Air Pollution', *Environment*, 29: 10–15.

'Draft Report of the Second Session of the IPCC Task Force on IPCC Structure', IPCC/TF/3rd/Doc. 3.

Ducrotoy, J. (1997). 'Scientific Management in Europe: The Case of the North Sea', in L. Brooks and S. VanDeveer (eds), *Saving the Seas – Values, Scientists, and International Governance* (Maryland: Maryland Sea Grant College).

ENDS Report, articles; (1993a). 'UK likely to be hard hit by revised SO_2 protocol', 218, March; 'Governments protect British Coal in talks on new SO_2 target', 222, July; 'UK leads objections to new agreement on SO_2', 224, September.

ENDS Report (1986), 'Opening Skirmishes on the Health of the North Sea',

141, October.

ENDS Report (1993b). 'UK Leads Objectives to New Agreement on SO$_2$', 224, September.

Esbjerg North Sea Conference Declaration (1995) (Copenhagen: Danish Environmental Protection Agency).

Fløistad, B. (1990). *The International Council for the Exploration of the Sea (ICES) and the Providing of Legitimate Advice in Fisheries Management* (Lysaker: The Fridtjof Nansen Institute, R:003–1990).

Friedheim, R. (1996). 'Moderation in Pursuit of Justice: Explaining Japan's Failure in the International Whaling Negotiations', *Ocean Development and International Law*, 27: 349–78.

—— (ed.) (forthcoming), *Towards A Sustainable Whaling Regime*, (Seattle, WA: University of Washington Press).

Gambell, R. (1995). 'Management of whaling in coastal communities', in A.S. Blix, L. Walløe and Ø. Ulltang (eds), *Whales, Seals, Fish and Man* (Amsterdam: Elsevier Science).

—— (1997). 'The International Whaling Commission Today', in G. Petursdottir (ed.), *Whaling the North Atlantic*, pp. 47–66 (Reykjavik: University of Iceland, Fisheries Research Institute).

Gates, W. L., Mitchell, J. F. B., Boer, G. J., Cubash, U. and Meleshko, V. P. (1992). 'Climate Modelling, Climate Prediction and Model Validation', in J. T. Houghton, B. A. Callander and S. K. Varney (eds), *Climate Change 1992: The Supplement Report to The IPCC Scientific Assessment* (Cambridge: Cambridge University Press).

Gehring, T. (1994). *Dynamic International Regimes: Institutions for International Environmental Governance* (Berlin: Peter Lang).

Gilbert, N. (1976). 'The Transformation of Research Findings into Scientific Knowledge', *Social Studies of Science*, 6: 281–307.

Global Environmental Change Report (GECR) (1992) 'The New Ozone Accord: "The Strongest Package of Law ... But Not Enough"'. (Massachusetts: Cutter Information Corporation).

Global Environmental Change Report (GECR) (1995a): 'IPCC Debates Economic Models', 8 September. (Massachusetts: Cutter Information Corporation).

Global Environmental Change Report (GECR), (1995b): 'CFC Phaseout Compliance Addressed in Vienna'. (Massachusetts: Cutter Information Corporation).

Global Environmental Change Report (GECR) (1997) 'Industry Weighs in on Climate Change', 13 June. (Massachusetts: Cutter Information Corporation).

Gray, J. (1990). 'Statistics and the Precautionary Principle', *Marine Pollution Bulletin*, 21: 174–6.

Green Globe Yearbook (1996). Oxford: Oxford University Press, for the

Fridtjof Nansen Institute.

Green Globe Yearbook (1997). Oxford: Oxford University Press, for the Fridtjof Nansen Institute

Grubb, M. (1989). *The Greenhouse Effect: Negotiating Targets* (London: Royal Institute of International Affairs).

—— (1996). 'Purpose and Function of IPCC', *Nature*, 379, 11 January: 108.

Gulland, J. (1998). 'The end of whaling?', *New Scientist*, 29 October, 120 (1663): 42–8.

Gupta, J. (1997). *The Climate Change Convention and Developing Countries: From Conflict to Consensus?* (Dordrecht: Kluwer Academic).

Haas, P. M. (1990). *Saving the Mediterranean: The Politics of International Environmental Cooperation* (New York: Columbia University Press).

—— (1991). 'Policy Responses to Stratospheric Ozone Depletion', *Global Environmental Change*, June, 224–34.

—— (1992a). 'Introduction: Epistemic Communities and International Policy Coordination', *International Organization*, 46: 1–37.

—— (1992b). 'Banning Chlorofluorocarbons: Epistemic Community Efforts to Protect Stratospheric Ozone', *International Organization*, 46: 187–225.

—— (1993a). 'Stratospheric Ozone: Regime Formation in Stages', In O. R. Young and G. Osherenko (eds), *Polar Politics: Creating International Environmental Regimes* (Ithaca: Cornell University Press).

—— (1993b). 'Protecting the Baltic and North Seas', In P. Haas, R. O. Keohane and M. Levy (eds), *Institutions for the Earth: Sources of Effective International Environmental Protection* (Cambridge, MA: MIT Press).

Haas, P. M., Keohane, R.O. and Levy, M. (eds) (1993). *Institutions for the Earth, Sources of Effective Environmental Protection* (Cambridge, MA: MIT Press).

Haigh, N. (1989). 'New Tools for European Air Pollution Control', *International Environmental Affairs*, 1: 26–38.

Hajer, M. A. (1995). *The Politics of Environmental Discourse: Ecological Modernization and the Policy Process* (Oxford and New York: Oxford University Press).

Hasenclever, A., Mayer, P. and Rittberger V. (1997). *Theories of International Regimes* (Cambridge: Cambridge University Press).

Hayward, P. (1990). 'The Oslo and Paris Commissions', Special North Sea Issue of *International Journal of Coastal and Estuarine Law*, edited by D. Freestone and T. Ijlstra: 91–101.

Hey, E. (1991). 'The Precautionary Approach – Implications of the Revision of the Oslo and Paris Conventions', *Marine Policy*, 15: 244–54.

Hey, E., Ijlstra, T., and Nollkaemper, A. (1993). 'The 1992 Paris Convention for the Protection of the Marine Environment of the North-East

Atlantic: A Critical Analysis', *International Journal of Marine and Coastal Law*, 8: 1-76.

High North Web News, IWC inter-sessional meeting, 8 December, 1997.

Hoel, A. H. (1985). *The International Whaling Commission 1972–84: New Members, New Concerns* (The Fridtjof Nansen Institute. R:003–1985 – in Norwegian).

Holt, S. (1985). 'Whale Mining, Whale Saving', *Marine Policy*, 9: 192–214.

Houghton, J. T., Meira Filho, L. G., Bruce, J., Hoesang Lee, Callender, B. A., Haites, E., Harris, N., Kattenberg, A. and Maskell, K. (eds) (1994). *Climate Change 1994: Radiative Forcing of Climate Change and An Evaluation of the IPCC IS92 Emission Scenarios*, reports of Working Groups I and III of the Intergovernmental Panel on Climate Change (Cambridge: Cambridge University Press).

Houghton, J. T., Meira Filho, L. G., Callender, B. A., Harris, N., Kattenberg, A. and Maskell, K. (eds) (1995). *Climate Change 1995: The Science of Climate Change*. Contribution of Working Group I to the Second Assessment Report of the Intergovernmental Panel on Climate Change (Cambridge: Cambridge University Press).

Houghton, J. T., Callander, B. A. and Varney, S. K. (1992). *Climate Change 1992. The Supplementary Report to the IPCC Scientific Assessment* (Cambridge: Cambridge University Press. Published for the Intergovernmental Panel on Climate Change).

Houghton, J. T., Jenkins, G. J. and Ephraums, J. J. (eds) (1990). *Climate Change. The IPCC Scientific Assessment* (Cambridge: Cambridge University Press).

—— (eds) (1990). *Scientific Assessment of Climate Change – Report of Working Group 1* (Cambridge: Cambridge University Press).

ICES Information (1993). 'How Polluted is the North Sea, and What Are We Doing about It?' (interview with Jean-Paul Ducrotoy, NSTF Secretary), 22 September.

International Commission on Whaling (ICW) (1975) *Twenty-Fifth Report of the Commission* (London: Office of the Commission).

International Convention for the Regulation of Whaling, Washington, DC. Articles signed on 2 December 1946.

International Whaling Commission (IWC) 'Rules of Procedure and Financial Regulations' (London and Cambridge: IWC).

International Whaling Commission (IWC) (1992). *Forty-Second Report of the International Whaling Commission* (Cambridge: IWC)

Isaksen, I. S. A. (1992). 'The Role of Scientific Assessments on Climate Change and Ozone Depletion for the Negotiation of International Agreements', paper presented at the Workshop on International Environmental and Resource Agreements, 19–20 October, Soria Moria Conference Centre, Oslo.

Ivarson, J. V. (1994). 'Science, Sanctions and Cetaceans, Iceland and the Whaling Issue' (Reykjavik: Centre for International Studies, University of Iceland).

Jänicke, M. (1997). 'The Political System's Capacity for Environmental Policy', in M. Jänicke and H. Weidner (eds), *National Environmental Policies* (Berlin: Springer-Verlag).

Jasanoff, S. (1990). *The Fifth Branch: Science Advisers as Policymakers* (Cambridge, MA: Harvard University Press).

Kerr, R. A. (1997). 'The Right Climate for Assessment', *Science*, 277, 26 September: 1916–18.

Knauss, J. (1997). 'The International Whaling Commission – Its Past and Possible Future', *Ocean Development and International Law*, 28: 79–99.

Kuhn, T. S. (1970). *The Structure of Scientific Revolutions*, 2nd edn (Chicago: University of Chicago Press).

—— (1991). 'The Trouble with the Historical Philosophy of Science', Robert and Maureen Rothschild Distinguished Lecture, 19 November, Harvard University.

Latour, B. and Woolgar, S. (1979). *Laboratory Life: The Construction of Scientific Facts* (Princeton, NJ: Princeton University Press).

Lee, K. N. (1993). *Compass and Gyroscope. Integrating Science and Politics for the Environment* (Washington, DC: Island Press).

Levy, M. (1993). 'European Acid Rain: The Power of Tote Board Diplomacy', in P. M. Haas, R. O. Keohane and M. Levy (eds), *Institutions for the Earth: Sources of Effective Environmental Protection* (Cambridge, MA: MIT Press).

—— (1995). 'International Co-operation to Combat Acid Rain', in *Green Globe Yearbook 1995* (Oxford: Oxford University Press, for the Fridtjof Nansen Institute).

Levy, M., Young, O. R. and Zürn, M. (1995). 'The Study of International Regimes', *European Journal of International Relations*, 1: 267–330.

Lindzen, R. (1990). 'Some Coolness Concerning Global Warming', *Bulletin of the American Meteorological Society*, 71: 288–99.

Litfin, K. (1991). 'Ozone Politics: Power and Knowledge in the Montreal Protocol', Paper prepared for the 1991 Meeting of the International Studies Association, 20–23 March, Vancouver.

—— (1994). *Ozone Discourses: Science and Politics in Global Environmental Cooperation* (New York: Columbia University Press).

—— (1995). 'Framing Science: Precautionary Discourse and the Ozone Treaties', *Millennium*, 24: 251–79.

Lunde, L. (1991). *Science or Politics in the Global Greenhouse? A Study of the Development towards Scientific Consensus on Climate Change* (Lysaker: The Fridtjof Nansen Institute, EED Report 1991/8).

MacTegart, W. J., Sheldon, G. W. and Griffiths, D.C. (eds) (1990). *Impacts Assessment of Climate Change – Report of Working Group II* (Canberra: Australian Government Publishing Service).

March, J. G. and Olsen, J. P. (1995). *Democratic Governance* (New York: The Free Press).

Marine Pollution Bulletin (1990). 'The Third International North Sea Conference', 215: 223.

Masood, E. (1995). 'Temperature Rises in Dispute over Costing Climate Change', *Nature*, 378, 30 November: 429.

—— (1996aa). 'Head of Climate Group Rejects Claims of Political Influence', 381, 6 June: 455.

—— (1996a). 'Climate Report Subject to Scientific Cleansing', *Nature*, 381, 13 June: 546.

—— (1996b). 'Companies Cool to Tactics of Global Warming Lobby', *Nature*, 383, 10 October: 470.

—— (1996c) 'Industry Warms to "Flexible" Carbon Cuts', *Nature*, 383, 24 October: 657.

Masood, E. and Ochert, A. (1995). 'UN Climate Change Report Turns up the Heat', *Nature*, 378, 9 November: 119.

Masterman, M. (1970). 'The Nature of a Paradigm', in I. Lakatos and A. Musgrave (eds), *Criticism and the Growth of Knowledge* (Cambridge: Cambridge University Press).

Maxwell, J. H. and Weiner, S. L. (1993). 'Green Consciousness or Dollar Diplomacy? The British Response to the Threat of Ozone Depletion', *International Environmental Affairs*, 5: 19–41.

McCormick, J. (1989). *Acid Earth* (London: Earthscan).

McHugh, J. L. (1974). 'The Role and History of the Whaling Commission', in W. E. Schevill (ed.), *The Whale Problem: A Status Report* (Cambridge, MA: Harvard University Press).

—— (1990). 'Communication Gaps Undermine Reports on Global Warming', *New Scientist*, 23 June. 126: 27.

MacKenzie, D. (1989). 'How to Use Science and Influence People', *New Scientist*, 122: 69–70.

'Measurement Campaigns of the Oslo and Paris Commissions' (1988). Paper produced for the first meeting of the North Sea Task Force, The Hague, 7–9 December.

Mensbrugghe, Y. (1990). 'Legal Status of International North Sea Declarations', Special North Sea Issue of *International Journal of Coastal and Estuarine Law*, edited by D. Freestone and T. Ijlstra: 15–23.

Meyer, A. (1995). 'Economics of Climate Change', *Nature*, 378, 30 November: 433.

Miles, E. L. (1989), 'Scientific and Technological Knowledge and International Cooperation in Resource Management', in S. Andresen and W.

Østreng (eds), *International Resource Management: The Role of Science and Politics* (London: Belhaven Press).

Miles, E. L., Underdal, A., Andresen, S., Skjærseth, J. B., Wettestad, J., Carlin, E. and Curlier, M. (forthcoming). *Explaining Regime Effectiveness. Confronting Theory with Evidence* (Cambridge, MA: MIT Press).

Mitchell, R. (1998). 'Discourse and Sovereignty: Interests, Science and Morality in the Regulation of Whaling', *Global Governance*, 4: 275–93.

Morisette, P. M., Darmstadter, J., Plantinga, A. J. and Toman, M. A. (1991). 'Prospects for a Global Greenhouse Gas Accord. Lessons from Other Agreements', *Global Environmental Change*, June: 209–23.

Mulkay, M. (1978). 'Consensus in Science', *Sociology of Science*, 17: 107–22.

New Scientist (1990). Comment, 'A Climate of Reason', 8 September, 127: 25.

Nollkaemper, A. (1991). 'The Precautionary Principle in International Environmental Law', *Marine Pollution Bulletin*, 22: 107–10.

—— (1993). *The Legal Regime for Transboundary Water Pollution : Between Discretion and Constraint* (Dordrecht: Martinus Nijhoff/Graham & Trotman).

Nordberg, L. (1993). 'Combating Air Pollution', LRTAP 'non-paper', March.

Oden, S. (1968). 'The Acidification of Air and Precipitation and Its Consequences in the Natural Environment', in *Ecology Committee Bulletin*, No. 1 (Stockholm: Swedish National Science Research Council).

Østreng, W. (1989). 'Polar Science and Politics: Close Twins or Opposite Poles in International Cooperation?', in S. Andresen and W. Østreng (eds), *International Resource Management: The Role of Science and Politics* (London: Belhaven Press).

Pallemaerts, M. (1992). 'The North Sea Ministerial Declarations from Bremen to the Hague: Does the Process Generate any Substance?', *International Journal of Coastal and Estuarine Law*, 7: 1–26.

Park, C. (1987). *Acid Rain – Rhetoric and Reality* (London: Methuen).

Parson, E. A. (1991). *Protecting the Ozone Layer: The Evolution and Impact of International Institutions* (Cambridge, MA: Kennedy School of Government, Harvard University, CSIA Discussion Paper 92–02).

—— (1993). 'Protecting the Ozone Layer', in P. M. Haas, R. O. Keohane and M. Levy (eds), *Institutions for the Earth: Sources of Effective Environmental Protection* (Cambridge, MA: MIT Press).

Paterson, M. (1992). 'Global Warming', in C. Thomas (ed.), *The Environment in International Relations* (London: Royal Institute of International Affairs).

Pearce, D. W., Cline, W. R., Achauta, A. N., Frankhauser, S. Pachauri, R. K., Tol, R. S. J. and Vellinga, P. (1995). 'The Social Costs of Climate

Change: Greenhouse Damage and the Benefits of Control', in J. B. Bruce, H. Lee and E. F. Haites (eds), *Climate Change 1995: Economic and Social Dimensions of Climate Change*, contribution of Working Group III to the Second Assessment Report of the Intergovernmental Panel on Climate Change (Cambridge: Cambridge University Press).

Pearce, F. (1994). 'Frankenstein Syndrome Hits Climate Treaty', *New Scientist*, 11 June, 142: 5.

—— (1997). 'Greenhouse Wars', *New Scientist*, 19 July 154: 38–43.

Popper, K. (1963). 'Science: Conjectures and Refutations', in K. Popper, *Conjectures and Refutations* (London: Routledge and Kegan Paul).

—— (1968). *The Logic of Discovery*, 2nd edn (New York: Harper and Row).

—— (1970). 'Normal Science and its Dangers', in I. Lakatos and A. Musgrave (eds), *Criticism and the Growth of Knowledge* (Cambridge: Cambridge University Press).

'Quality Status of the North Sea' reports (1984; 1987; 1993). Prepared by the Scientific and Technical Working Group to the International Conference on the Protection of the North Sea.

Reid, P. (1990). 'The Work of the North Sea Task Force', Special North Sea Issue of the *International Journal of Coastal and Estuarine Law*, edited by D. Freestone and T. Ijlstra: 80–9.

Reports of the International Whaling Commission, (1950–96) (London and Cambridge: IWC).

Røssum, J. (1984). *The Negotiations over Reduction of the Catch Quota in Antartica. The International Whaling Commission 1960–65*, unpublished master's thesis, Department of Political Science, University of Oslo. (In Norwegian).

Sætevik, S. (1988). *Environmental Cooperation between the North Sea States* (London: Belhaven Press).

Sand, P. (1990) 'Regional Approaches to Transboundary Air Pollution', in J. Helm (ed.), *Energy: Production, Consumption and Consequences* (Washington: National Academy Press).

Scarff, E. (1977). 'The International Management of Whales, Dolphins and Porpoises: An Interdisciplinary Assessment', *Ecology Law Quarterly*, 6: 323–571.

Schweder, T. (1993). 'Intransigence, Incompetence or Political Expediency? Dutch Scientists in the International Whaling Commission in the 1950s: Injection of Uncertainty'. Unpublished paper, Department of Economics, University of Oslo, Norway.

Scott, W. R. (1981). *Organizations: Rational, Natural, and Open Systems* (Englewood Cliffs, NJ: Prentice-Hall).

Sebenius, J. K. (1984). *Negotiating the Law of the Sea* (Cambridge, MA: Harvard University Press).

Shackley, S. and Skodvin, T. (1995). 'IPCC Gazing and the Interpretative Social Sciences', *Global Environmental Change*, 5: 175–80.

Shapin, S. (1993). 'Mertonian Concessions'. Book review, *Science*, 259, 5 February: 839–41.

Singer, F. (ed.) (1992). *The Greenhouse Debate Continued: An Analysis and Critique of the IPCC Climate Assessment* (San Francisco: ICS Press).

Skjærseth, J. B. (1991). *Effektivitet, problem-typer og løsningskapasitet: En studie av Oslo samarbeidets takling av dumping i Nordsjøen og Nordøstatlanteren* (Lysaker: The Fridtjof Nansen Institute).

—— (1992). 'The "Successful" Ozone-Layer Negotiations. Are there any Lessons to be Learned?', *Global Environmental Change*, 2, December: 292–301.

—— (1996). 'The Impact of Environmental Institutions: Implementing North Sea Pollution Control', paper prepared for the 37th Annual Convention of the International Studies Association, April, San Diego, CA.

—— (1998). *The Making and Implementation of North Sea Pollution Commitments: Institutions, Rationality, and Norms* (Lysaker: The Fridtjof Nansen Institute. Doctoral dissertation).

Skodvin, T. (1998). *Structure and Agent in the Scientific Diplomacy of Climate Change* (Oslo: CICERO. Doctoral dissertation).

—— (1999). 'Structure and Agent in the Scientific Diplomacy of Climate Change: An Empirical Case Study of the Intergovernmental Panel on Climate Change (IPCC)'. Dr. polit. thesis in political science, Department of Political Science, University of Oslo. Accepted for publication by Kluwer Academic Publishers (Dordrecht).

Spencer, L. with BoCluverk, J. and Morais, R. C. (1991). 'The Not So Peaceful World of Greenpeace', *Forbes*, 11 November: 174–80.

Stenstadvold, M. (1991). 'The Evolution of Cooperation. A Case Study of the NOx Protocol', unpublished thesis, University of Oslo (in Norwegian).

Stoett, P. (1995). 'The International Whaling Commission: From Traditional Concerns to an Expanding Agenda'. *Environmental Politics*, 14: 130–5.

Stokke, O. S. and Vidas, D. (1996). *Governing the Antarctic: The Effectiveness and Legitimacy of the Antarctic Treaty System* (Cambridge: Cambridge University Press).

Sundquist, J. L. (1978). 'Research Brokerage: The Weak Link', in L. E. Lynn (ed.), *Knowledge and Policy: The Uncertain Connection* (Washington, DC: National Academy of Sciences).

Susskind, L. E. (1994). *Environmental Diplomacy. Negotiating More Effective Global Agreements* (New York and Oxford: Oxford University Press).

Thaulow, H. (1989). *Nordsjøavtalen – for lite miljøvern for pengene!* Note (Oslo: Norwegian Institute for Water Research).

The IPCC Response Strategies – Report of Working Group III (1990). (Covelo, CA: Island Press).

The Oslo and Paris Commissions (1984). *The First Decade: International Cooperation in Protecting Our Environment* (London: The Oslo and Paris Commissions).

Tønnesen, J. and Johnsen, A. (1982). *The History of Modern Whaling* (London: C. Hurst).

Underdal, A. (1987). 'International Cooperation: Transforming "Needs" into "Deeds"', *Journal of Peace Research*, 24: 167–83.

—— (1989). 'The Politics of Science in International Resource Management: A Summary', in S. Andresen and W. Østreng (eds), *International Resource Management: The Role of Science and Politics* (London: Belhaven Press).

—— (1994). 'Progress in the Absence of Substantive Joint Decisions? Notes on the Dynamics of Regime Formation Processes', in T. Hanisch (ed.), *Climate Change and The Agenda for Research* (Boulder, CO: Westview Press).

—— (1999) 'One Question, Two Answers', in E. L. Miles *et al.* (eds), *Explaining Regime Effectiveness: Confronting Theory with Evidence*, ch. 1.

UN/ECE internet LRTAP information, September 1997.

United Nations Framework Convention on Climate Change. Agreed upon in Rio, June 1992. Published by the UNEP/WMO Information Unit on Climate Change (IUCC) on behalf of the Interim Secretariat of the Convention, Geneva, Switzerland.

Weale, A. (1992). *The New Politics of Pollution* (Manchester: Manchester University Press).

Weiss, P. (1996). 'Industry Group Assails Climate Chapter', *Science*, 272, 21 June: 1734.

Wetstone, G. (1987). 'A History of the Acid Rain Issue', in H. Brooks and C. L. Cooper (eds), *Science for Public Policy* (Oxford: Oxford University Press).

Wetstone, G. and Rosencrantz, A. (1983), *Acid Rain in Europe and North America* (Washington, DC, Environmental Law Institute).

Wettestad, J. (1989). *Uncertain Science and Matching Policies: Science, Politics and the Organization of North Sea Cooperation* (Lysaker: the Fridtjof Nansen Institute).

—— (1992). 'The "Effectiveness" of the Paris Convention on Marine Pollution from Land-Based Sources', *International Environmental Affairs*, 12: 101–21.

—— (1994). 'International Acid Politics: The UN ECE-Convention on

Long-range Transboundary Air Pollution (LRTAP)', in S. Andresen, T. Skodvin, A. Underdal and J. Wettestad, *'Scientific' Management of the Environment? Science, Politics and Institutional Design* (Lysaker: the Fridtjof Nansen Institute, R:006–1994)

—— (1994b). 'Combating Land-based Marine Pollution in the North-East Atlantic: The Paris Convention (PARCON) and the North Sea Conferences'. In S.Andresen, T.Skodvin, A.Underdal, and J.Wettestad, *'Scientific' Management of the Environment? Science, Politics and Institutional Design* (Lysaker: the Fridtjof Nansen Institute, R:006–1994).

—— (1994c). 'Science, Politics and Institutional Design: The Case of the North-East Atlantic Land-Based Pollution Regime', *Marine Policy*, 18: 219–33.

—— (1995). 'Science, Politics and Institutional Design: Some Initial Notes on the Long-Range Transboundary Air Pollution Regime'. *Journal of Environment and Development*, 4, summer: 165–85.

—— (1996). *'Acid Lessons? Assessing and Explaining LRTAP Implementation and Effectiveness'* (Laxenburg: IIASA, WP-96-18 March).

—— (1998), 'Participation in NOx Policy-Making and Implementation in the Netherlands, UK, and Norway: Different Approaches, but Similar Results?', in D. G. Victor, K. Raustiala and E.B. Skolnikoff (eds), *The Implementation and Effectiveness of International Environmental Commitments*, pp. 381–431 (Cambridge, MA: MIT Press).

—— (1999a). 'Increasing Concern and Improving Design: OSCON, PARCON, and the North Sea Conferences', in J. Wettestad, *Designing Effective Environmental Regimes* (Cheltenham: Edward Elgar).

—— (1999b). 'More Discursive Diplomacy than "Dashing Design"? The Convention on Long-range Transboundary Air Pollution (LRTAP)', in J. Wettestad, *Designing Effective Environmental Regimes* (Cheltenham: Edward Elgar).

WMO (1985). 'Report of the International Conference on the Assessment of the Role of Carbon Dioxide and of Other Greenhouse Gases in Climate Variations and Associated Impacts', in Villach, Austria, 9–15 October (Geneva: WMO Report No. 661).

—— (1992). *WMO and the Ozone Issue.* (Geneva: WMO Report No. 778).

—— (1994). *Scientific Assessment of Ozone Depletion: 1994* (Geneva: WMO Report No. 37).

WMO/UNEP IPCC (1988). Report of the First Session of the WMO/UNEP intergovernmental Panel on Climate Change, 9–11 November, Geneva, Switzerland.

—— (1989). Report of the Second Session of the WMO/UNEP Intergovernmental Panel on Climate Change, 28–30 June, Nairobi, Kenya.

—— (1990a). 'Policymaker Summary of the IPCC Special Committee of the Participation of Developing Countries', August.

—— (1990b). Report of the Third Session of the WMO/UNEP Intergovernmental Panel on Climate Change, 5–7 February, Washington DC, USA.

—— (1990c). Report of the Fourth Session of the WMO/UNEP Intergovernmental Panel on Climate Change, 27–30 August, Sundsvall, Sweden.

—— (1991a). Report of the Fifth Session of the WMO/UNEP Intergovernmental Panel on Climate Change, 13–15 March, Geneva, Switzerland.

—— (1991b) Report of the Sixth Session of the WMO/UNEP Intergovernmental Panel on Climate Change, 29–31 October, Geneva, Switzerland.

—— (1992a). Draft Report to the Seventh Session of the WMO/UNEP Intergovernmental Panel on Climate Change, 10–12 February, Geneva, Switzerland.

—— (1992b). Report of the Eighth Session of the WMO/UNEP Intergovernmental Panel on Climate Change, 11–13 November, Harare, Zimbabwe.

—— (1993). Draft Report to the Ninth Session of the WMO/UNEP Intergovernmental Panel on Climate Change, 29–30 June, Geneva, Switzerland.

—— (1994), Draft Report to the Tenth Session of the WMO/UNEP Intergovernmental Panel on Climate Change, 10–12 November, Geneva, Switzerland.

—— (1995). Report of the Eleventh Session of the WMO/UNEP Intergovernmental Panel on Climate Change, 11–15 December, Rome, Italy.

—— (1996). Report of the Twelfth Session of the WMO/UNEP Intergovernmental Panel on Climate Change, 11–13 September, Mexico City, Mexico.

—— (1998). Draft Report to the Fourteenth Session of the WMO/UNEP Intergovernmental Panel on Climate Change, 1–3 October, Vienna, Austria.

Wuster, H. (1992). 'The Convention on Long-Range Transboudary Air Pollution: Its Achievements and its Potential', in T. Schneider (ed.), *Acidification Research, Evaluation and Policy Applications* (Amsterdam: Elsevier).

Wynne, B. and Shackley, S. (1997). 'Global Warming Potentials: Ambiguity or Precision as an Aid to Policy?', *Climate Research*, 8: 89–106.

Young, O. R. (1989). 'Science and Social Institutions: Lessons for International Resource Regimes', in S. Andresen and W. Østreng (eds), *International Resource Management: The Role of Science and Politics* (London: Belhaven Press).

Young, O. R. and Osherenko, G. (eds) (1993). *Polar Politics. Creating International Environmental Regimes* (Ithaca: Cornell University Press).

—— (1998). *Creating Regimes: Arctic Accords and International Gover-*

nance (Ithaca: Cornell University Press).

Ziman, J. (1968). *Public Knowledge: The Social Dimension of Science* (Cambridge: Cambridge University Press).

—— (1984). *An Introduction to Science Studies: The Philosophical and Social Aspects of Science and Technology* (Cambridge: Cambridge University Press).

Index